AIRCREW

'And then our weary, battered column, short 24 bombers, but still holding the close formation that had brought the remainder through by sheer air discipline and gunnery, turned in to the target. I knew that our bombardiers were as grim as death while they synchronized their sights on the great ME-109 assembly shops lying below us in a curve of the winding Blue Danube, close to the outskirts of Regensburg ... Our bombs were away. We turned from the target toward the snow-capped Alps. I looked back and saw a beautiful sight – a rectangular pillar of smoke rising from the ME-109 plant. Only one burst was over and into the town. Even from this great height I could see that we had smeared the objective. The price? Cheap, 200 airmen.'

BY THE SAME AUTHOR

The Technique of Television Announcing
Four Men Went to War

AIRCREW

THE STORY OF THE MEN
WHO FLEW THE BOMBERS

BRUCE LEWIS

WEIDENFELD & NICOLSON

First published in Great Britain in 1991 by Leo Cooper
Paperback edition published in 2000 by Cassell
This paperback edition published in 2022 by Weidenfeld & Nicolson
an imprint of The Orion Publishing Group Ltd
Carmelite House, 50 Victoria Embankment
London EC4Y 0DZ

An Hachette UK Company

3 5 7 9 10 8 6 4 2

A CIP catalogue record for this book
is available from the British Library.

ISBN (Mass Market Paperback) 978 1 4746 2628 6
ISBN (eBook) 978 1 4746 2629 3
ISBN (Audio) 978 1 4746 2630 9

Printed in Great Britain by Clays Ltd, Elcograf S.p.A.

MIX
Paper from
responsible sources
FSC® C104740

www.orionbooks.co.uk
www.weidenfeldandnicolson.co.uk

To Miki with Love

Contents

Contents

Glossary

ABC: Airborne Cigar. Powerful transmitters carried by Lancasters of 101 Squadron to jam enemy instructions to Luftwaffe night fighters.

ASI: Airspeed Indicator.

ATA: The Air Transport Auxiliary whose pilots, both men and women, ferried aircraft from the factories to the squadrons.

Bullseye: Code name for participation by an OTU trainee crew in a bombing raid. Often with a 'screen' or experienced pilot.

Circuits and Bumps: A training exercise in which a pilot took off in an aircraft, circled the airfield and landed – repeating the exercise over and over again until he was completely familiar with the flying characteristics of that particular machine.

Cookie: The standard 4,000 lb blast bomb carried by RAF Bomber Command. It was an unstreamlined drum made from thin mild steel and filled with molten RDX explosive. The casing made up only 20% of the weight. There was also an 8,000 lb version.

DR: Dead Reckoning; basic navigation without the help of radar or radio aids.

ETA: Estimated Time of Arrival.

FIDO: Fog Intensive Dispersal Operation. Pipes laid either side of the runway had petrol pumped through them under pressure. This was ignited and blazed upwards through perforations in the pipes. It was an effective, if costly, method of dispersing fog in the vicinity of the airfield.

Freya: Luftwaffe code for their ground radar used to detect approaching bomber forces.

Gee: Bomber-navigation radar, dependent on pulses received from ground stations in England.

George: Automatic pilot.

Grand Slam: 22,000 lb bomb. The largest bomb ever carried in

World War Two. Designed by Barnes Wallis, only the Lancaster could deliver it.

Ground Cigar: Powerful transmitters sited in England and manned by German-speaking operators, men and women, broadcasting false instructions to enemy night fighters.

H2S: The first self-contained airborne navigational radar needing no ground stations.

IFF: Identification Friend or Foe. An automatic transmitter giving aircraft a distinctive shape or 'blip' on a radar screen, distinguishing it from enemy 'blips'.

Kammhuber Line: Named after its instigator, Generalmajor Josef Kammhuber, it was a defensive line of searchlights, flak guns and ground-controlled night-fighters, stretching from Denmark in the north down the entire length of the enemy-occupied coast. It finally comprised over 200 separate 'boxes' each with is own control centre. British bombers had to pass through this defensive screen both on the outward leg, and when returning from a raid.

Knickebein: (Crooked Leg). Code-name for a system of radio navigational beams used by the Luftwaffe to bomb British cities at night in 1940. By the autumn of that year British scientists had learned the secrets of its operation and introduced countermeasures which included 'bending' the beam.

Lichtenstein or **Li:** Luftwaffe code for their AI (Airborne Interception) radar equipment.

LMF: Lack of Moral Fibre. A cruel tag applied to aircrew who could no longer face up to the demands of operational flying.

Monica: Code-name for radar equipment used in RAF bombers to detect enemy night-fighters approaching from the rear. Hastily discontinued when it was discovered these same night fighters were 'homing in' on Monica's radar emissions.

MU: Maintenance Unit.

Naxos: Luftwaffe code for their version of 'Serrate'.

Nickels: Leaflet raids carried out in the early stages of the war. Operations known cynically in the RAF as 'Bumphleteering'.

Oboe: Radio beam navigation system. Two ground stations transmitted beams which intersected at the target. It was so accurate that crews could bomb 'blind' with it, but it was limited in range to about 350 miles. Effective over the industrial haze of the Ruhr.

OTU: Operational Training Unit. Originally the last stage before joining a squadron, but later becoming, at most, the penultimate state, when . . . **HCU**: Heavy Conversion Units were introduced. At these crews were familiarised with the big four-engine bombers, usually Halifaxes. There was a further stage at . . . **LFS**: Lancaster Finishing School, for those crews fortunate enough to be selected to fly 'Lancs'.

Perfectos: Refined radar equipment fitted in night intruder Mosquitoes which triggered the Luftwaffe version of IFF signals in their night-fighters. The successor to **Serrate**.

RDF: Radio Direction Finding.

Serrate: Radar receiver used for detecting German night-fighter radar emissions and carried by night intruder Beaufighters.

SABS: Stabilizing Automatic Bomb Sight.

Ship: American term for an aircraft.

Special Operator or 'Special': The eighth member of crews flying with 101 Squadron. German speaking, the Special operated ABC equipment.

Tallboy: 12,000 lb deep-penetration 'earthquake' bomb. Also the brain-child of Barnes Wallis, Lancasters of 617 Squadron were specially adapted to the job of carrying it.

Tame Boar, (Zahme Sau): German code name for infiltration of the bomber stream by twin-engine night-fighters, Messerschmitt 110s and Junkers 88s. Guided into the stream by ground control, the interception was then carried out by the individual aircraft using their Lichtenstein radar.

U/S: Unserviceable. Occasionally caused misunderstanding among servicemen from the United States.

WAAF: Women's Auxiliary Air Force. Members of this force participated in most of the RAF skilled trades except flying.

Wild Boar, (Wilde Sau): German code name for Luftwaffe nightfighters, (often single-engine day fighters pressed into night service), which massed high over the target to pick off RAF bombers silhouetted by the searchlights and flames. This method was rapidly introduced by the Germans after the dropping of 'Window' over Hamburg in July, 1943, scrambled their radar systems.

Window: Metal strips cut to the same lengths as the wavelengths of German ground radar transmitters. When dropped from bombers at regular, timed, intervals it could either swamp the enemy radar screens, or, used more selectively, create a false impression of a major raid approaching, and even, as on D-day, simulate the advance of a vast seaborne invasion.

Wurzburg: Code-name for two versions of Luftwaffe ground radar control systems. The smaller of the two installations was used to direct master searchlights and flak guns, while **Wurzburg Reise**, (Giant Wurzburg), accurately detected individual bombers, the information then being passed to night-fighters equipped with Lichtenstein.

X-Verfahren: Code-name for a more advanced system of radio navigational beams operated by Heinkel 111s of Kampfgruppe 100, acting as pathfinders to the main force. Most successful on the raid against Coventry, it was afterwards rendered less effective by British countermeasures. (This system is often wrongly referred to as **X-Gerat**, a term which covered the airborne equipment only).

Introduction

I am aware of the number, some would say plethora, of books that have been published on the subject of the Allied Bombing Campaign in Europe during the Second World War. Many of these concentrate in detail on the strategic and tactical aspects of this campaign, and also on the remarkable application of radar that made possible the successful bombing of Germany by night. I have learned a great deal, particularly about high level policy, from reading carefully researched publications, often written by authors who were not even born at the time.

However, as one who flew with Bomber Command, and who retains an undying respect for my companions of those days, I sometimes feel, because of the way the subject is presented, that there is a danger of the 'machine' and the 'electronic wizardry' taking precedence in people's minds over the human beings who actually crewed the bombers. To say, for example: 57 of our aircraft failed to return on 21/22 January, 1944, is rather different from reporting that over 400 airmen were lost on that night.

So, in an attempt to redress the balance a little, this book is a combination of first-hand experiences told to me by a number of one-time aircrew members, mixed with a few personal memories, and a background filled in by a fair amount of research. Overall, I hope it throws some light on the tasks that these young volunteers undertook, and which they fulfilled to the best of their ability under terribly dangerous circumstances.

I have included a section on the exploits of men of the United States 8th Army Air Force in addition to those of the RAF's Bomber Command – we were all airmen who flew to war over Europe in the 'Heavies', and were in it for the same purpose – to kick out the Nazis.

Many thanks to all those kind people who made this book

possible, including that painstaking historian, Martin Middlebrook, who has generously allowed me to refer to his definitive work *The Bomber Command War Diaries*. Also the staff of The Memorial Library Second Air Division USAAF for giving me so much help during my visit to Norwich. I am grateful for Mr Andrew Renwick's careful guidance in the Photographic Department of the RAF Museum, Hendon, and to his colleague, Mr David Ring, who rendered valuable help at the eleventh hour. Lastly, and particularly, those 'ex-bomber types', who told me without a trace of self-promotion, what happened to them while flying in the wartime skies over Europe.

The original edition of *Aircrew* had already gone to print, when on the night of 16 January 1991, the world learned of the outbreak of the Gulf War. The US Air Force and the Royal Air Force, along with the air forces of other nations, were again engaged in combat against a merciless tyrant who, without provocation had occupied the territory of a small peaceful nation.

Viewing our television screen, listening to the radio and reading the newspapers, we marvelled at the meticulous planning, the miraculous technology, the sheer weight and bombing accuracy that characterized this allied onslaught mounted with the authority of the United Nations. After only a few hours it was clear this was the most devastating air battle since World War Two.

News of 'intelligent' missiles and the application of hi-tech that can guide a bomb through a doorway left us breathless; yet it was obvious that the participation of highly skilled aircrew showing extraordinary courage in the face of enemy fire was still the supreme ingredient – just as it had been in times past.

Seeing on TV the British and American pilots and navigators returning from sorties – the way they looked and the words they spoke – my thoughts went back half a century to those other aircrew, quite a bit younger, more hastily trained, possibly less articulate, who flew against the tyrant of their day.

Although the similarities were striking, one difference was evident. The new aircrew had no inhibitions about admitting fear, or that they sometimes shed tears. Sadly, such transparent honesty would not have been understood in our war.

During Bomber Command's unremitting campaign against the enemy, lasting without respite from the first day of war in September 1939, until May 1945, for any given hundred aircrew these were the grim statistics:

Killed on Operations	51
Killed in Crashes in England	9
Seriously Injured	3
Prisoners of War	12
Evaded Capture	1
Survived Unharmed	24

55,500 Bomber Command aircrew lost their lives, a rate of loss never before borne by a military force of comparable size in the history of the world.

As Alastair Revie, an army officer, wrote: '... The price paid in human terms for the strategic and tactical bombing of Germany – the major innovation of World War Two – was almost unthinkable. In all, more bomber crewmen died between 1939 and 1945 than infantry officers in the slaughter of the trenches of World War One'.

The casualties suffered by American aircrews of the 8th USAAF in their air battles over Europe were almost identical with those of the RAF's Bomber Command, but these were sustained over a shorter period of time, and so, in that sense, were even greater.

Since the publication of the first edition of Aircrew I have, to my surprise and delight, received a steady flow of letters from readers. I doubt that I deserve the kind words penned by so many. On the other hand, the criticism of my errors gently pointed out by some of my correspondents has been richly deserved. There is no doubt this new edition benefits from a number of corrections resulting from their constructive help.

It has been a pleasure to hear from ex-aircrew, from writers and historians, and also from members of the younger generation who have expressed interest in what is now aviation history; their quest for knowledge makes certain that the events that took place in those times will never be forgotten.

Loyalty to the type of aircraft in which men flew remains as strong as ever. Although I received no support for the ill-fated Manchester, a number of readers who flew the giant Stirling claim that they owe their lives to its rugged strength and unequalled ability to take punishment.

To counter my criticism of the seating arrangements in the Halifax I have been assured that the escape hatches in this bomber were better sited than those in the Lancaster. According to my informants – per seven-man crew attempting to jump from these aircraft in an emergency, on average 2.45 survived from Halifaxes, and only 1.3 from Lancasters.

One of my regrets down the years has been the loss of contact with the members of the two crews with whom I flew during the Second World War. After sharing so many dangers in our youth it seemed a pity that, when we came to hang up our operational flying boots, we should merely shake hands, bid each other farewell and never meet again.

Now, as a result of wide distribution of my book and help from 101 Squadron Association, I have made contact with some of my surviving comrades from those days – and what a joy that has been. I am particularly grateful to Orion, the publishers of this latest paperback edition for the opportunity to include additional photographs kindly provided by Jack West, living in Australia; Jim Bursell's widow, Jean, and family, from New Zealand; Peter Clifford, in Sussex; and our navigator, Colin Pyle, now residing in Edinburgh.

Bringing together old friends and meeting new ones has made the writing of *Aircrew* rewarding enough in itself. If, in its latest form, this book gives pleasure to a wider group of readers then I shall be more than content.

Bruce Lewis

AIRCREW

ONE

In The Beginning

It was my 18th birthday when I walked into the recruiting office and volunteered for Flying Duties with the Royal Air Force. Bomber Command had already been fighting a lonely, bitter war against Germany for over two years and was, at that time, going through a bad patch. Aircraft losses were mounting and results were disappointing. In Britain many powerful voices were murmuring that the money lavished on the bomber offensive could be better spent elsewhere in the pursuit of victory. I, of course, like the rest of the British public, knew nothing of these political undercurrents.

Most of us who were to fly in the four-engine 'Heavies' – the Lancasters and Halifaxes that sustained the great onslaught against the enemy in the later years of the war – were either still at school, or starting out on our first jobs, when war was declared against Germany on 3 September, 1939.

Yet from that very first day of hostilities crews were climbing into their slab-sided, matt black Armstrong Whitworth Whitleys, while others struggled to board the less cumbersome, but unbelievably cramped Handley Page Hampdens – with fuselages only three feet across at the widest point!

Luckiest, from the standpoint of flying the best RAF bomber then available, were those crews who manned the remarkable Vickers Wellington. Basically it was a metal and wood basket covered in canvas. It was everything that a warplane should be – strong, reliable, able to absorb untold punishment and regarded with real affection by the men who flew in her. They nicknamed her the 'Wimpey'. Designed by Barnes Wallis, the genius whose name is irrevocably linked with Bomber Command, the 'Wimpey' was the only aircraft among those early bombers to be still on active service at the end of the war.

This trio of twin-engine bombers, pitifully lacking in defensive armament, painfully slow, yet remarkably rugged, was the mainstay of Bomber Command's offensive against Germany in the early years of the war. In the beginning they were crewed by men who had made flying their career in the peacetime RAF. The training they had received had ill-prepared them for the arduous duties that lay ahead – especially in the essential skills of navigation by night.

These professional airmen alone carried the war to the doorstep of the enemy. From among the few survivors of that era emerged the leaders of the many who were to follow – outstanding flyers including Guy Gibson of Dam Buster fame, Leonard Cheshire who won his Victoria Cross for numerous acts of supreme courage rather than for a single incident, and Don Bennett, leader of the Pathfinder Force, a superb pilot and brilliant navigator.

Franklin D. Roosevelt, the American President, had appealed to all European nations to refrain from 'unrestricted aerial warfare on civilian populations or unfortified towns'. Britain, in her immediate reply to the President, had promised that 'indiscriminate attack on civilian populations as such will never form part of our policy'. Undoubtedly this was sincerely meant at the time, but in the light of what was to happen as the war progressed no statement could have presaged a more bitter irony.

Even so, as darkness fell on that first night of war, ten Whitleys, three from 51 Squadron and seven from 58 Squadron, took off from their grass runways and set course to the east. The Whitley was the only RAF bomber specially designed to fly at night. The crews had been trained accordingly, but under conditions of peace, when it was comparatively simple to navigate from one well-lit town to another while flying over home territory.

It is remarkable, in the light of later operational strategy, that these poor old kites, pushing their way through the night at all of 120 mph, visited between them Hamburg, Bremen and no less than nine other cities in the Ruhr during the course of that one mission. Of course, they did not drop a single bomb on the Germans – instead they rained down 5½ million leaflets!

Marshal of the Royal Air Force Sir Arthur Harris, whose name is synonymous with Bomber Command, spoke for many in the

RAF – particularly those aircrew who had to risk their lives dropping these bits of paper:

> In the earliest stages of the war we were not allowed to bomb anything on land, and our only possible targets were therefore warships, which we could attack only by day. Our losses from enemy fighters and flak were prohibitive and we therefore desisted before we had done ourselves or the enemy much harm. Meanwhile the Whitleys and Hampdens were put to the questionable employ of dropping pamphlets all over Europe, a game in which we never had the slightest faith. My personal view is that the only thing achieved was largely to supply the Continent's requirements of toilet paper for the five long years of war.

As Sir Arthur said, our losses were prohibitive. After a series of hard lessons, Bomber Command had to admit that the theory of the successful 'self-defending bomber' *operating by day* had been no more than a peacetime pipe-dream. Even the concentrated fire from Wellingtons flying in close formation had proved inadequate in warding off attacks from German single-engine fighters.

The climax was reached on 18 December, 1939, when twenty-two Wellingtons flew on an armed reconnaissance sortie over Wilhelmshaven. At 13,000 feet they could see and be seen for miles through a cloudless sky. The crews were obliged to break formation to a certain extent because of the intense flak. Unknown to them, for the first time a German ground controller was operating an experimental 'Freya' radar station.

This controller had detected the British bombers when they were still 70 miles from their target. As they turned for home, the waiting fighters tore into their ranks with vicious beam attacks. The Luftwaffe pilots had quickly learned that an approach from this quarter left the Wellington at its most vulnerable. After a running battle only ten of the twenty-two bombers remained. It was small consolation that gunners in the Wellingtons managed to shoot down two of the German fighters.

Five out of a force of twelve Wellingtons had been shot down in the same area only four days previously. So, out of thirty-four bombers dispatched on those two raids, exactly half had been lost. Eighty-five aircrew did not return to their squadrons.

As a result of these disastrous set-backs, and in view of further tragic losses sustained during the short but hopeless Norwegian campaign the following April, a change of policy was forced on Bomber Command. It was vital to conserve the small number of bombers and the limited supply of crews then on squadron strength. It was difficult to gauge when the full Nazi onslaught in the West would begin, or exactly what form it would take.

If the Wehrmacht marched against France, every bomber the RAF possessed would be needed to harry the enemy's lines of communication. Or, should the Luftwaffe engage in an all-out bombing offensive against Britain, then plans were ready to strike at German airfields and supply depots. Schemes to destroy industrial centres, oil refineries and storage facilities had also been worked out in detail.

Meanwhile, by the turn of the year Hampdens and Wellingtons were joining the night-flying Whitleys on 'Bumphleteering' raids, as the crews called them. At least the airmen were gaining experience in flying over enemy territory in the dark. Navigation was based on 'dead reckoning', radio 'fixes' when not too far from base, and, on moonlit nights, observation of ground features such as lakes, rivers and coastal landmarks. In addition it was sometimes possible to take 'star shots' with the sextant, a time-honoured aid to navigation at sea, but only of limited value in the air because of problems caused by the speed and motion of the aircraft.

On pitch black nights, in freezing temperatures, it was a case of 'dead reckoning', working out *in theory* just where you were by making use of forecast winds, and *nothing* else. As likely as not, even the radio would be out of action, its aerial a useless icicle. Yet even these crude facilities were usually sufficient to get a crew somewhere over Germany and back again to England on a 'bumph chucking' trip. Exactly where the leaflets fell was not critical. Later, when specific targets for bombing raids had to be located, it was another matter. Then, and only after a long period of self-delusion by Bomber Command, did the gross inaccuracies of night-time navigation across Europe become shatteringly obvious.

It was no fault of the men who flew those early missions that aircraft so often failed to reach their targets. With the lack of direction-finding aids it was rather like, as one navigator put it, 'sitting in a freezing cold stair cupboard with the door shut and the Hoover running and trying to do calculus.' Never in the history of war was a man called upon to carry out such complicated calculations in the midst of battle.

When I flew in bombers as a wireless operator I was able to observe at close quarters the unimaginable stress under which a navigator worked for long periods of time. He had to maintain an almost superhuman detachment, even when the enemy was doing his best to destroy the aircraft in which he was working, and when his pilot was twisting and turning and diving and climbing in a corkscrewing effort to escape that destruction.

In those earlier days of war, before the Germans had honed their night defence system into the deadly weapon that it later became, the most terrifying enemy the bomber crews had to face was appalling weather. 1940/41 produced the worst winter in living memory. The men flying the Wellingtons, Whitleys and Hampdens had to struggle through endless blankets of fog and fight fierce head-winds that reduced the forward speed of the already slow aircraft to almost nothing.

Ice was the worst menace. It formed in thick layers on the wings. It turned hydraulic systems to jelly; gun turrets, bomb doors, undercarriages all stopped working. It formed an opaque sheen over Perspex windows, making it impossible to see out. Ice played havoc with instruments and the radio.

Frostbite was not uncommon among those who flew in these pioneer bombers. Hands were encased first of all in a silk glove, over this a woollen glove, and finally a thick leather gauntlet. In order to carry out some essential duties, plotting a course on a chart for instance, writing up a signals log, or accurately tapping out a message on a morse key, this protective clothing had to be removed. If a bare hand inadvertently touched a metal part of the aircraft it would freeze to that object immediately.

I remember one of my first night cross-countries in a Wellington, while training at OTU. We had each been provided with a pack of sandwiches wrapped in grease-proof paper with an outer cover of newspaper. In addition we were given a small tin of concentrated orange juice. It must have been around 3 am when I felt the need for refreshment. I reached for the fire axe and aimed a blow at the top of the tin, making a suitable hole through which to pour the liquid. It was a waste of time. The orange juice had frozen into a solid block. Unwrapping the sandwiches I discovered they were encased in a frosty covering of crystals and were as hard as stone. When I hit them with the axe, sharp splinters of bread flew all over the cabin. We were flying in an airborne refrigerator.

Although this book concentrates on the aircrew who flew in the heavy bombers of Bomber Command and the American 8th Air Force, it would be churlish not to say a word about a couple of machines flown by men of the RAF in the initial stages of the war. One of these was the Bristol Blenheim.

The Blenheim was generally unable to join its bigger brothers under the protective cover of darkness. Its range was limited and, when the strategic bombing policy began in earnest, its bomb-carrying capacity was too restricted. It carried only 1000 lbs of bombs, compared with up to 7000 lbs lifted by a Whitley. Yet in spite of these shortcomings, the twin-engine Blenheim was a compact, business-like *medium* bomber, which, a few years earlier, had been acclaimed a world beater. It was Britain's first modern, all-metal stressed-skin military aircraft. It was faster than any other RAF bomber of those days, which was just as well, because its defensive armament was disgracefully inadequate.

So the men who flew in Blenheims, pilot, observer and wireless operator/air gunner, had to go on facing the perils of daylight operations. Once the 'phoney' war was over and all-out bombing began, the crews of the Blenheims kept up an unremitting attack on enemy-occupied channel ports and targets near the coast. Any gentlemanly agreement relating to bombing restrictions had come to an end when the Germans bombed Rotterdam on 15 May, 1940. During the Battle of Britain Blenheim squadrons played a vital role in making sure that England was not invaded by the Germans. They, and the crews of Wellingtons, destroyed hundreds of motorised barges concentrated by the enemy for that purpose.

The stalwart Bristol Blenheim remained in action until August, 1942, when its intruder role over Europe was taken on by the American-built Douglas Boston flown by RAF crews. But the Blenheim continued to serve overseas long after this time.

In those early days Britain had yet another bomber, the Fairey Battle. Also manned by a crew of three, the aircraft was classed as a *light* bomber. It was powered by a single Merlin engine. Ten squadrons of Battles, of which the RAF had more than any other bomber, were sent to France at the outbreak of war, along with a number of Blenheims. They formed the Advanced Air Striking Force in support of the French Army, and were no longer part of Bomber Command. In fact, Bomber Command only rarely used the Battle in an operational capacity.

The Fairey Battle looked so advanced, so clean in outline, more like a long, elegant fighter than a bomber, that no one could fail to be impressed by its appearance. As a schoolboy my favourite Dinky Toy was a model of a Fairey Battle. Later I thanked God that I was born too late to fly in combat in one of those underpowered, unprotected machines. The courage of the crews who flew to their death in Battles has never been fully acknowledged.

In the Spring of 1940, when the Germans invaded the Low Countries, the Advanced Air Striking Force was thrown into the battle to try to stem the enemy onslaught. They bombed supply columns and lines of communication. The losses among the Battles and Blenheims reached horrific proportions. They were shot out of the sky, either by withering fire from the mobile flak batteries, or as a result of relentless attacks by Messerschmitt 109 fighters, whose superior fire-power and speed left the Battles, in particular, with almost no hope of survival.

On 12 May, 1940, the CO of 12 Squadron told his men that it was vital to destroy two large bridges that spanned the Albert Canal near Maastricht in Holland. This was the only chance of stemming the Wehrmacht's headlong advance. Making no bones of the fact that the mission was suicidal, he called for volunteers. Every pilot, observer and wireless operator/air gunner in the squadron stepped forward.

Six crews were picked for the job. The Battles took off. In spite of intense opposition, one of the bridges was hit and partly destroyed. None of the aircraft returned from that mission. One of the pilots, 21-year-old Flying Officer D.E Garland, and his observer, Sergeant T. Gray were each posthumously awarded the Victoria Cross – the first to be won by the RAF in the Second World War. Their wireless operator/air gunner, Leading Aircraftman L. R. Reynolds, who also died, received no such recognition.

9

This was the quality of aircrew transferred from Bomber Command to other duties. The command could ill afford to lose such men.

Over the course of the coming years the frittering away of men and machines was to continue in other ways. Crews, after being expensively trained in Bomber Command's own operational training units, were then not infrequently transferred to Coastal Command, or sent overseas.

Thus the efforts to build up Bomber Command's strength until it was equal to the immense task it had set itself, that of bringing Germany to her knees by strategic bombing, was constantly frustrated by factors quite unrelated to losses caused through enemy action.

I witnessed one or two examples of this 'filching' during my training. On one occasion some of us were asked if we would be prepared to transfer for duties with the army, serving as wireless operators in tanks fighting in the Western Desert. A few of our number volunteered to go, relishing the chance of immediate action. These young men were unhappy at the prospect of at least another year's training in the RAF before seeing active service.

By the end of the Battle of Britain the Luftwaffe, too, had been taught by our fighter pilots that daylight bombing attacks were too costly in men and machines, even when the German bombers were accompanied by large fleets of escorting fighters. From then on, until their services were required the following year in Russia, the Heinkels, Dorniers and Junkers also sought the cover of night to bomb British cities.

Previously, during the Battle of Britain, the German bomber force had concentrated on trying to destroy the RAF fighter fields in south-east England. Such was the intensity of the onslaught that Fighter Command was at one time in a critical situation.

On the night of 25/26 August, 1940, a force of forty-three British bombers, made up of Whitleys, Hampdens and Wellingtons, bombed Berlin. Six of the Hampdens, flying to the limit of their fuel capacity, were lost. Material damage to the cloud-covered city was negligible, yet the psychological effect on the Nazi leader was profound. The effrontery shown by British airmen in daring to fly

10

600 miles into the Fatherland to drop high explosive on the Third Reich's capital city was too much for Adolf Hitler. Angrily he ordered his Luftwaffe chief, Hermann Göring, to retaliate with all his strength against London – only a few miles away from his front-line airfields in France.

Göring was anxious to restore his tarnished prestige. Previously he had confidently told Hitler that the RAF fighter force would be smashed in two weeks. This had not happened. On the contrary, because of the activities of that same fighter force, Luftwaffe bombers and their escorting fighters had fallen from the British skies in their hundreds since early August. And now another of the Reichsmarschall's famous boasts, that 'not a single bomb will fall on Germany', had been blown apart by Bomber Command.

The commander-in-chief of the Luftwaffe eagerly ordered round-the-clock bombing of London in the belief that the RAF's stock of Spitfires and Hurricanes was almost depleted. Calculating that his enemy had only about a hundred fighters left, he underestimated by at least ten times. Also, by switching tactics at this crucial stage, by bombing the city and leaving the RAF airfields and control centres unmolested, he relieved Fighter Command of its most worrying problem, and in so doing he lost the battle.

Obliged in the end to concentrate on night bombing, the Luftwaffe inflicted severe suffering on the people of London. By the end of the year 13,000 citizens had been killed and a further 16,000 seriously injured. Many homes were destroyed, especially in the poorer areas of the East End. Numerous historic buildings were reduced to rubble. The docks suffered badly too, but Britain had other ports. In addition, much of Britain's war industry was situated elsewhere, well away from London, particularly in the Midlands and the North.

Far from lowering civilian morale or causing panic, the common hardships inflicted by the bombing united Londoners in their determination to win through in the end. This indomitable spirit was equally evident among the people of all the 'blitzed' cities of Britain, Birmingham, Liverpool, Plymouth, Bristol, Swansea and Coventry, which in a single night lost 500 people, and a further 1,200 injured. 60,000 buildings were destroyed or damaged, a third of the city's factories were put out of action, and the ancient cathedral ruined. Yet, when 10,000 people were offered transport to leave the devastated city on the following day, only about 300 took up the offer.

There were no arguments at that time about it being morally wrong to bomb Germany. Such academic 'afterthoughts' only emerged when victory was in sight.

In their early night raids on the British Isles the German crews had three advantages: short flying distances to their targets; little effective interference from Britain's primitive night defences; and an ingenious but simple system of intersecting radio beams that guided the Luftwaffe bombers to their targets. The first of these, the Knickebein, was soon countered by British scientists, but then a more accurate device known as *X-Verfahren* was introduced by the Germans and used to devastating effect against Coventry.

One member of our family had good reason to remember the consequences of what she insisted afterwards was the result of our scientists 'bending the beam'. This was a common expression at the time among the civilian population for what was supposedly being done by the 'boffins' to divert the German bombers from their targets.

Auntie Annie lived on her own in a remote hill farm high on the mountains above the town of Llangollen in North Wales. One night the 'Jerries' started to bomb Auntie Annie. Showing great courage, my Uncle Trevor, who lived in the valley, commandeered a wheel chair and lugged it up the mountainside to rescue the old lady. As he said afterwards, 'With bombs exploding all round, I would never have believed it possible to come down a mountain so quickly, while guiding a wheelchair occupied by an elderly relative.'

An official postmortem on the raid came to the conclusion that the intended target had been the Mersey docks in Liverpool. It was a bright moonlight night at the time of the attack, and on that particular mountain there are large outcroppings of dark grey rock. It was thought that the German crews, thanks to a little 'scientific misdirection', had mistaken these dark patches for clusters of shipping moored in the River Mersey. I am pleased to report that both my aunt and her farm escaped without serious damage. Many rocks were badly splintered and two sheep were killed.

It is interesting to examine the positions occupied by the various crew members in Luftwaffe bombers. In the Junkers 88, for example, all four airmen occupied the same cockpit in the nose. The pilot sat high on the left, with the navigator close beside him or prone when bomb-aiming. The flight engineer was stationed just behind the pilot. He was also responsible for manning the upper rear gun. The wireless operator was to the engineer's right, from where, when necessary, he could struggle down to fire the lower rear gun at the back end of the bombsight gondola. Similar seating arrangements also applied in Heinkels and Dorniers.

So German crews flew into battle literally shoulder to shoulder. This feature had been introduced into Luftwaffe bomber designs for two reasons. One was to facilitate crew communication, both visual and oral. The other was a belief that flying in such close proximity would help to sustain morale. Panic, it was thought, would be less likely to break out in the chummy environment of a shared cabin.

As a result of hard experience gained in the Battle of Britain, armament was substantially increased. At one time the unfortunate engineer was made responsible for manning no less than five separate hand-held guns. There must have been moments when the clatter and confusion in the 'cosy cabin', especially when a wounded comrade fell into your lap, produced a totally different effect on morale from that envisaged by the chairborne psychologists.

By contrast, crew members of RAF night bombers, with the exception of the Hampden, were more isolated. The gunners, particularly, led a lonely life in their power-operated turrets – a form of defensive armament not used on German bombers. Navigators and wireless operators worked in close proximity, as of course did the pilot and second pilot, until the latter was replaced by the flight engineer when the four-engined 'Heavies' took to the air. The bomb-aimer, when he arrived on the scene later in the war and took over responsibility from the navigator for dropping the bombs, usually stayed in his nose compartment except during take-off and landing. Aircrew kept in touch with each other via 'intercom' – an electrical inter-communication system.

Bomber Command may have been suffering disappointments

and frustrations at that time, but these were shared by the German flyers too. Colonel Werner Baumbach, one of Germany's finest bomber pilots, wrote:

> Hitler talked about 'extirpating' the English towns, and propaganda coined the word 'coventrizing' for the maximum degree of destruction which was deemed to have been inflicted on Coventry. In this night-bombing during that winter London figured pre-eminently in the German communiques and reports on the progress of the Luftwaffe's 'wearing-down' strategy – which was *not* in fact achieving its purpose . . . The mining of the Thames estuary and the Wash and attacks on shipping on moonlight nights were continued. Night bombing of various targets was intensified, though the English fighters and AA defences were continuously improving while the efficiency of the Luftwaffe was rapidly decreasing. . . .
>
> At the beginning of 1941 the Luftwaffe High Command had to admit that England could not be reduced to impotence solely by night bombing, carried out as it was by inadequate forces . . . the German air war against her had failed.
>
> *The battle over England cannot be compared even remotely with what was to happen to Germany from 1942 onwards.*

This was the assessment of a Luftwaffe pilot who was later to become 'General of Bombers'.

Inadequate those German raids against England may seem with hindsight, yet they inflicted more damage than Bomber Command was able to match when attacking targets in Germany during that period. In one raid on Berlin most of the bombs fell in the surrounding countryside, a few of which destroyed some farms. The topical joke in the German capital was: 'Now they are trying to starve us out!'

Nothing daunted, as the winter of 1940 set in, RAF bombers continued to beat their way across Germany in defiance of the worsening weather. On occasion the targets were never found, or places were bombed up to a hundred miles from the designated aiming point – without the crews ever realizing they were in error. Blacked-out Germany remained mysterious, remote and vast beneath them. The signposts of radar, which were to become the guides of the future, were almost undreamed of then.

Compared with the colossal tonnage of later years, the weight

14

of bombs dropped on Germany by the RAF in 1940 was negligible. Yet the efforts of those valiant pioneers were far from wasted. Their attacks on the enemy brought a fierce satisfaction to those inhabitants of Britain who had suffered from the Luftwaffe's bombing. It is true that official propaganda made the effect of these raids on the Third Reich seem far more devastating than it really was. A publication issued by His Majesty's Stationery Office called *Bomber Command* presented a glowing report of what was being achieved. While admitting that our bomber force was not yet as big as the RAF would wish, it was, it said, nonetheless producing remarkable results. The book contained an inspiring map, captioned: 'Attack at the Heart: The Raids on Germany'. It covered an area from the Baltic, south as far as Munich, and east beyond Dresden and Stettin. Against every major town and city in Germany were printed clusters of bombs in varying sizes. These bombs were grouped according to the number of raids supposed to have taken place on each target. Symbols represented munition works, power stations, aerodromes, seaplane bases, aircraft works, oil refineries, railways, docks and waterways, naval ships, and an all-embracing symbol entitled 'various objectives'. Without doubt all these missions had been mounted, but how many targets had been *hit*, and by what number of aircraft, was not detailed.

The book was notable for some excellent photographs of Whitleys, Hampdens, Wellingtons and Blenheims, and crew members at their various stations inside the aircraft. There were action shots of bombs falling (by day of course), and aerial views of apparent damage to enemy installations by high explosive. It is significant that the 'damage' had to be pinpointed by arrows drawn across the photographs, in contrast to reconnaissance pictures taken in the later stages of the war when the devastation was all too obvious.

Even the smallest raid occasionally had an effect on the recipients out of all proportion to its destructive value. An outstanding example was a mission reported by an American correspondent, William L. Shirer. He was living in Berlin at the time when the USA was still neutral. During that period Germany also had a non-aggression pact with the Soviet Union. He wrote:

At this point in the conversation, say the German minutes, the

Führer called attention to the late hour and stated that in view of the possibility of English air raid attacks it would be better to break off the talk now, since the main issues had probably been sufficiently discussed.

That night Molotov gave a gala banquet to his hosts at the Russian Embassy on the Unter den Linden. Hitler, apparently exhausted and still irritated by the afternoon's ordeal, did not put in an appearance.

The British did. I had wondered why their bombers had not appeared over Berlin, as they had almost every night, to remind the Soviet Commissar on his first evening in the capital that, whatever the Germans told him, Britain was still in the war and kicking. Some of us, I confess, had waited hopefully for the planes, but they had not come. Officials in the Wilhelmstrasse, who had feared the worst, were visibly relieved. But not for long.

On the evening of November 13, [1940], the British came over early. It gets dark in Berlin about 4 pm at this time of the year, and shortly after 9 o'clock the air-raid sirens began to whine and then you could hear the thunder of the flak guns and, in between, the hum of the bombers overhead . . . Molotov had just proposed a friendly toast and Ribbentrop [the Nazi Foreign Minister] had risen to his feet to reply when the air-raid warning was sounded and the guests scattered to shelter.

In the safety of the underground shelter of the Foreign Ministry conversation continued between the Germans and the Russians. . . . Molotov stated that the Germans were assuming that the war against England had already actually been won. If therefore [as Hitler had maintained] Germany was waging a life and death struggle against England, he could only construe this as meaning that Germany was fighting 'for life' and England 'for death'.

This sarcasm may have gone over the head of Ribbentrop, a man of monumental denseness, but Molotov took no chances. To the German's constant reiteration that Britain was finished, the Commissar finally replied, 'If that is so, why are we in this shelter, and whose are those bombs which fall?'

(From *The Rise and Fall of the Third Reich*.)

Winston Churchill wrote that the air raid was actually timed for this occasion:

We had heard of the conference beforehand, and though not invited to join in the discussions did not wish to be entirely left out of the proceedings.

16

How small that raid must have been, when compared with the massed onslaughts of later years, can be seen by consulting the 'Bomber Command War Diaries':

> 13/14 November, 1940. 72 Hampdens, Wellingtons and Whitleys to 5 targets. *1 Hampden was mistakenly shot down by a Spitfire soon after its take-off.* A further Hampden and Whitley were lost. Only 15 aircraft reached primary targets.

Fifteen bombers spread over five targets hardly represents a weighty attack, especially on a city as large as Berlin. It is likely that falling shell fragments from the defending anti-aircraft guns caused at least as much distress as the British bombs.

Yet Bomber Command never gave up trying. The following night fifty aircraft set off for Berlin again. Only half that number reported reaching the city. Ten aircraft – four Hampdens, four Whitleys and two Wellingtons, were lost from this and other bombing missions that night, the heaviest night loss sustained by the RAF up to that time. Forty-six airmen of Bomber Command would not fly again.

At the beginning of 1941 Bomber Command planned to concentrate on bombing oil-processing plants as soon as the weather improved. From mid-February this became possible and the attacks began. But, as so often happened with Bomber Command campaigns, the force had to be diverted to other matters, in this instance after only one month. Britain, who the previous year had repulsed the German attempts to subdue her airpower, was now in dire peril at sea. Her vital lifeline with America, the shipping that plied back and forth across the Atlantic, was in imminent danger of being cut. Vessels were being torpedoed and bombed and shelled to the bottom of the ocean at an alarming rate. U-boats, long range Focke-Wulfe Kondors, and fast, heavily armed surface-raiders were all taking their toll.

Bomber Command was asked to forget the synthetic oil targets for the present and concentrate its efforts on bombing the shipyards building the submarines in ports such as Hamburg, Kiel and Bremen, also inland targets like Mannheim – home of the marine diesel engine. In addition, airfields as far apart as Norway and France had to be attacked in order to frustrate the activities

17

of the huge, four-engine Kondors which had been ranging far out
into the Atlantic, well beyond the reach of RAF fighters.

This was not all. When the battleships *Scharnhorst* and *Gneisenau*
docked in Brest, the port was bombed continuously, preventing
the two warships from returning to the Atlantic

The bases from which the U-boats embarked on their raids,
Bordeaux, St Nazaire and Lorient, were attacked time after time.
The Germans, using slave labour, were forced to construct massive
concrete U-boat pens as a result of these operations. Towards the
end of the war Dr Barnes Wallis put a weapon into the hands of
Bomber Command that would demolish these hitherto impreg-
nable fortifications.

At the beginning of this phase, small numbers of the new generation of big bombers began to arrive on some squadrons. Four of
the twin-engined Avro Manchesters and three four-engined Handley Page Halifaxes joined eighty-one of the older aircraft in a raid
on Hamburg's Blohm & Voss U-boat yards. This was in mid-
March, 1941. A month earlier the cumbersome four-engined Short
Stirling had flown on its first operation.

The ageing Whitleys and Hampdens would continue to play
their part for more than another year, but like old soldiers they
honourably began to fade away during this period. Not so the
robust, trouble-free Wellington which had become the mainstay
of Bomber Command and would remain in this role for some time
to come.

Now, a year and a half after the outbreak of war, the fresh
volunteer crews were beginning to join the squadrons to take their
place beside flyers who had carried the war to the enemy since the
beginning. These were the young men who had trained as aircrew
cadets, some abroad under the Empire Air Training Scheme,
others in Britain. All had come together to form themselves into
crews at Operational Training Units in the British Isles.

Most of the chapters that follow are based on first-hand accounts
told to me by some of these men, many who were no more than
boys when they volunteered for flying duties. In some instances
dialogue has been included. Purists may object to this on the
grounds that no conversation can be accurately reported after a
lapse of half a century. In reply I would suggest that we are not

dealing here with ordinary conversation, but recalling remarks sometimes made under circumstances of extreme emergency and danger, leading to heightened emotion, stress and fear. At such times, what is sensed, seen, smelt and heard, including the spoken word, can often be etched indelibly on the memory. In relating events, both in the air and on the ground, these one-time aircrew sometimes brought an added vitality to their recollections by remembering what they or their companions had said on certain occasions. Statements or orders from superior officers were also recalled when those words bore a particular significance. To have ignored these snatches of quoted dialogue would, I believe, have reduced the sense of atmosphere unique to those days, and, worse, broken faith with men who have taken the trouble to tell me about their experiences.

TWO

The Pilot/Navigator

In the earlier part of the war, RAF training for pilots followed much the same pattern as that which had existed in peacetime. Instruction up to the stage where a pupil was able to demonstrate his competence in handling a single-engine aircraft, coupled with a knowledge of related subjects such as navigation and theory of flight, had varied little over the years. In Chapter Six we shall be following a pilot cadet through this initial phase of his training in more detail.

After the award of his 'Wings', continuity of training, at least for the potential bomber pilot, sometimes went adrift during those earlier days. Lack of specialization, or a shortage in certain aircrew categories, meant that less experienced pilots were occasionally used to perform other flying duties, particularly as navigators, for which they were not fully qualified. While struggling in these unfamiliar roles time slipped by, denying them the chance to build up valuable operational hours as pilots and captains of their own aircraft.

This situation existed mainly through a shortage of bombers and a scarcity of trained navigators. The story of how this affected one volunteer, who became 'the bomber pilot who never was', is related below:

Leslie Biddlecombe, who lived in Orpington, was educated at Highfield College, Leigh-on-Sea. At 19 he was a clerk at the Lombard Street branch of the Westminster Bank. He was a tall, thin, pale-skinned young man. On the day war was declared he walked into an army recruiting office on Bromley Common, having decided to join the Buffs. The office was empty. Although he waited for some time, nobody turned up. He went home disillusioned. A small circumstance, but it changed the course of his life. He made up his mind to volunteer for flying duties with the RAF instead.

It was not until the following July (1940) that he was summoned to RAF Uxbridge. Accompanied by his father, Leslie was interviewed by a Wing Commander. He remembers little of what was said at the meeting, but he does recall that both he and his father were impressed with the Wing Commander's bright blue eyes!

Having been found acceptable, it was then necessary to undergo a stringent medical examination. To pass 'Fit Aircrew A1' was a guarantee of fitness above the standard demanded by any other branch of the Services. The difficulty in Leslie's case was that he had suffered with asthma since the age of six. At school he had been unable to play football or take part in any of the more strenuous sports. Wednesday afternoons were set aside for outside activities, but, as often as not, he spent the time with his mother at the cinema.

However, he decided to bluff his way through as best he could. He was going to answer no to asthma when they ran through the list of ailments – any one of which automatically disqualified an applicant. He felt he had a chance of deceiving the RAF doctors because he had been told that asthma was undetectable unless actually in spasm. What worried him most was the breath control test. In this one was required to blow down a rubber pipe and hold some mercury steady in a glass tube for a minimum length of time. Before the event, he had assiduously practised deep breathing and holding his breath. When the time came he kept the mercury in position for about 1½ minutes, which was acceptable, and had no particular trouble with any of the other tests.

Enlisted as an Aircraftman 2nd Class, Aircrew Cadet, his first two weeks in the RAF were spent in a Receiving Centre at Babbacombe in Devon. Here he was kitted out with his uniform. Billeted with others in the once posh Sefton Hotel, Leslie found the accommodation less luxurious than the exterior of the building suggested. Stripped down to the bare boards, it contained no more than rows of iron-framed beds.

It was here that they suffered their first casualty. The cadets received some inoculations and were warned not to indulge in any alcohol for the time being. Unfortunately, one of their number

21

could not resist sampling the local cider. He imbibed liberally after being jabbed – and died.

Then followed a hectic period at the Initial Training Wing in Paignton – long sessions of lectures on navigation, meteorology, theory of flight, morse and RAF law. Classroom studies were punctuated by periods of strenuous physical exercises and foot drill. Leslie revelled in all this activity and enjoyed a fitness he had never known before. The stuffy days spent in the bank were completely forgotten. 'Lights Out' was at 9 o'clock in the evening but the cadets were so tired by the end of the day that no one objected to early bed.

After six weeks the course entrained for the Elementary Flying Training School at Burnaston in Derbyshire. Those cadets who had successfully completed basic training – by no means all of them – were now promoted to Leading Aircraftmen. The time had arrived to learn to fly an aeroplane.

The majority of teenagers during the 1930s and '40s had very little money to spend on themselves, and were limited in their choice of spare-time activities. Leslie knew nothing of mechanical matters, had never seen an aircraft at close quarters, and had no idea how to drive a car. So all this was a novel experience – the gateway to a new and adventurous world.

They were taken up in Miles Magisters – single-engine monoplanes with two open cockpits, one for the instructor, the other for his pupil. The aircraft, of course, was fitted with dual controls. Presumably to instil a sense of respect for this machine, it was explained that it had at least one advantage over the Tiger Moth, the RAF's other basic trainer – the Magister, they said, had brakes!

In those first overwhelming moments, overcome by the miracle of flying through the air at 3,000 feet, Leslie gripped the 'stick' for dear life with both hands. The pilot, who was in complete control, urged him to relax and take things more easily. After a surprisingly short time he found he was getting the hang of the controls – he actually enjoyed doing some straight and level flying, a little gliding and climbing, even a few gentle turns.

Leslie was aware that some of the pupils, although putting on brave faces, were worried about their ability to pass the course. Others seemed sublimely confident. One cadet complained about

22

the way his instructor ordered him to execute certain manoeuvres in the air, and then made it impossible for him to carry out these instructions by moving the controls in the opposite direction. 'Tomorrow,' he said, 'I'm going to take things into my own hands and force the controls the way I want them to go!' Within a few days he had been 'washed out' and posted away.

Leslie was among the less confident pupils. He was uncertain whether or not he was making satisfactory progress. One of his consolations was his immunity to air-sickness (yet, strangely, he is sea-sick on the calmest of waters). His greatest shock came when, without warning, his instructor put the Magister into a spin. A moment before, strapped into the open cockpit, he had felt content and secure with the aircraft in level flight.

In an instant his sense of well-being was shattered as he was thrust forward and saw the earth rushing up towards him. 1,000 feet was lost in no time. As the pilot pulled out, he asked his pupil if he was all right. Leslie called back down the speaking tube, and said, with an assurance that he was far from feeling, 'Yes thanks, sir. I'm fine!'

'Excellent!' said his instructor, who promptly pulled the stick back and fell away into a second spin! Another 1,000 feet disappeared from the altimeter. Now only 800/900 feet above the ground, Leslie was mightily relieved when he realized no further spins were contemplated.

Not long afterwards he was carrying out this aerobatic manocuvre himself – grit teeth and haul back on stick – a little apprehensive for fear of overdoing it. Then a firm push forward on the stick . . . coming out of the spin . . . rush of blood to the head as G forces exert pressure . . . no ill effects . . . feeling fine.

Flying brought its own brand of tiredness – a deep, all-pervading weariness that Leslie had never experienced before. It was enough to sit sprawled in the mess in the evenings, listening to the fascinating variety of dialects spoken by his fellow cadets. Some, from certain areas of northern England particularly, were difficult to understand. On the other hand, volunteers from overseas, from the colonies, expressed themselves in fresh and colourful speech that was easy to follow.

During these moments of relaxation, he was filled with a happy contentment for the opportunities the war had brought him. Under normal circumstances he would never have met so many interesting companions who had come from such a variety of different places. It was stimulating, exciting, and so much better than anything he had ever hoped to experience in civvy street

Leslie was taught by two flying instructors during this period. After a time he came to the conclusion that the first of these was not a good teacher. He was sure that the man's ability to instruct was impaired by his fear of flying with pupils. The potential dangers of trying to teach cadets the intricacies of flying, and correcting their errors, with only 3,000 feet leeway between themselves and the ground, had obviously played on his nerves. Leslie was sure that, because of this pilot's apprehensions, he was not receiving the best instruction

The second instructor, a Flying Officer, certainly knew his stuff. But, as time went on, Leslie became more and more certain that this officer was not satisfied with his progress. He dreaded the thought that, perhaps, he too might soon join the ranks of the 'washed out'. One day he was accompanied by a civilian pilot who asked him to stall the aircraft. This he did successfully. After some more flying he told him to complete a circuit and bring the Magister in to land. The civilian flyer then reported: 'Nothing wrong with this man. Time he went solo.'

Leslie had undergone no more than eleven hours' instruction. Yet he thought the length of time taken to solo was rather excessive. In later years he was consoled to learn that the Duke of Edinburgh had soloed after the same number of hours. In fact, the time he had taken was somewhat better than average for RAF pupils during that period.

At that time the Luftwaffe carried out several air raids in the area. Protesting cadets were herded into concrete shelters that were crowded, dusty and hot. Most of them would have preferred to have stayed in bed. One night they thought they were in for a direct attack when a number of flares dropped on their airfield. The actual bombing, however, took place further north in the vicinity of some steelworks

Training at EFTS being satisfactorily concluded, Leslie was

24

posted to Brize Norton. Nearly all trainee pilots in the RAF fervently hoped to finish up flying fighters – especially during the Battle of Britain, when the 'First of the Few' were saving the nation in their Spitfires and Hurricanes. But as soon as he arrived at this new station, he guessed he had been selected for bombers. The training aircraft were *twin*-engine Air-speed Oxfords.

He remembers a brisk, efficient Flying Officer instructor who warned him straightaway, pointing to an Oxford, 'Don't try spinning that thing or you'll dive straight into the deck!' Training included 'circuits and bumps', cross-country navigation flights, beam approach exercises – a new technique at that time – low-level practice, forced-landing procedure and emergency flying on one engine. All valuable 'gen' for a future bomber pilot.

A catastrophe befell Leslie while he was at Brize Norton. Someone stole his parachute. He had to replace this expensive pack of silk, and it cost him £40. This was a fortune. An LAC's net pay barely exceeded a £1 per week in those days.

Another disaster of a much more serious nature occurred at this time. One morning he shared an Oxford with a fellow trainee called Bickford. He heartily disliked those moments when Bickford was at the controls indulging in what Leslie considered to be impossibly tight turns. That evening 'goose flares' were lit, and night flying was ordered for the first time. At the end of the exercise Bickford was missing. The officer in charge ordered a search. They found his dead body lying in a damp field. His aircraft had dived straight into the ground.

There was a lighter side. Like the other trainees, Leslie enjoyed attending the local dances. Easily identified as 'aircrew in the making' by the white flashes in their forage caps, they were popular with the girls of the district. It was during one such 'do' that he met Joan, an attractive girl from Witney. It was not long before they became engaged. He thought nothing of walking the seven miles from his girlfriend's home back to the RAF base after a rapturous evening.

The completion of training at Brize Norton, just before Christmas, 1940, was a highlight in Leslie's flying career. This was the moment when he was promoted to Sergeant and awarded his pilot's wings. Unusually, there was no ceremonial 'passing out' parade to mark the occasion.

He had done well. His overall pass mark was 73.5%. If he had managed to attain 75%, then he would have been awarded a Pilot's 'B' Licence – useful for peacetime flying.

Before leaving, he was told to report for an interview to assess his suitability for a commission. The presiding Squadron Leader asked him what school he had attended. 'Highfield College, Leigh-on-Sea, sir.' The officer looked at him with an air of pitying disdain. 'Never heard of it.' That was the end of the interview and, for the time being, Leslie remained a Sergeant.

He now expected to be posted to an Operational Training Unit to gain experience on the type of bomber he would be flying on operations. Instead he was posted to No 2 Air Navigation School at Cranage.

The system in those days, later discontinued, was for 'sprog' pilots to fly as 'second dickies' to more experienced 'skippers' until they became proficient enough to warrant their own aircraft and crew. Apart from taking his turn at the controls, a second pilot was also expected to help out with the navigation. This, it was explained, was the reason for his posting to Cranage.

This part of his training was, more or less, a waste of time. Lecturers dealt with the theory of getting an aircraft from one point to another – reading off the rectified airspeed, correcting for altitude and temperature differences to find the true air speed, then applying the actual windspeed to give the ground speed of the aircraft. Rightly, it was emphasized that calculations involving all these factors had to be meticulous. This was the only way a given course could be followed accurately.

It was all classroom stuff, fair enough in its limited way, but barely touching on the many extra problems brought about by darkness, adverse weather conditions and enemy action when flying over hostile territory. At best it was a revision of what he had already been told in earlier training.

Air navigation practice in lumbering twin-engine Avro Ansons – 'flying greenhouses' the RAF called them – was, for the most part, a farce. The men who piloted these aircraft were nearly all 'tour-expired' veterans. They were thoroughly 'brassed off'. They

26

had no interest in co-operating with 'sprog' navigators in the fur-
therance of their training. One of their few interests lay in 'beating
up' those pubs where they happened to know the barmaid. To
attempt serious navigation under those circumstances was not a
practical proposition.

Not surprisingly Leslie, too, was more than a little 'brassed off'.
As a recently qualified pilot, he never had an opportunity to keep
his hand in at Cranage by taking over the controls of an aircraft.

1941 had dawned and the weather was freezing cold. The heating
facilities in Ansons were primitive indeed. What with one thing
and another he was pleased when the day came to pack his kit
and leave for the Operational Training Unit at Cottesmore.

With a thrill of excitement he saw that the hard-standings were
occupied by Handley Page Hampdens. Smaller and lighter than
its twin-engined contemporaries, the Wellington and Whitley, it
was really a medium, rather than a heavy bomber.

Powered by two Bristol Pegasus XVIII engines of 980 hp each,
it is surprising how wildly, as with other aircraft of the day, the
performance and bomb-carrying capacity were exaggerated in the
press and popular publications. (Sometimes these figures are still
quoted in books about the history of bombers). In the case of the
Hampden these were virtually doubled. One book brought out in
the early '40s described the Hampden as having a top speed of
265 mph, cruising at 217 mph, and with a bomb load of 4,000
lbs. The Hampden was known in the RAF to exceed the operational speed of the Whitley by 10 mph and we have already
established that the Whitley flew, in favourable circumstances, at
120 mph! As for bombs, 2,000 lbs was really more than enough.
Even the great Guy Gibson was apprehensive about such a load:

> None of us had ever done it before and we did not even know
> whether our Hampdens would unstick with 2,000 lbs of bombs.

By the time Leslie flew on operations the normal load for a
Hampden was down to 1,500 lbs – two 500 lb HEs and two 250
lb HEs being a typical package. It is incredible that, only four
years later, slightly modified Avro Lancasters were each capable
of carrying 22,000 lbs in the shape of a single 'Grand Slam' bomb
– more than the total weight of bombs lifted by a squadron of

27

fourteen Hampdens. Yet the Lancaster, itself not a specially large aircraft, had a net weight only three times that of a Hampden.

The day after Leslie arrived at Cottesmore he attended a lecture given for the new intake of aircrew. The officer went to the trouble to emphasize what a safe aircraft the Hampden was to fly. Any rumours heard to the contrary should be discounted as idle gossip. At that moment they heard the sound of a tremendous crash outside the window. A Hampden had taken off and dived into the ground, smashing itself to smithereens.

In spite of this dramatic introduction, he found the Hampden was indeed a pleasant aircraft to fly, with gentle, 'forgiving' characteristics. But it *was* cramped. When his instructor took him up for the first time, Leslie had to squat down behind him and look over his shoulder. This was the only way to glean some idea of how to handle the bomber. In an aircraft about half the width of a family saloon car it was impossible to sit side by side.

Later on, during cross-country exercises, he took it in turns with a fellow pupil to fly either as pilot, or as navigator/bomb aimer. Because of the confined interior they could not swap roles while flying. The pilots only had a few weeks to get to know their aircraft, learn to navigate in a restricted space – beneath the pilot's feet – and carry out a little bombing practice with a World War One bomb sight.

There was no attempt to form crews at this stage, something which became normal practice at OTUs later on. Leslie never knew with whom he would be flying next. Sometimes he was unlucky enough to be paired with one of the 'mad' characters on his course. Mouland-Begbie could handle a Hampden better than most, but over the bombing range he enjoyed easing back on the stick and stalling the aircraft. This had an unfortunate effect on his colleague who was trying to aim the bombs – he would be pinned to the deck unable to move!

Rishworth, another 'bonkers' type, liked nothing more than riding his Hampden like a horse, bucking it up and down through the skies by pushing the control column backwards and forwards. Whenever he saw an inviting hole in the strata he could never resist diving through it. Sadly, neither Rishworth nor Mouland-

Begbie survived OTU. They were killed before they ever reached the squadrons.

Once, when at the controls of a Hampden, he had a narrow escape himself. Coming in to land he misjudged his approach and had to make an instant decision – either to attempt to overshoot and go round the circuit again, or try to land two-thirds of the way along the runway. He was in 'fine pitch', so decided to put the bomber down on the concrete strip and hope for the best. He thought he had got away with it as he swung the aircraft round to port, but unfortunately the airfield boundary hedge on his starboard side was just too close, and tore off the aircraft's entire twin-tail unit. (If the reader cares to study photographs of a Hampden, he will see how slender was the boom to which the tail was attached). The horn warning the pilot that the tail-wheel was still retracted blared its strident note continuously. This was not surprising, because the wheel was buried deep inside the hedge.

Leslie and the rest of the crew climbed out of the remaining section of the Hampden and stomped across the airfield to take whatever 'medicine' the CO decided to dole out.

A new kind of endorsement had recently been introduced by the RAF. It was a form of mild reproof, making full allowance for inexperience. Leslie got away with nothing more than this. However, he and the others had been spotted by some 'admin' types as they had walked away from the wreck and crossed in front of Station HQ. They received an entirely separate chastisement – nothing to do with crashing an aircraft, but for being improperly dressed. They had omitted to wear their caps! As punishment for this 'crime' they were obliged to march round and round a hangar for one hour. All ex-aircrew will recognize this as a fair illustration of the two distinctly 'different' 'RAFs'.

Something now occurred at Cottesmore, the horror of which has remained in Leslie's memory to this day. A blazing Whitley, one of the few on the strength of the OTU, succeeded in landing on the airfield. The fire-tender, the ambulance, and every available person on the station rushed to the scene. They saw members of the crew clambering free – all except the rear gunner who was trapped in his turret. Helpless, they watched as the poor boy became engulfed in flames. Nothing could save him. His agony

29

was unbearable to see – he was pleading for help. An officer, his face set, raised his pistol, took careful aim and fired. The boy's agony was over.

Still shocked, Leslie later went round to visit two of the air gunner's pals in their billet. As he entered, he was astounded to see both airmen sitting on their beds, laughing uncontrollably. They had been studying a tiny piece of charred cloth no bigger than a half-crown. 'Look,' they said, the tears rolling down their cheeks, 'that's all that's left of him.' This was his first experience of raw hysteria.

As soon as he had clocked up sufficient hours, he was posted to a squadron at Hemswell. Almost before he knew what was happening he was on a night operation to Mannheim. Flying as navigator, he had to guide the bomber to the target, drop the bombs, and man the hand-held Vickers 'K' gun poking out of the aircraft's nose. The following day his papers arrived and he was given a severe dressing-down. There were two squadrons stationed at Hemswell and he had flown with the wrong one – 144 Squadron, instead of 61 Squadron, to which he had actually been posted.

Now at last he became a member of a regular crew, skippered by Pilot Officer John Graham. Sergeant 'Ginger' Hughes was the wireless operator/air gunner. The lower/rear gun position was manned by a quiet, reliable New Zealander, Sergeant 'Kiwi' Nuttall.

Leslie was 2nd pilot, navigator, bomb aimer and front gunner. The first and last of these duties were academic: in the event of the 1st pilot being killed or wounded it would have been virtually impossible to take his place for the reasons already given. As for the front gun, it was most unlikely that any German fighter pilot would be so insane as to mount a frontal attack at night.

Within a short time both squadrons were transferred to North Luffenham. It is worth noting that 144 Squadron flew more raids than any other Hampden squadron, and suffered the highest losses. This included a 100% loss during a raid in the area of Heligoland.

61 Squadron went from strength to strength and finished the war with the second highest number of raids in Bomber Command. It actually chalked up more Lancaster raids than any other squad-

ron. While flying with 61 Squadron, Flight-Lieutenant William Reid won his Victoria Cross on a flight to Düsseldorf on the night 3/4 November, 1943. But this was more than two years after Leslie's brief flying career with the RAF had come to an end.

Pilot Officer John Graham was a competent and cheerful captain who went out of his way to look after his crew. Leslie had no opportunity to fly his bomber on operations, yet he felt neither resentment nor anxiety. He had every confidence in John's ability, and was quite prepared to wait until he had completed ten trips before becoming a 1st pilot himself. Meanwhile, he was grateful to be flying in any capacity.

They worked well as a team and flew to Aachen, Hanover, Karlsruhe twice, Frankfurt and Cologne without encountering too much trouble. Leslie applied whatever he had learned during training to get them to these targets. It was a matter of crossing the English coast at the correct point, and then checking the position once the enemy coast was reached. Ginger never failed to get him some useful radio bearings while crossing the sea. As for arriving at the target, he always prayed that someone else would get there first and light it up for them. This implied a touching belief that the first man in had found the right place!

Returning from a raid, they always kept on the alert, even after reaching Britain. The Hampden, with its slim fuselage and twin rudders, was too easily mistaken for either the Luftwaffe's Messerschmitt 110 or the Dornier 17. A number of Hampdens returning from operations against the enemy, sometimes almost within sight of their home bases, had been shot down either by their own AA batteries or by RAF fighter pilots deficient in aircraft recognition skills. [See page 18]

They never sighted an *enemy* night fighter during these missions. Leslie put this down to the modest height at which they flew – not more than 11,000 feet. (The books of the period, of course, quoted the Hampden's service ceiling as 22,700 feet!) Wellingtons, however, operated at around 14,000 feet and possibly ran into more fighter opposition.

The flak looked deceptively pretty, like a colourful firework display when viewed from a distance, but was deadly, and frightening to fly through. At that low height the AA gunners fired high-velocity, low-calibre tracer shells. When flak struck the bomber it reminded Leslie of someone throwing gravel. One of the most startling experiences was when they ploughed their way through an electrical storm. Lightning flashes crackled all round the metal frame of the cabin.

His seventh mission was to the great northern port of Kiel. On the night of 8 August 1941, Graham and his crew, accompanied by forty-nine other Hampdens and four Whitleys, flew straight over the North Sea towards Denmark. Leslie remembers well that the briefing officer had told them their objective was the German battleship *Scharnhorst*. This is interesting, because the *Scharnhorst* and *Gneisenau* where both in Brest at the time.

They had been advised to fly down the east coast of Denmark in order to reach the target. By doing this, they were assured, they would avoid the flak. This proved to be untrue. Nevertheless, they pressed on and arrived over the docks at their usual height of 11,000 feet.

As they lined up for their bombing run, a searchlight caught them in its beam. Within a fraction of time this column of intense light was joined by two others of equal brilliance. They had been caught in a dreaded cone. Leslie, blinded, lay in the bomb-aimer's position in the transparent nose. In seconds the flak was hitting them, badly damaging their port wing. John pushed the stick forward and sent the bomber into a steep dive. The altimeter spun in reverse as they fell away from the searchlights and flak. Pulling out of the dive must have been too much for the weakened wing. It failed to support the aircraft, still loaded with bombs. Moments later they crashed.

Leslie remembers struggling to his hands and knees and crawling out through a gap in the side of the Hampden. He could hear groans coming from both John and Ginger. John had broken his back, while Ginger was in agony from a terrible head wound. Kiwi, in the lower gun position, was dead. He had probably been killed by flak before hitting the ground. Miraculously, although in the most vulnerable part of the aircraft, Leslie had escaped with no more than a sprained ankle and a scratch on his nose.

Within a few moments some Luftwaffe soldiers from a nearby anti-aircraft site arrived on the scene. In a state of shock, Leslie called to them in the only words of German that he knew: *'Dein icht mein ganzes herz!'* . . . 'You are my heart's delight!' The Germans laughed and treated the three survivors with consideration. The lives of both John Graham and Ginger Hughes were saved by skilled surgery carried out in Lübeck hospital. Leslie Biddlecombe became a prisoner of war for nearly four years.

The Bomber Command War Diaries mention the reactions of some German military veterans from the First World War who witnessed that raid on Kiel. They said that the flak barrage was so intense, it reminded them of the Western Front offensives of 1914–1918.

It is certain that young men who volunteered for flying duties during that period and were assigned to bombers suffered from inadequate and hurried training that fell far short of proper preparation for their onerous tasks. Newly qualified pilots were used, certainly when flying in Hampdens, in a capacity for which they were only minimally prepared – that is as navigators, while in Whitleys or Wellingtons, where the second pilot took over the controls from time to time, they were still wastefully underemployed.

It was illogical for pilots to be paired in aircraft that could only carry a small bomb load. In the later stages of the bomber offensive a single unmodified Lancaster, flown by one pilot and a crew of six, could carry up to 18,000 lbs of bombs. In order to lift that same load it would have required twelve Hampdens with combined crews totalling forty-eight airmen, *twenty-four of them qualified pilots*. In current terminology – hardly cost-effective!

True comparison between the earlier days of Bomber Command's operations and those that followed later in the war is barely possible anyway. A given weight of bombs dropped in 1944 did infinitely more damage than a comparable weight dropped in 1941. In the beginning RAF bombs were of such inferior construction that the explosive element accounted for little more than a quarter of their weight, the difference being made up of heavy metal casing. The Amatol explosive, used by the British since World War One, was not nearly so effective as that employed by the Germans, who, in any case, packed twice as much explosive into their bombs.

33

The crowning irony was that aircrew were expected to throw away their lives while fighting, not only with inefficient weapons, but with ones that were often defective. A large percentage of those early bombs failed to explode on impact.

Added to this, as we have seen, was the frequent failure of crews to find their targets through lack of navigation aids. Even if the target was found, the chances of hitting it were reduced because of antiquated bomb-sights. Is it fair to assume, then, that the campaign in those early days was a pitiful waste of time? Nothing could be further from the truth. Without the fortitude and bravery of men such as Flight Sergeant (later Warrant Officer) Leslie Biddlecombe, the massive bombing offensive of the future could never have come about. It was the pioneering spirit of these early volunteers that laid the foundations for what was to come – an onslaught on the enemy such as the world had never seen. They showed the world that, in spite of Göring's boast to the contrary, British bombers could range, night after night, far and wide over German territory.

Britain then stood alone, her cities bombed by the Luftwaffe, her home army impotent, her ships at the mercy of U-boats. Only Bomber Command carried the war to Germany. This was done as well as it could be done at the time. The exploits of the young bomber crews gave heart to the British people. Their deeds brought comfort to a nation under siege. Furthermore, they inspired those of us who were to follow.

THREE

The Air Gunner

The professional air gunner emerged as a distinct aircrew category in World War Two. In the previous war a bombing plane's defence was in the hands of the observer who operated under very difficult conditions. For example, in the British B.E.2 he sat in an open cockpit in front of the pilot, surrounded by a confusion of struts and wires, while the engine limited his field of fire immediately ahead. Flying suits were, of course, unheated and the intense cold not only affected the physical efficiency of the men, but also caused stoppages in their guns when the lubrication systems froze.

By the outbreak of the Second World War the RAF had developed the power-operated turret. It was then best utilized in the Vickers Wellington which mounted two .303 Browning machine guns in a nose turret, and four .303 Browning machine guns in the tail turret. Later, beam guns were added to frustrate side-on attacks. After the development of the four-engine 'heavies' the mid-upper turret became standard additional defensive equipment. Later we shall see how the Americans brought the 'art' of air gunnery to its ultimate peak, when, in daylight skies over occupied Europe, their aptly named Fortresses and Liberators fought their way through to the target in spite of the fiercest opposition from cannon and rocket-firing Luftwaffe fighters.

At first air gunners were usually of low rank, often no more than LAC. Soon, however, the minimum rank, as for all aircrew, was established as Sergeant. It was possible for a volunteer air gunner to reach operational squadron service more quickly than in any other flying category. The actual gunnery course took only six weeks. It was said, with some justification, that the rear gunner occupied the most dangerous position in the plane. It was certainly the loneliest, and the coldest. Yet occasionally it was an advantage to be situated aft; as Reg Scarth discovered – on two occasions.

Tough, restless and stocky, with a clipped northern accent, Reg Scarth finally hauled himself into the rear turret of a Vickers Wellington in 1943. He went an unusually roundabout way to get there. But for his determination to fly, he might well have remained as an administrator in the RAF.

Having volunteered for aircrew duties, he should have finished up as a pilot, which was what he was selected for. In fact he almost certainly would have become a pilot if it had not been for his stockiness. Then he could have trained as a navigator, but his restlessness got in the way of that. Instead, Reg became an air gunner, for which his toughness suited him well. Eventually he attained the rank of Squadron Leader.

Reg was born in Osset, Yorkshire, on 15 September, 1922, and joined the RAF as an apprentice in July, 1938, shortly before his 16th birthday. He was posted to Ruislip where he trained in the Records Office. He qualified in September, 1939, the month Britain and France declared war on Germany, and began work as an RAF clerk at Church Fenton.

It was not very long before restlessness set in. Volunteering for duties overseas, he expected to finish up in France like most other servicemen at that period of the war. Instead he was posted to Rhodesia. Life was pleasant enough – good climate, a full social life, and plenty of sport. By 1942 he had been promoted Sergeant.

In South-East Africa the war seemed a long way off. It was this that worried him more and more as time went by. Reading between the lines in newspaper and radio reports, he felt certain there must be a serious shortage of aircrew back in England. Yet there he was living in safety and comfort in a billet remote from the war. So he volunteered for flying duties. As a veteran of four years standing in the RAF, he sailed through his initial training, being excused much of what the raw recruits had to undergo.

At EFTS he thoroughly enjoyed himself learning the basics of flying in tiny De Havilland Tiger Moths. These delightful little biplanes were like machines from a bygone age. They could be spun and stalled with impunity, and however much pupils mistreated them, their wood and canvas construction nearly always stood up to the strain. Reg was convinced he had found his vocation – he was a natural pilot. But when he reached SFTS at

Cranborne, near Salisbury (now Harare) he was faced with one of the most frustrating situations of his life. Here the advanced training aircraft were rugged North American Harvards. Built on a much more generous scale than the diminutive Tiger Moth, they were also very noisy, with large, 'ungeared', single radial engines.

Reg was convinced he could handle the Harvard, or any other aircraft for that matter. Eagerly he strode out to the flights alongside his instructor. Full of enthusiasm he hauled himself up the metal side of the fuselage, stepped over the lip of the cockpit and sank out of sight into its depths. To his dismay, at 5 feet 4 inches, his head was below the level of the windscreen. He was unable to see out. Even worse than that, the rudder bar was beyond the reach of his feet!

For a moment his chagrin knew no bounds. He cursed all idiot aircraft designers who based their cockpit dimensions on the measurements of giant Texans. Then his mind raced – seeking a solution. Explaining the problem to his sympathetic instructor, he rushed off to the Sergeants' Mess and grabbed a couple of cushions. Returning to the Harvard, he placed one behind his back to move himself forward towards the pedals, and then sat on the other which he placed underneath his parachute. 'All right now,' he assured the pilot, 'Let's go!'

But it was not all right. It proved quite impractical to try to control the aircraft in an efficient manner when perched so precariously. Those in authority were very sorry; they admired this man who had voluntarily forfeited a safe post in order to go to war. They did their best to allay his bitter disappointment, and offered him a variety of alternatives: either to join a long queue of cadets waiting to complete their pilot training on Oxfords – aircraft in which the seats were adjustable, and where the pilot sat in a cabin with all-round visibility, rather than a small confined cockpit, or train as a navigator, or forget the whole thing and return to his ground trade as an administrator.

Reg had made up his mind to fight in the air in some capacity, so his answer to the last alternative was a brief, 'No thanks.' Yet he knew for sure that the other two offers would lead to delays and extended periods of further training. Navigators particularly, unlike in the earlier years, were now receiving a long and compre-

hensive course. The war might well be over by the time he qualified.

After a moment's thought, he asked: 'Any vacancies for air
gunners?'

'Always.'

'How long to wait?'

'Immediate acceptance.'

'Duration of course?'

'Six weeks.'

'That's for me,' said Reg.

His erstwhile mates safely back in the office must have found
his behaviour quite incomprehensible. Reg, on the other hand,
was perfectly happy to be moving positively in the direction he
wanted to go – back to England to see some action.

Gunnery School at Gwelo Moffat was stimulating enough.
Flying in Oxfords fitted with turrets, he blasted away at drogues,
long sausage-shaped canvas objects towed by intrepid airmen in
airborne tugs. He studied the mysteries of 'deflection', dismantled
Browning .303 machine guns, and re-assembled them until he
could do it in his sleep. He fired at targets on the ground and
studied film of fighters approaching from all conceivable angles.
Mentally he absorbed the shapes of models, representing friendly
and enemy planes, which hung from the ceilings of every classroom.

After the six-week intensive course he had qualified. Proudly
sporting his new air gunner's brevet above his left breast pocket,
a single silvery-white wing and the letters AG surrounded by a
laurel wreath, he arrived in Cape Town, South Africa. He was
billeted in a vast transit camp crammed full of servicemen waiting to board ships bound for many destinations. There were
two parades each day at 8am and 6pm. After roll call the names
of those who were to sail that afternoon, or the following morning, would be read out.

Reg, who had found himself a girlfriend, soon became fed up
with this monotonous routine. He got into the habit of staying
overnight at the girl's home on the other side of town. After all it
was safer – he might well have been mugged returning to camp

38

late at night! Each morning and evening he telephoned the camp for the latest shipping news.

When his turn did come it was actually his girl, working in a shop, who first broke the news. She told him he would be embarking on the troopship *Staffordshire* the following day. So much for wartime security in Cape Town.

But no one had told him where he was going. He assumed, and hoped, that the voyage would end in an English port, but having experienced the vagaries of posting procedures during his years in 'admin', he was prepared for anything, or almost anything. What actually happened was outside his wildest speculations.

Reg's group was made up of forty aircrew, all senior NCOs. These airmen had learned their specialized skills at great expense to the British taxpayer. Even in those days it cost thousands of pounds to train a flyer in any category. The idea was that, once they were qualified, they should then fight the enemy in the air.

So how were they employed? As soon as the *Staffordshire* put to sea they were signed on ship's articles to carry out 'trooping' duties. This involved calling at small ports along the West African coast collecting native 'troops'. The military knowledge that had been imparted to these unfortunate blacks was limited. They had been told from which end of a rifle the bullet emerged, and very little else. They had not the remotest idea who the enemy was, and their desire to fight anyone was less than enthusiastic.

This unhappy complement of 'passengers' was shipped up to Freetown and disembarked. Then Reg and his boys sailed back for more 'recruits'.

He celebrated his 20th birthday on 15 September, 1942, in Lagos. Having regard for his years of service in the RAF, he was the senior man of his group. Occasionally he had to act as policeman, both on and off the ship. Once, with an Askari escort he went ashore to round up 150 native deserters. After scouring several unsavoury locations he returned to the *Staffordshire* with a handful of deserters. Unfortunately, the compliment of prisoners was outweighed by the number of escorting troops who had disappeared!

Another time, perhaps not surprisingly, three of his fellow aircrew sergeants had gone ashore and got drunk. They were reported to be causing a disturbance in a hotel and Reg was detailed to bring them back to the ship. With a revolver strapped to his waist he strode into the hotel, determined to restore peace and order. At that moment the local Gendarmerie arrived. Mistaken for one of the revellers, Reg received a smack on the back of the head from a truncheon. He woke up later in a gaol from which he was released the following day.

Matters came to a head when they again docked in Freetown with another two or three thousand troops. Orders were issued to take the troops north to Bathurst, in readiness for an assault on the German U-boat base at Dakar. Reg, with the wholehearted support of his comrades, felt the time had arrived to lodge an official complaint.

He explained to a Flight Lieutenant that he, and many of the others, had been in Africa for two and a half years. They had trained to do a job that would help Britain's war effort, yet their services were not being utilized in a proper manner. The effect of this protest was dramatic. Coded signals sped back and forth between RAF Freetown and the Air Ministry in London. An indignant Group Captain came on board.

'This is all wrong,' he protested. 'You boys are desperately needed back home. They are crying out for aircrew. Why the hell are you wasting your time here?'

It had worked! In double quick time they were ferried from the *Staffordshire* to the SS *Orion,* a one-time P&O luxury cruise liner. Within the hour the small contingent of flyers had set sail for England with an escort of eight warships.

Reg was impressed by the promptness in which matters had been arranged. Especially comforting was the presence of their formidable naval protectors, who ranged around them like watchful sea-dogs. His astonishment, therefore, was all the greater when one morning he woke to find the 'navy' had disappeared. The warships had 'turned right' into the Mediterranean, leaving the *Orion* to face the troubled 'home waters' alone.

They rounded the northern coast of Ireland in a tremendous gale. At one point a large four-engine aircraft was spotted. A high ranking 'brown job' [RAF term for an army type] called to everyone within hearing, 'It's all right, it's a "friendly"!' Reg, who

40

knew better, headed for the nearest machine gun. The Focke Wulf Kondor flew over the liner at a safe height and dropped one small bomb. It splashed into the sea, missing them by about 200 yards.

Within hours they had docked in Liverpool and were soon away on disembarkation leave. After this Reg was sent to 15 OTU at Harwell. Flying under training as rear gunner in Wellingtons, fate intervened before he really had a chance to get to know his new crew. Taking part in a cross-country exercise, the bomber, for some unknown reason, began to lose height rapidly. The bomb aimer, bracing his feet against the instrument panel, assisted the pilot in heaving back on the control column. To the relief of the crew an airfield was spotted through the darkness. Attempts to contact the control tower on R/T met with no response. However, someone on the ground was operating an Aldis signal lamp. It was flashing a welcoming 'Green'. With the Wellington behaving unpredictably they wasted no time in preparing to land.

Unknown to them, the airfield was at that time in use for training glider pilots. They were learning to fly the giant troop-carrying Horsas which were constructed almost entirely of wood.

Invisible without identification lights, a Horsa was coming in to land at that precise moment. The green ground-light was flashing for *its* benefit. Reg's bomber was immediately overhead, the crew unaware of the glider's presence. At about 150 feet the Wellington crashed down on to the Horsa.

The Horsa disintegrated in a flurry of flying wood splinters, the impact killing both the glider pilot and his pupil. The Wellington hit the concrete with tremendous force, slewed off the runway, crushing a Jeep and injuring its driver. Every member of Reg's crew, the bomb aimer, pilot, navigator and wireless/operator, was injured. Only Reg, in his rear turret, escaped unhurt. Facing backwards, he had felt the initial impact when the bomber hit the glider. Believing they had landed, he relaxed completely. It was this lack of tension, he believed, that saved him from injury when they hit the ground.

In the well-proved RAF tradition Reg was detailed for flying again almost immediately – this time joining a crew made up mostly of Canadians. He was pleased to discover that his skipper, Squadron Leader Piddington, was an experienced pilot about to return for his second tour of operations. It was good luck, he thought, to team up with a man who had flown so many times against the enemy. A surer guarantee of survival than flying with a 'sprog' pilot, anyway.

Back on night cross-country training flights, it was not long before Reg had a bit more excitement. Crews had been warned to keep an eye open for enemy night intruders – the all-too-potent, twin-engine Junkers 88. On this particular night they were flying over the Bristol/Taunton area when a twin-engine fighter suddenly dived at them. It did not fire, but as it broke away Reg raked its belly with his four Brownings.

On landing back at base all hell was let loose. The attacking aircraft had not been a Ju88, but a 'friendly' night fighter – a Bristol Beaufighter. The shaken pilot landed at his squadron and filed his report immediately. Angry messages were exchanged between Fighter Command and Bomber Command. Each blamed the other for the incident. In the end Reg was exonerated. It was established that the fighter pilot was guilty of an error of judgement in swooping in at night on an RAF bomber – especially the easily identifiable 'Wimpey', with its characteristic 'Wellington boot' silhouette.

Most OTUs were now equipped with Wellingtons, on which crews came together for the first time. This gave them an opportunity to work as a team – practising by day and night on cross-country navigation and wireless exercises, fighter affiliation, circuits and 'bumps', and, on the ground, ditching and crash procedures. Meanwhile specialist flight leaders continued to polish up aircrew's skills within their particular categories, either on the turret firing ranges, in the signals cabin, or at the flight, bombing and navigation simulators.

By this time, with the bomber offensive building in strength and effectiveness, and with the new four-engine bombers taking over more and more from the earlier two-engine types, an extra phase had been introduced into aircrew training. This was the establishment of HCUs – Heavy Conversion Units, in which crews converted to four-engine aircraft.

They also took two additional members on to the team, a flight engineer to look after the increased demands imposed by the extra

42

machinery, and a second gunner to man the mid-upper turret. Unpardonably, the extra turret, in common with that at the rear on these new generation 'heavies', sprouted nothing more effective than the derisory .303 with which RAF bomber crews had tried to defend themselves since the start of the war, and which would remain as their sole protection until the end. How many bomber crew lives could have been saved, given adequate defensive fire-power, can never be estimated.

Arriving at the RAF's HCU at Topcliffe, after completing their course at Harwell, Squadron Leader Piddington's crew converted on to the four-engine Handley Page Halifax. It was, of course, considerably bigger than anything they had flown before, but as Reg remarked at the time, 'The gunners still sit in their turrets, the navigator at his desk, the wireless operator in front of his radio, the "driver" behind his controls, the bomb aimer stretched out in the nose. The only real difference is that we now have an extra "bod", the engineer, to help keep us up in the air – and, we all have a bit more room!'

Not unexpectedly they finished up in a Halifax Squadron – a Canadian one. 427 (Lion) Squadron was stationed at Leeming in Yorkshire and had recently converted from Wellingtons to Hali-faxes. By the end of the war no squadron in 6 Group had carried out more raids. The squadron was rather pleased with itself because it had been 'adopted' by MGM Studios in Hollywood. One star in particular, Greer Garson of *Mrs Miniver* fame, kept in close contact with them, sending letters and food parcels at regular intervals.

They completed a few operations without serious incident, but had an unusual experience when returning from Düsseldorf on the night of 11/12 June, 1943. A large raid this, and the first in which more than 200 Halifaxes had taken part. Suddenly they were attacked by a Messerschmitt 109. It was the usual situation – an agile fighter, armed with lethal 20 mm cannon, against a lumbering bomber whose guns, as often as not, lacked the range even to reach the fighter, let alone cause it damage.

There was only one defence – to 'corkscrew' out of danger. Reg had that moment shouted over the intercom telling his skipper to do just that when an amazing thing happened. A burst of tracer hosed out of the blackness towards the Messerschmitt and sent it plummeting towards the earth. For a bare instant Reg spotted the aircraft that had come to their rescue – a twin-engined, well-proportioned aircraft with pointed wings and a single fin. He recognized it at once. It was the incredibly fast RAF De Havilland Mosquito out on night intruder patrol. Its task was to seek out and destroy enemy fighters over Germany. But to do this at the very instant when the fighter was attacking a bomber must have been rare indeed. After that Reg was convinced they were a lucky crew!

Shortly after this, their skipper was promoted to Wing Commander and sent as CO, with his crew, to 429 [Bison] Squadron, another Canadian unit. Here they were in the process of changing over to Halifaxes from Wellingtons, one of the last in 6 Group to do so. By the time the transfer of aircraft had been completed they would have lost more Wellingtons on operations than any other squadron in the Group.

The Wellington had almost run its honourable course with Bomber Command. By October, 1943, it would have flown its final major operation in Europe. During its long tour of duty since the beginning of the war the 'Wimpey' had clocked up more sorties than those flown by Whitleys, Hampdens, the unfortunate Stirlings and the ill-fated Manchesters all added together.

The deal for Piddington, the new CO of 429, was that he should return to flying Wellingtons until the conversion to the larger aircraft had been completed. After this, he and his crew, if they survived, would go back to flying Halifaxes. Morale in 429 had been shaken at that time. The squadron had lost three COs in the previous eight weeks. Wing Commander Piddington was ordered to restrict his personal trips to the minimum.

Air Chief Marshal Sir Arthur Harris had taken over as the chief of Bomber Command in February of the previous year, when the numerical strength in aircraft had been little more than it was at the outbreak of war. During 1942 he had nurtured and expanded his force until now, in 1943, he felt in a position to mount a series of powerful 'battles'. From March until July, he had concentrated his main blows against the Ruhr – Germany's vast industrial area, made up of many towns in the country's mid-west. This heavily

44

defended part of the Fatherland was known to the bomber crews as 'Happy Valley'.

Reg and his crew had carried out most of their raids so far over 'Happy Valley'. Now, in late July, Harris launched his 'Battle of Hamburg', a devastating series of attacks on Europe's biggest port and Germany's second largest city, housing one and three-quarter million people. It was planned to complete the operation in a concentration of four heavy raids spread over ten days. The new CO of 429 decided to fly with his crew on the second of these missions – on 27/28 July, 1943.

At briefing, Piddington pointed out the importance of the raid, the large number of aircraft taking part and, because of this, the need to maintain strict flying discipline within the bomber stream. He stressed how vital it was to stick to the timings that had been set down.

On a cheering note he emphasised the success of 'Window', a radar counter-measure which had been used for the first time three nights previously over Hamburg. 'Window' consisted of metallic strips which, when dropped in thousands from the bombers, completely foxed the enemy's defences, both on the ground and in the air. AA guns, searchlights, and night fighters became 'blind'. The radar screens from which these defences had previously been directed were now blotted out by clouds of tinsel.

But for the timid argument that this device could have been turned round by the Germans and used in raids against Britain, (hardly a major threat with the Luftwaffe's bombers fully engaged in Russia) 'Window' could have been employed by Bomber Command as long ago as April of the previous year. It has been estimated that 'Window' saved 100–130 RAF bombers, a minimum of 700 aircrew, during those ten nights of the 'Battle of Hamburg'.

All of which makes what follows particularly ironical. Piddington's crew were lucky in having an especially fine Wellington. Aircraft, like people, varied enormously in the way they behaved, even among the same type. The CO's 'Wimpey' must have been about the fastest ever built. In spite of his warnings to the squadron to maintain strict timing, they arrived over the target early. Fully aware of the dangers of orbiting Hamburg, the CO decided to start his bombing run without delay.

Reg, ever watchful in his rear turret, guns swinging up and down, port and starboard, spotted an Me 109 with its navigation lights switched on on the starboard beam. As he opened fire the fighter's companion, unnoticed, came in dead astern and blasted the Wellington without mercy. It was a clever trick which sent the bomber reeling towards the ground with no hope of recovery.

They had become victims of the new tactics forced on the Luftwaffe by the introduction of 'Window'. *Wilde Sau* [Wild Boar] was the code name for freelance single-seater fighters now given their head to seek out and destroy the bombers without assistance from radar.

After a moment's struggle, Reg slid open the doors of the turret. Grabbing inside the fuselage, he hauled his 'chute from the rack, dragging it round and slamming it onto his chest harness. The hydraulics were out of action. Sweating in spite of the cold, he rotated the turret by hand and fell out backwards into space.

How long he was unconscious he does not know. When he woke up, he was drifting through the night spinning gently. In his haste to leave the aircraft he had not realized that only one hook of his harness was attached to the parachute, which was why he was rotating.

There were several other things that he did not know at the time. One was that this attack on Hamburg was the most devastating raid to date, at least forty thousand citizens meeting their deaths in the terrifying firestorm that ensued. Nor did he know that, apart from himself and the wireless operator, the rest of the crew had been killed.

He drifted down some way to the north of Hamburg, landing in the middle of a decoy area – a system of shallow channels that the Germans filled with kerosene and set on fire to simulate a target. Fortunately for Reg it was not being used that night. After hiding his 'chute, cutting off the tops of his flying boots and checking through his escape kit, he started heading north by north-west hoping to reach Denmark. He was already suffering from one frustration; the escape kit contained all the usual aids: water purifying tablets, Horlicks tablets, benzedrine tablets, compass,

46

mini-razor, and of course the exquisitely printed silk maps. But the maps were useless. They only showed the Franco/Spanish border area!

As he was trudging over Luneburg Heath an amazing thing happened. He had been hopping from tuft to tuft avoiding the boggy ground. At one point his foot slipped into the mire. Bending down to extricate himself, he noticed a sealed buff envelope lying in the grass. Tearing it open, he found it contained an RAF map of the location through which he was then travelling! He has spent the rest of his life trying to puzzle out how it got there.

Walking only by night, hiding and resting by day, eating fruit, potatoes, turnips and broad beans, he drank as much milk as he needed from the churns placed conveniently at the entrances to farm lanes. Soon he reached the broad Kiel Ship Canal. Sitting down on a bank he watched the shipping – U-boats, merchantmen, naval vessels of various kinds including an E-boat that passed quite close to him. Reg gave the crew a friendly wave and they waved back. The fact that he was wearing RAF battledress, an air gunner's brevet, and Flight Sergeant's tapes and crown on his sleeves did not seem to strike any of the Germans as unusual. The blue-grey uniform was probably enough to create a satisfactory overall image.

As dusk fell he started to walk along the towpath. In the distance he could see a large bridge spanning the canal, but could also make out the silhouettes of sentries patrolling it. Between him and the bridge a ship was moored. Dodging behind a bush, he lay down to think things over. After a while there was the sound of people approaching, but from opposite directions. The two sets of footsteps came to a halt in front of his hiding place. They belonged to a couple of sentries who had met for a chat and a smoke. The meeting went on interminably, and Reg, weary beyond words, especially German words, fell fast asleep. When he awoke, dawn was breaking and the sentries had gone. The throb of the ship's engines broke into his consciousness and he hurried along the path. It was an awful moment. The ship, already clear of the bank, was gathering speed; flying from her stern was the flag of neutral Sweden.

Disconsolately he retracted his steps. Narrowly avoiding a set-to with a bull by diving through a hedge, he finished up at a small railway station called Goebbels. There was a goods train waiting at the platform so he smuggled himself into one of the sentry-box-like cabins that were attached to the back of the wagons. Before long the train chugged off and did not stop until it reached the small town of Hohenwestedt.

Here, unfortunately, a girl porter opened the door of his hideaway and discovered him huddled on the floor. As she rushed off to raise the alarm Reg ran out of the station and into the town. He was some way along the High Street when the station staff caught up with him and escorted him back to the station master's office. Soon they were joined by a little policeman in a spiked helmet, and the local schoolmaster who acted as interpreter. They treated him respectfully enough, and, although insisting that he turn out his pockets, found nothing of significance, not even the steel file concealed in his tobacco pouch.

Taken to the town jail, he was left on his own. Removing a metal door from a small stove in the corner of the cell, Reg used it as a tool to hack away at the plaster on the outside wall. By about 11 o'clock that night he had succeeded in gouging out a reasonably large hole in the inner brickwork, but then he heard footsteps in the corridor outside. It was the female porter. She had brought him black bread, jam, and a mug of coffee. Suddenly, as they heard more footsteps outside, the girl dived into the blanket cupboard taking the supper with her. A man entered the cell, carrying an identical meal. He was in a friendly, chatty mood and sat with Reg while he ate his food. 'You know,' the German said, 'You should not have dropped any bombs on Hamburg, you should drop them all on Berlin instead!'

After he had gone, the girl came out of the cupboard and handed Reg his second supper. What she thought of her fellow countryman's remarks would never be known. After his double ration, he gave up on the brickwork and fell asleep. Next morning he woke to the sound of 'Raus! Raus!' It was yesterday's friendly policeman who appeared to have had a personality change, shouting, gesticulating, and shoving him out into the corridor. Then he realized that the show was for the benefit of two Luftwaffe guards who had come to collect him.

As he went down the police station steps he felt a heavy boot in his back to help him on his way. This time it was one of the guards. They bundled him into a car. As it sped away, the man who had kicked him apologised for his behaviour, and said, 'I'm sorry but we have to put on a performance for the locals!' Reg had remained at liberty for the best part of a month, and during the fighter attack had sustained wounds to his face and head. The Luftwaffe cleaned him up and gave him proper medical attention, including the removal of several bits of shrapnel. After this he was put on a train heading south.

At Luneburg there was a delay. On the platform a Red Cross canteen had been set up and he and his escort helped themselves to coffee. One of the helpers turned out to be an English woman who was married to a German. She was hungry for news about Britain. All she had heard for nearly four years was Nazi propaganda in the German press. Reg was happy to assure her that her country was not a heap of rubble, the people were far from starving and the allies were well on the way to winning the war.

At Dulag Luft, near Frankfurt-am-Main, he felt as if he was taking part in an RAF training film. His interrogators were classic examples of all that he had been warned about. First the 'friendly' type asking for information 'on behalf of the Red Cross'. 'It is necessary to know these things so your poor parents' minds can be put at rest.' Then the bullyboy: 'We can find no evidence that you are an RAF flyer. Unless you can give us details about your squadron, we shall have you shot as a spy.' Reg knew this was all bluff, at least he hoped it was and that his persecutor had 'read the script'!

Having surmounted the first two hurdles, he now looked forward to the concluding part of the 'film', where unsuspecting aircrew were wined and dined and had glamorous female company lavished on them as part of a softening-up process. To Reg's disappointment the last 'reel' must have been lost, and he never received what he considered to be his just reward for keeping his trap shut.

In the company of about seventy other aircrew, he was sent to Stalag 4B at Muhlburg, near Leipzig. This camp, which was in a filthy state, had been occupied by French, Belgian and Slav

49

prisoners. As soon as the RAF contingent arrived they created hell and the place was cleaned up. Within a very short time the camp was properly organized, with arrangements for football, theatre, bridge, chess, and many other group activities, including, of course, an escape committee. Several escapes were made, but most were unsuccessful, the absconders being brought back to camp within two days. A few of the escapees were never seen again.

Reg made his attempted break for freedom at the beginning of June, 1944. A group of prisoners were going to break out over the 'wire' at night. He and his friend Bob were about 50 yards behind the leading escapees when someone fell over the trip wire. This set off the alarm and within moments there was pandemonium with guard dogs howling and Germans yelling and running in all directions. Fortunately for Reg and Bob they managed to scurry back to their hut undetected and so avoided an uncomfortable session in the 'slammer'.

In September a contingent of paratroops captured after Arnhem, arrived in transit. Reg, Bob and a Cornishman named Jack Pauly swapped identities with three of the paras. This was to enable the flyers to get out of the camp on working parties. At the main gate they were interrogated and Jack's true identity was discovered, but his two companions got away with their masquerade. Sent to Kemlitz, they were then split up and served in working parties on opposite sides of the town. Reg was with eight paratroopers and, because he was an experienced 'Kriegie' and by now reasonably fluent in German, they elected him their 'Confidence Man'.

Their place of work, a chemical factory, was situated about half an hour from the billet. To impress the Germans, Reg and his commando always marched with absolute precision on their way to and from the factory. Their task was to load trucks standing at railway sidings alongside the works. It presented a golden opportunity to sabotage the system. The paras simply swapped the destination labels on the wagons – what should have gone east went west and vice versa. It took the authorities the best part of two months to discover the cause of the chaos.

The Stabsfeldwebel in charge was a singularly decent man. For instance he allowed them to listen to the English news on his

50

radio. In his wisdom, while letting them remain in the same billet, he sent Reg and the paras to work in a timber mill about eight miles away at Rersdorf. They travelled there each day, leaving at 6.30 am, on a train packed with foreign workers. The saw mill was the next target for sabotage. The paras slaved away, piling the wood into the works at such a rate that eventually they seized up the giant flywheels, and broke the thick pulley belts. Production was brought to a standstill for over two days.

This incurred not only the extreme displeasure of the Germans, but also upset some of the long-term POWs who, until the arrival of Reg and his paras, had looked on employment in the mill as a comparatively cushy number. However, the efforts of the commando were considerably augmented when a Flying Fortress unloaded its bombs on the mill shortly afterwards. Reg, lying flat on the ground, was shaken by the explosions and the huge logs flying through the air in all directions. About 20% of the bombs were delayed action and these continued to go off over the following two days.

One Unteroffizier had a particular loathing for Reg and his men. Work was scheduled to stop at 7 pm, but on this occasion he kept them at it well into the night. The commandos made sure that the ice-encrusted baulks of timber were dumped in a position that completely blocked the only exit for the train. The next day the Unteroffizier threatened to send Reg to Buchenwald – a name which meant nothing to him at the time.

The 'incorrigibles' were taken to HQ at Stalag 4F for close interrogation. Although this turned out to be a wasted exercise for the Germans, a finger-printing session was much more revealing. As soon as Reg's dabs were on the sheet it was a case of 'Who are you?' It was established that he was certainly not Private R. O'Brian of the Paratroops, but definitely was Flight Sergeant R. Scarth of the RAF. He wondered if this time he had pushed his luck too far.

Next morning Reg lay in his bed and refused to join the working party. When the Unteroffizier came storming in demanding that he report for duty, Reg told him, 'I am a Flight Sergeant, and as you are aware, because of my rank the Geneva Convention absolves me from working for the enemy.' In a fury the officer drew his revolver – 'I will count up to 5. If you are not outside by then, I shall shoot you!' 'If you do,' replied Reg, 'then you will have my friends to reckon with.' The German glanced over his shoulder and saw eight grim-faced paratroops standing in a row behind him. He flounced out of the hut re-holstering his gun.

One of the paras stayed behind to keep an eye on Reg while the others went back to work. In the afternoon two stony-eyed SS troopers came and collected him and took him back to HQ. He was confronted by the CO, an Austrian Captain who, in the past, had been pleased to trade certain German commodities which Reg and the others needed in exchange for the English cigarettes. The Captain thought the best thing he could do for his 'problem' prisoner was to get him back to his original camp as quickly as possible, before less amiable people started to shape his future. So Reg returned to Stalag 4B and spent 28 days in the 'slammer'. Eventually, the POWs were liberated by the advancing Russians.

During the period when Reg had been masquerading as para-trooper Bob O'Brian, who was a married man, he had thought it expedient to invent a wife for himself. Five years previously he had met a girl in Leeds called Peggy and, although they had not seen each other since 1939, they had kept up a correspondence even during his time as a POW. She must have been surprised to receive a letter, in Reg's familiar handwriting, addressed to Mrs O'Brian, starting 'My Darling Wife', and signed, 'Your adoring husband, Bob'.

She contacted the Red Cross people who soon put two and two together. They surmised that Flight Sergeant Scarth had changed his identity for a definite purpose, probably in an attempt to escape. Peggy, who had no idea where Reg's parents lived, carried out some clever detective work and traced them to their home village of Tingly in Yorkshire. Reg had been writing to them as Uncle Fred and Auntie Marian. Soon, unknown to Reg of course, Peggy was visiting his parents regularly – they had become firm friends and were naturally drawn together by a mutual bond.

When Reg came home after the war he was astonished to find that Peggy had her feet tucked firmly under his parents' table. They were married soon afterwards!

FOUR

The Flight Engineer

There was nothing complicated about the two-engine RAF bombers flying at the beginning of the war. A competent pilot had no difficulty in keeping an eye on the limited number of instruments arrayed before him and would quickly spot any indications of trouble. But if, for example, he failed to notice a drop in oil pressure, then it was likely that his 'second dickie', his co-pilot, would speedily draw his attention to the fault, except in the case of the Hampden, where, as we have already seen, the second pilot was isolated below his skipper's feet, busy with navigation!

With the advent of the true 'heavy' bombers, the four-engine Stirlings, Halifaxes and Lancasters, a new era of technical complexity had arrived. In these much bigger, more sophisticated machines an array of panels, one for each of the engines, was covered in a confusing collection of dials and switches and warning lights, all needing to be watched every moment that the aircraft was in the air. These were in addition to the normal flying instruments and were set in a position away from the pilot's line of vision. At this time it had also been decided to abolish the role of second pilot.

Obviously an extra member of the bomber team was needed to take care of these increased responsibilities. So it was that the Flight Engineer was introduced. Pilots, bomb aimers, navigators, wireless operators and gunners were, by and large, all trained in their flying duties from scratch after volunteering from civilian life. But the flight engineer was more likely to have been in the RAF already, having served an apprenticeship in one of the engineering trades. Because of this he was usually the only 'regular', or career serviceman, in the crew. Yet, just like the others, he too would have volunteered to fly. Such a volunteer was John Roberts.

53

One of my most memorable days at school was when we travelled on an outing by bus to Southampton waters. Apart from gawping in amazement at all the giant ocean liners, including the magnificent *Queen Mary*, we also visited the RAF seaplane base at Calshot, in the Solent. I did not know, as I admired the swan-like outline of a Short Bros Singapore flying boat drawn up on the concrete slipway, that there was a young RAF apprentice named John Roberts at work on the 560 hp Rolls-Royce Kestrel engines that powered those beautiful 'boats'. There was not much difference in our ages, and, if I had known him then, I am sure I would have envied him.

John Roberts was born on 10 September, 1922, at Clacton-on-Sea, after his father's ill health had obliged the family to move there from London. Mr Roberts had suffered terribly on the Somme during the First World War – he had been gassed, sustained a hole in his head from a shrapnel wound, and was paralysed down one side of his body. Yet, on occasion, father and son would go up to London on a day's outing. On the way they enjoyed watching the brightly coloured biplanes circling overhead. Indeed, John was probably inspired to volunteer for the RAF more through seeing these aircraft than for any other reason, although, at that time, he had no particular desire to actually fly in them.

At the County High School he had been good at chemistry, geography and English. It was the time of Munich and, in spite of Prime Minister Chamberlain's attempts to appease Hitler, a spirit of patriotism was growing among the youngsters of Britain. Like several of the brighter pupils in his class he was accepted into the RAF as a boy apprentice at the age of fifteen. That was in August, 1938.

John soon discovered that his new life at RAF Halton was no sinecure. The pay was minuscule. The discipline bore down on the lads both during working hours and in their leisure time. The apprentices were referred to by the older airmen as 'Trenchard's Brats', after Lord Trenchard, the 'father' of the Royal Air Force. It was he who had fought to retain a service independent from the navy and the army, and who had the foresight to see the value of building a force based on technical skills.

In spite of all, John lapped up the instruction he received. He developed new confidence as his knowledge and competence grew. With the outbreak of war, the apprentices' worth was recognized. They were proud to be known as 'The Brats' – and it became a term synonymous with ability based on sound training. This group, imbued with the 'Air Force Spirit', formed a strong foundation without which the RAF could not have functioned in war.

With the war a new sense of urgency prevailed. The apprenticeship course was shortened by a year. Passing out as a Fitter 2E, John got on with his job of maintaining aero engines, including the Kestrels fitted in tandem to the Singapores. By 1943 he had been promoted to corporal and had developed an ever-increasing itch to fly, so when he saw an Air Ministry memo inviting volunteers for the new aircrew category of flight engineer he applied at once.

His training for the new job bordered on the bizarre. First of all he was posted to St Athan in South Wales. A six-week ground course in the duties of a flight engineer did little more than emphasize the importance of keeping an eye on the petrol gauges when flying in four-engine aircraft. He discovered a Halifax bomber hidden away in a hangar and assumed that, at some stage in the instruction, the pupils would be given a detailed briefing on this aircraft. In fact they never set foot inside the fuselage!

Then he went on a short journey further along the Welsh coast to RAF Pembrey, near Llanelly, for another course, this time in air gunnery. Oddly enough, none of it took place in the air! The embryo flight engineers' gunnery training was limited to practice in Boulton Paul turrets anchored to concrete blocks on the ground. He felt relieved that he was not going to become an air gunner. Cramming his 6 foot 2 inch frame into a Perspex 'bubble' was not far short of purgatory.

Sharing this course were a number of wireless operators and John was amused to find that the engineers were generally better at gunnery than the 'sparks'. He imagined this was because the engineers, used to noisy machinery, were less affected by the racket inside the turrets as the guns were being fired.

Unfortunately an unsympathetic permanent staff at Pembrey, from Station Warrant Officer down, made life unpleasant for the aircrew cadets. This state of affairs existed in a few RAF camps, nearly always the ones furthest removed from war activities. It arose through a sense of grievance that these upstart 'sprogs' were getting more money and quicker promotion than people who had been around for years. The fact that 60% of Bomber Command aircrew became casualties did not, presumably, enter the equation. It never seemed to strike these disgruntled types that they were at perfect liberty to volunteer for flying duties themselves

At Pembrey the staff made certain that, when the day's training had finished, the cadets were kept hanging about long enough to make sure they missed the evening train to Llanelly. Every opportunity was taken to inflict punishment for 'petty crimes'. One of John's pals was confined to camp for a week because he had a shoelace missing during a kit inspection.

Unlike the flight engineers, the wireless operators did receive gunnery practice in the air. To add insult to deprivation, after days of intensive instruction, those cadets who were ex-fitters were ordered to carry out maintenance work on the training aircraft over the weekend. Corporal Roberts' temper finally boiled over.

As senior cadet he ordered the others to down tools and then marched them back to the billet. He had started a mutiny. There were few permanent staff on the camp at the weekend and a lone junior duty officer, for whom John felt quite sorry, pleaded with them not to cause trouble. A compromise was reached. John agreed to call off the 'mutiny', but only on the understanding that there would be no more maintenance work. Nothing further was heard about the incident and the engineers were not instructed to service any more aircraft.

It was with relief that John left Pembrey for the Halifax Heavy Conversion Unit at RAF Marston Moor. He had been awarded his FE aircrew winged brevet and promoted Sergeant although he had still not flown for a single minute! Almost at once he joined a crew and knew, without doubt, that he would be flying within days, if not hours. At last the chance had come to learn something about the aircraft he was supposed to 'take care of' while it was in flight.

Occupied with these pleasurable thoughts, he was sitting in a classroom trying to concentrate on an exercise in mental arithmetic. The door opened and a Squadron Leader came in.

'Chap called Roberts here?'

'Yes, Sir'.

'Right Roberts. On your way. You're posted to a special duty squadron!'

'But, Sir. I've only just arrived here. I've just joined my new crew. I've had no training in the air!'

'Don't worry about that, Sergeant Roberts. You'll get plenty of experience on the squadron!'

And that was that. Within hours he had arrived at 161 Special Duties Squadron, Tempsford, near Cambridge.

161 Squadron had an interesting history. It had been formed in February, 1942, from a nucleus provided by the King's Flight. It operated with a variety of aircraft over the war years, including Whitleys, Halifaxes, Stirlings, Lysanders and Hudsons.

The squadron's duties involved delivering supplies and agents to Resistance units on the Continent. The smaller Hudsons and Lysanders actually landed on fields in enemy-occupied territory to collect agents – a risky business which often resulted in high casualties.

By the time John took up his duties the Whitleys had been withdrawn from service and the Halifaxes were performing the main 'dropping' operations. Stirling 1Vs took over this role in mid '44.

RAF Tempsford was shared by two squadrons. The other, 138, was engaged in similar work, but often operated further afield, even flying as far as Poland. Foreign aircrew were much in evidence on 138 Squadron, particularly Poles and Czechoslovakians. Again, losses were sometimes severe.

It is not difficult to imagine John's bewilderment. When he arrived at his new squadron he knew nothing of the clandestine affairs in which Tempsford was involved. The more questions he asked, the more blank faces he encountered. Security was impressively tight. Later, after he had been on 161 for some time, he realized that even the ground staff working on the aircraft had little idea of the squadron's true function.

The Squadron Leader had been right – experience came fast.

On the day of his arrival he was sent up to perform the flight engineer's role of air-testing a Halifax's engines. The ink had hardly dried in his log book, as he proudly wrote up his very first flight in an aeroplane, before he was ordered up again on a night-test.

The following day his name was among those listed for operations. The interesting thing about John's log book entries is the absence of any target destinations. Only the duration of the flights is recorded with no mention of where they had been. On his first mission, for instance, on 12 May, 1943, there is an entry showing that they flew for just over 7 hours. John remembered this as a longish trip to southern France.

He remembered, also, that he made something of a *faux pas* on this first 'op'. The Halifaxes of 161 had had their mid-upper turrets removed. They had intruded well down into the fuselage amidships taking up too much room. Below this point, a large round hole had been cut in the floor of the aircraft, covered by semi-circular doors. Through this aperture the parachuting agents made their exit. Various items of equipment for the Resistance fighters were also despatched this way – weapons, explosives, torch batteries and even pigeons in boxes, each with their own little parachute.

After leaving the dropping zone, it was customary for the crews to fly on to an area some distance away and then throw out leaflets. By doing this it was hoped that the Germans might be fooled as to the true purpose of their mission. On this night Pilot Officer Affleck, John's new skipper, called over the intercom, 'OK, Robby, time to get back down the kite and chuck out some bits of bumph.' John immediately made his way along the noisy, dark, vibrating, unfamiliar fuselage. He found a large brown paper parcel and unwrapped it. Inside were smaller parcels; these he also unwrapped. Inside each of these were even smaller parcels. When those were unwrapped he discovered they contained blocks of leaflets, rather like brand new banknotes, each bundle neatly tied together with string. Fishing out his penknife he cut all the pieces of string. Then he struggled across to the large hatch-covers over the hole in the floor. As he lifted these lids, in preparation for dispatching the leaflets, an unexpected thing happened. Far from leaving the aircraft, the inrush of air scattered the sheets throughout the interior, covering the occupants in paper. As the

58

wireless operator said later, 'The effect was positively autumnal!' No one had thought to tell John that there was a small chute provided for the purpose of ejecting leaflets. After all, no one would have believed that until the previous day, he had never flown in an aeroplane!

He soon grew to like the Halifax, which, apart from the 'drop hole' and the missing turret, was very little modified from the Main Force bombers. Static lines ran along the interior for the parachutists and there was a fairing over the tailwheel to prevent possible injury to those who jumped. Above all, he developed an admiration for the 1390 hp Merlin XXs which transcended the respect he had held for any other aero engine. As an engineer he rated them near perfect for reliability and performance under all conditions.

161 Squadron carried fewer aircrew because of the specialist nature of the operations. There was no bomb aimer, and only one gunner, in the rear turret. Sometimes, when agents were to be dropped, the crew was joined by a 'despatcher'.

John found the missions fascinating, if decidedly hair-raising. Over the drop zone on a moonlit night it was almost like watching a film – reflections from the wet oilskins worn by the freedom fighters; the occasional flashing torch; the car in the distance with headlights blazing; obviously speeding to the scene – presumably driven by Gestapo.

Seeing rainbows at night amazed and puzzled him. Previously he had always believed this was a scientific impossibility. Glowing red flames in the River Rhône, near Avignon, a reflection from their eight exhausts, two per engine, caused him a great deal of worry and highlighted the aircraft's vulnerability. If the flames were that obvious at cruising speed, he thought, they must show up like blazing beacons with the throttles wide open.

He was lucky to be teamed with a very experienced skipper. The previous year Pilot Officer Affleck had been involved in a dramatic mission to bring out some agents from France. In an attempt to take off from a small field, his Lockheed Hudson had become bogged down in the mud. Luckily Resistance fighters and local gendarmerie, aided by oxen with strong ropes, managed to drag the aircraft free. He became airborne without a moment to spare and so avoided capture by the Germans.

The modus operandi of 161 Squadron was almost the exact opposite from that practised by the rest of Bomber Command. Whereas the Main Stream bombers normally flew high, the higher the better, 161 flew to the dropping zone 'hugging the deck'. This was to avoid detection by enemy radar. On reaching their destination they had to climb to 1,500 feet, still a low height by any standards, in order to ensure safe parachute descents.

Another difference – bombers operated in a protective stream, relying on safety in numbers. Also, as we have learned, from August, 1943, onwards, they shovelled out 'Window' in vast quantities. But 161 Squadron aircraft flew alone to their 'target' hoping to attract as little attention as possible.

Agents and vital supplies were carried to Norway, Denmark, Holland, Belgium and France. John was convinced that the trip across the Zuider Zee into Holland was the most hazardous because all the small islands seemed to bristle with flak emplacements. Aircrew flew 'on the water' to try to keep out of trouble. One night there was an awe-inspiring instance when this technique was carried too far.

Affleck's crew had their own Halifax, T for Tommy, in which they had every faith and cherished above all other aircraft. One night they lent it to a Flying Officer 'Dinga' Bell and his crew. These ungrateful types treated poor old T for Tommy so badly it was never quite the same again. Flying at wave-top height over the Zuider Zee, 'Dinga' Bell actually ploughed the Halifax into the water. Survival seemed impossible. Yet, jettisoning every container they somehow managed to struggle out of the sea and stagger back to base. This was all the more remarkable as the two port wooden propellers were smashed to matchwood, leaving only the stumps. The bomb-bay and the rear turret were full of seaweed!

Agents arrived at Tempsford in large black limousines driven by women of the WRAC. Officially aircrew were not supposed to speak to these undercover operators apart from the routine instructions given over the drop zone. However, sharing common dangers created a comradely atmosphere in which more than idle banter was sometimes exchanged. The airmen were the only people to whom these men and women could speak without fear of betrayal, before they plunged into a world where a single unguarded word could send them, and others, to their deaths.

Tempsford is mentioned in a remarkable book, *Six Faces of Courage*, by Professor M. R. D. Foot, where he illustrates the exploits of half-a-dozen agents. He describes how one of these men, Harry Peuleve, was dropped by a Halifax of 161 Squadron into a field near Nîmes, in France. He was parachuted too close to the ground and broke his leg. Unable even to hobble, Peuleve was discovered by a farmer and his family who gave him shelter for the night. The following day he was taken to a discreet hospital ward in Nîmes. The book goes on to describe how the fracture was so severe that a surgeon, who took care to ask no questions, had to be called in to set it. This was a major operation, and an anaesthetist was available; but Peuleve insisted on being operated on without anaesthetic – to avoid any possibility of giving secrets away while unconscious.

On one occasion John and his crew had to 'deliver' a group of young Belgian agents. The weather conditions were foul, and the Halifax was being buffeted all over the sky – albeit, as always, only a few feet from the ground. One of the flight engineer's most important tasks was to keep a careful eye on the fuel gauges, and switch on the aircraft's petrol wing-tanks in plenty of time before they ran dry; the gauges were rarely 100% accurate. To make the procedure a little more difficult, the manufacturers had located the fuel-cocks under the rest-bed.

John was not in his best mood as he knelt on the aircraft's juddering floor and struggled to carry out the adjustment. The Belgians sitting on the rest-bed hardly made the task easier. Nearing the dropping area the hatch-covers were opened in readiness. Suddenly, the interior was lit up by a blinding light. They had inadvertently flown over an airfield near Bapaume and were momentarily caught in a searchlight beam.

As the Germans opened fire, their guns must have been depressed to the lowest notch in an effort to hit the hedge-hopping intruder. It seemed to John that all they were achieving was the demolition of their own hangars. Seconds later the surrounding darkness had swallowed up the Halifax which soon reached its destination, marked by a pinpoint of light shining up from the ground, as a torch flashed the letters of the day.

John's philosophy at this time was that he and the boys were doing a good job. He hoped he might be spared a little longer so he could continue his work. Work was the key factor – keeping himself busy at all times took his mind off the constant danger. Never-ending mental arithmetic, calculating fuel consumption, without help from a calculator, was the constant lot of a flight engineer. There was no time to brood.

He felt certain that fate would catch up with him sooner or later. The chances of completing a tour were too remote to be considered seriously. Having come to this conclusion, he made the most of each day as it came along with absolutely no regrets. He found it impossible to join in what he considered the false bon-homie indulged in by many aircrew. As the crew wagon made its way out to the aircraft, the flyers would rend the air with raucous jokes and mock insults, assuring each other that 'they were definitely for the chop this time'. John would sit silently in his seat, lost in his own thoughts.

When his best pal was shot down, he made no attempt to hide his feelings under a cloak of indifference. It was an almost unbearable tragedy and that was all there was to it.

John, who never considered himself a natural engineer, (he would much rather have been a botanist) went to endless pains to avoid making any mistakes when flying. During the course of his career in the RAF which extended from 1938 until 1960, he only knowingly made one error as a flight engineer – not a bad record. One night on return from an 'op' he was distracted by the possibility of enemy intruders in the vicinity of his home base. On that occasion he forgot to release the mechanical safety locks that held up the undercarriage. These acted as a safeguard in the event of the hydraulics being damaged. When Affleck tried to lower the wheels, they would not come down. Once John had realised the problem and removed the locks they landed safely.

He always had great faith in the standard of ground maintenance. The Halifaxes were looked after with meticulous care. He knew, better than most, how expertly the fitters had been trained. The faith that Trenchard had in his 'Brats' had been well-founded

62

– it was the ex-Halton boys, hugely reinforced by wartime conscripts and volunteers, who kept the kites flying, often working on bombers under appalling weather conditions in the open air.

The regulations laid down by the RAF for servicing the four-engine 'Heavies' were second to none. John sometimes felt that the inspections went too far. He believed that a number of the Daily Inspections bordered on the finicky – but if this was a fault, then it was a comforting one. [See Odell Dobson's experiences in Chapter 10].

Two American Air Force Liberators arrived at Tempsford to take up operational duties. To John these aircraft looked impressively workmanlike, already noted for their long range. Their crews behaved in a professional manner, showing interest in the radar equipment installed in the Halifaxes – equipment that the Liberators did not possess. That night they both took off on a mission to Poland. Only one returned. The following day the survivor flew away from the airfield never to be seen again.

There was an American, a typical Brooklyn boy, who had joined the RAF and flew with the squadron as a Sergeant wireless operator. On a mission to Montluçon in Central France, the aircraft in which he was flying crashed. Escaping without injury, he was placed on a truck on top of the pile of containers which he and his crew had just dropped, and carted off to Montluçon. Hidden by underground workers, he soon settled in and made the best of his new circumstances. He even found himself a French girlfriend.

News eventually filtered back to the squadron, and his Wing Commander flew over in a single-engine Lysander, landed, picked him up and brought him back to Tempsford. One of the last things the French asked their new-found American friend before he left was 'Please tell the RAF never to bomb us'.

Not long after this incident, 161 Squadron were briefed for a mission to drop more containers in the same locality. It was the night of 15/16 September, 1943. They were just arriving, at low level as usual, when, to quote from the Bomber Command War Diaries, the following happened:

209 Halifaxes, 120 Stirlings, 40 Lancasters, and 5 American For-

tress B-17s took part in a moonlit raid on the Dunlop rubber factory at Montluçon in Central France. The pathfinders marked the target accurately and the Master Bomber, Wing Commander D. F. E. C. Deane, brought the Main Force in well to carry out some accurate bombing. Every building in the factory was hit and a large fire was started.

The report omits to mention that as the bombs rained down a clutch of poor old Halifaxes from 161 Squadron was trying to get on with the work of dropping containers! Nor is there any quote about the reaction of the citizens of Montluçon to this unexpected attack.

Incidentally, the Sergeant from Brooklyn was asked by the American Eighth Air Force to leave the RAF and join them. He complied with this request and was immediately promoted to Colonel. The increase in pay alone must have been a heady experience!

The time came when Affleck's crew became the longest surviving on the squadron. Their durability was attributed to the quality of the crew, a seasoned pilot and, particularly, an outstanding navigator, Wilson McMaster. He, like his skipper, was on his second tour. He never failed to reach the drop zone accurately and on time, and then always plotted a safe course back to base. Flying so low, there was little help from electronic aids, although, like other navigators, he sometimes made good use of a radar device hidden in a tree 'somewhere in France' !

John could hardly believe his luck, when, after completing thirty-nine operations, his tour was over and he was still alive. It took a little while for the fact to sink in. Not only had he survived, but he had actually completed nine more missions than was normal for a first tour in Bomber Command. (In spite of its special-duty role 161 Squadron was still a Bomber Command squadron under the authority of 3 Group.) After Affleck had completed his second tour, John pressed on with another crew skippered by a cheerful New Zealander, Sergeant Wilkinson, and then completed his operational duties with Flying Officer Don Harborow and his crew.

On the night of 17 December 1943, while John was celebrating his good fortune on leave, 161 suffered probably its heaviest loss of the war. Western Europe was unexpectedly blanketed in a thick layer of fog. Apart from 25 Lancasters lost during a raid on Berlin, a further 30 bombers crashed while attempting to land back at their bases in England killing 148 aircrew, injuring 39, while 6 were presumed lost in the sea. 161 Squadron shared in this terrible toll. McMaster, navigating a new crew, brought them back to within a few miles of the emergency airstrip at Woodbridge, Suffolk. Crossing the coast under very low cloud the Halifax struck a radar mast slicing off a section of the wing and the port outboard engine. Struggling with the controls the pilot belly-landed the aircraft in mud on the River Deben. All the crew survived except McMaster. Apparently thrown clear, he was discovered shortly afterwards floating face down in shallow water. All attempts to resuscitate him, failed.

To John's surprise he was awarded the DFM, commissioned and sent to RAF Feltwell, a Lancaster Finishing School, as an instructor. The usual pattern, which was to reveal itself throughout his flying career, had cropped up again. Apart from his early apprenticeship not once did he receive training for any job that came his way. Now he was expected to teach others in an aircraft he had only seen flying in the distance!

His introduction to the Avro Lancaster was a revelation – to use his own words, 'It was a dream! It flew like a bird'.

Yet the greatest bomber of the Second World War had been born out of failure. With high hopes, the Avro Manchester had been launched early in 1941. Powered by two Rolls-Royce Vulture engines of 1760 hp, it proved a bitter disappointment. The Vultures were notoriously unreliable. Many aircrew lost their lives flying in these dangerous machines. There was nothing wrong with the aircraft itself, only its engines. Roy Chadwick, A. V. Roe's chief designer, was inspired to fit four Merlin engines in place of the two Vultures. The name Manchester died. With a wing span increased by 12 feet to accommodate the two extra engines, the Lancaster soared into the air – the 'Shining Sword', as Arthur Harris called it, had arrived.

Unlike the Halifax, where the flight engineer was stationed under the astrodome, on the Lancaster John found he was in closer proximity to the pilot, almost like a second pilot. With his Merlin

XXs, which had also powered the Halifaxes, he was perfectly content. Perhaps his most satisfying moment in the air came one day when an American B17 Flying Fortress took up formation alongside them. The American pilot indicated by signs that he would welcome a race. Reaching over to his switch panel, John cut two of the bomber's engines. Then opening the throttles on the two remaining motors, the Lancaster pulled steadily ahead of the Fortress!

John, who in 1946 married Lynne, a charming girl from the WAAF, remained in the RAF as a flight engineer until 1960. One of the highlights of his peacetime career was taking part in the Berlin airlift, when the entire population of the city was fed from the air for months by the Americans and British, until the Russians, who had blockaded the city, relented and removed the road barriers. Apart from food, the aircrews carried electrical generators, huge rolls of newspaper, and coal. John and the others were not very keen on coal as a cargo. But, joining the constant stream of planes, they did enjoy flying low over General Sokoloski's residence. He was the man who had ordered the blockade!

After 22 years in the RAF, John retired with the rank of Flight Lieutenant and became, not a botanist, but an antique dealer.

FIVE

The Bomb Aimer

The role of the bomb aimer, like that of the flight engineer, was created through the need for greater efficiency in bombing operations, utilizing the effectiveness of the four-engine bombers. Until the arrival of these larger aircraft, the business of dropping bombs had been left to the navigator. With increased specialization among aircrew, better aircraft, improved equipment, radar navigation aids, bigger and more potent bombs, the highly trained bomb aimer became the prime member of the crew at the moment of attack, guiding his pilot towards the aiming point.

Bomb aimers were sometimes recruited from the ranks of cadets washed out as pilots. After further rigorous training they passed out in their new role. Because of their long period of instruction, many of these men, apart from being skilled in their own job, had also accumulated a knowledge of navigation, and how to fly an aircraft – not a four-engine bomber, perhaps, but with enough know how to be useful in an emergency.

We suggested earlier that the rear gunner might have occupied the most dangerous position in the aircraft. There is no doubt, however, that over the target where the flak was normally at its thickest, the bomb aimer was exceptionally vulnerable. Stationed in the nose, which was constructed only of transparent perspex and a thin metal skin, he lay stretched full length along the floor of his small compartment, his face above the lens of the bomb-sight, his whole body exposed to any piece of white-hot, jagged shrapnel that might enter the front of his plane at any moment during that crucial bombing run. As a bomb aimer, Harold Chadwick worked out his own solution to this and other problems.

Over the years Harold Chadwick has carved out a way of life that, in many ways, is that of a 20th Century Robinson Crusoe. He lives in the foothills that look down on the Mediterranean coast of Southern Spain.

As companions he has a variety of animals – a very old horse, goats, turkeys, chickens, and many dogs and cats whom he and his wife, Cynthia, have rescued over a period of time from certain destruction. Harold's first action each morning is to climb down the deep well that he dug for himself and his family years ago when they first came to Spain. When he reaches water level he has a brief chat with his friend Ernie. Ernie is an eel. An old Andalucian farmer advised Harold to pop an eel into the well to keep the drinking water pure. Ernie, undoubtedly grateful for his permanent home, has never failed in his task. It would be beyond the grasp of Harold's Spanish neighbours to associate their friend, the 'funny' Englishman with the sharp jerky movements – *el hombre* who is never still, with Flight Lieutenant H. Chadwick, DFC, of 617 Squadron – one of the specially chosen bomb aimers who dropped the first of the mighty 'earthquake' bombs.

Harold Chadwick was born on 14 September, 1922, in Nottingham. Later on the family moved to Uttoxeter, and when he left school he went to work in Woolworths as a trainee manager. He did not take kindly to the routine, and anyway, his ambitions lay elsewhere.

During the First World War his father, also Harold Chadwick, had transferred from the cavalry to the RFC. As a scout pilot he flew Spads, Bristol Fighters, Sopwith Triplanes and SE5s – and was shot down twice. Harold senior was lucky to survive those years. Harold junior had always admired his father's exploits in the air and was determined to become a fighter pilot himself.

The Second World War was at the end of its first year, and the daylight phase of the Battle of Britain had just been fought and won by the Royal Air Force. As soon as Harold was 18 years old, the youngest permissible age to start aircrew training, he volunteered to fly with the RAF. Neville Crisp, who had been his friend at Alleynes Grammar School, applied at the same time. They were both accepted for training as pilots.

At an RAF station near Cambridge the new cadets were put through a flying aptitude test before graduating to Tiger Moths for their Initial Flying Training. This successfully completed, they were shipped over to Canada to take part in the Empire Air Training Scheme. The young trainees were sent on sister ships, former Dutch cargo vessels, and it was the alphabetical division by name that decided in which vessel they sailed. Chadwick and Crisp, therefore, had no problem in keeping together. They reached Nova Scotia without incident. The other ship was torpedoed by a German U-boat. There were no survivors.

Everything went well for Harold at first, flying Stearman PT17 biplanes and clocking up some sixty hours on these machines at Calgary, Alberta. Then, to his delight they were posted over the border to the USA for a session on Vultees, finally graduating on to the Harvard Advanced Trainer. But his Harvard instructor, an ex-Eagle Squadron flyer, must have suspected that his pupil was harbouring a 'guilty secret'. Taking him up one day he put the machine into every aerobatic manoeuvre known to man. After being thrown violently about the sky for minutes on end, the unfortunate Harold literally 'coughed up' his 'secret'. He was most horribly air sick.

But it was not just the result of aerobatics. All through his training, every time he took off he had thrown up. To make matters worse, this was nearly always accompanied by prolonged nose-bleeding. It was to his credit that he had managed to conceal his affliction for such a long time, and indeed had done so well on his course in spite of it. Now, with only days to go before receiving his wings, he had been found out.

His friend 'Spud' Crisp gained his wings as a pilot and eventually finished up flying Coastal Command Beaufighters. Distressed beyond measure as he watched his fellow cadets being rewarded for their efforts, Harold cast about for some way of continuing to fly. Like so many before him, he sought the shortest course that would qualify him for flying duties in *any* aircrew capacity. It was obvious that the officers in charge had no idea how serious his air sickness really was.

Back in Canada, at Picton, Ontario, he began training for a new aircrew category – a Nav/B. Essentially this was a bomb aimer with a working knowledge of navigation. The course was short, only 14 weeks. The navigation part of the syllabus had already been covered during pilot training, while the bombing practice was not particularly taxing. He passed out among the top three and received an immediate commission. At the same time he was awarded his bomb aimer's brevet – the single wing with a B surrounded by a laurel wreath.

Harold's air sickness never left him, nor did the nasal bleeding. Invariably, when returning from a mission over Germany he would be plagued with the stench of his own vomit, while his oxygen mask would be slimy with blood. Yet, lying in the dark isolation of the Lancaster's front compartment he was able to conceal his suffering from the rest of the crew. In spite of all, he was eventually to join the elite by becoming one of Bomber Command's most skilful bomb aimers.

He must have done particularly well on his course in Canada because he was retained as an instructor at Picton. After six months, however, he came back to Britain, and was posted to RAF Lichfield, an aircrew reception centre. It was now around the middle of 1943.

The time had come to find himself a crew. This involved a haphazard process of wandering around and trying to assess pilots, navigators, wireless operators and gunners purely from their appearance. It really was a case of 'pot-luck'. Nobody had any means of measuring another man's standard of competence in the air until such time as they flew together.

As time went on, more and more people formed themselves into crews, and he wondered if he might be left as odd man out. Then he spotted an 'old', grey-haired Sergeant pilot hanging about waiting for the NAAFI tea wagon to arrive. To Harold he looked steady and reliable. His name was Arthur Fearn, a man in his thirties, at least eleven years older than himself. They agreed to team up, and then between them brought together the other three members of the crew – Nav, Wop/AG and AG – an all-Sergent crew with the exception of Pilot Officer Harold Chadwick.

At Fradley OTU, still not far from Lichfield, they gained experience as a team, flying Wellingtons. Nearing the completion of their course, they were sent on a 'Nickel', the code name for a leaflet raid. Four Wellingtons with their trainee crews took off that night and dropped 'bumph' over Paris. Only Harold's crew and one other returned – a 50% loss.

70

They converted to Halifaxes at Swinderby HCU, collecting two more Sergeants, a Flight Engineer and Mid-Upper Gunner to man the extra positions. Unlike the Wellington, Harold was no longer in isolation; now he shared the nose position in the Halifax with the wireless operator and the navigator. His confidence in the crew was growing, especially in the ability of Arthur as a pilot. Arthur was not going to do anything silly, not with a wife and family to go home to.

Conversion to Lancasters when they reached 57 Squadron, at Scampton, in Lincolnshire, meant that Harold regained his solo position in the nose. On the 'Lanc' the navigator and wireless operator were stationed further aft in their own cabin.

57 Squadron had been operating steadily since the beginning of the war and had always suffered higher than average casualties. On top of that, Sergeant Fearn's crew had chosen just about the worst time to join an operational squadron. It was the Autumn of 1943 and 'Bomber Harris' was ready to throw his command into an unprecedented attack on Berlin, in a battle that was to be fought to the death through the coming winter and into March of the following year.

Their baptism came on 3 September. They were scheduled for a raid on 'Big City'. The Bomber Command Diaries state that because of the high casualty rates among Halifaxes and Stirlings in recent Berlin raids the heavy force was composed only of Lancasters. On some of the Berlin raids that followed, Halifaxes, and even the lumbering Stirlings, were used again to make up the numbers. It was not the most successful of attacks, many of the bombs falling short because of inaccurate marking. Twenty-two of the aircraft were lost out of a force of 316 Lancasters.

To Harold and the other inexperienced members of Arthur Fearn's crew the long trip across Germany seemed nothing less than awful. They witnessed Lancasters being shot from the sky, not only over the target but also on the flights there and back. Shocked by the night's events, they concluded that there was little hope of completing more than one or two such trips.

Yet, as the weeks went by they somehow survived, and, because of the date, Harold was to recall one incident as being particularly poignant. It was over Berlin yet again. They had just dropped

71

their bombs when a blazing Lancaster drifted across their path slightly above them. In what seemed like slow motion, the doomed aircraft slid over to port. He saw the rear door of the fuselage open and three figures tumble out into the flak-filled night. Within moments their chutes had billowed out. Then, still with four of the crew injured, trapped or dead inside, the stricken bomber plunged in an ever steepening dive into the target. It was Christmas Eve.

Being commissioned, Harold lived in different quarters from the NCOs. He slept in a corrugated-iron Nissen hut with beds for twelve officers. During his time with 57 Squadron, from his place in a corner of the hut, he saw every other bed change ownership at least twice as the occupants went missing. It was the duty of each WAAF batwoman to look after the domestic welfare of two junior officers. Harold felt sorry for these women, often 'motherly' types, who, with tears in their eyes, collected up a small bundle of possessions belonging to yet another of 'their officers' who would not be coming back.

Throughout that terrible winter Arthur Fearn's crew soldiered on. The losses mounted all the time until, on 24/25 March, 1944, Harris staged his last big raid on Berlin. It was to cost Bomber Command, on that single night, the loss of hundreds of aircrew as seventy-two aircraft were shot from the sky. And only five days later the command was to suffer its greatest tragedy ever – ninety-five bombers lost on a disastrous mission to Nuremberg. More aircraft ditched in the sea, and a further seventy-one were heavily damaged in crashes back in England. But Harold and the rest of Arthur Fearn's team had moved on to something more specialized by then, as we shall see shortly.

In all, Arthur Fearn and his crew completed nine raids on Berlin, interspersed with missions to other heavily defended targets such as Mannheim, twice, Frankfurt and Leipzig. Harold remembers one Berlin trip in particular. They were on their bombing run and Harold was guiding Arthur up to the aiming point: 'Left, left, steady . . . left, left . . . right . . . steady'. Harold pressed the 'tit': 'Bombs gone!'. But they had not gone. There was a total hang-up. Feverishly, with heavy flak bursting all round, and searchlights slicing perilously close, he checked his bomb panel a second time, re-setting each switch in turn. But the 4000-pound 'Cookie' and its surrounding canisters of incendiaries remained obstinately in place.

Arthur's voice came over the intercom: 'For God's sake get the bloody things sorted out. We can't stooge around this place all night!' Harold realized he would have to try releasing the load manually. Grabbing an emergency oxygen bottle and clawing his way back to the body of the Lancaster, he hastily removed the inspection covers above the bomb bay. But he was unable to reach the hooks that retained the 4000-pounder. Seizing the fire-axe he started chopping away at the aluminium floor. Arthur's voice came through again on the head-set: 'This is too bloody dicey. I'm going to get away from the target and head for home.'

Harold chopped and chopped with desperation. He knew well enough that the extra fuel consumed by carrying this load on a return flight could mean dry tanks before reaching England. Ditching in the sea with the extra weight of bombs would reduce their chances to nil. At last he made a hole large enough to start work on the actual retaining hooks. With the bomb doors open, he lay in the path of a howling gale. His hands were so frozen he feared the axe might slip from his grasp at any second. Eventually the great steel drum fell away, taking one of the bomb doors with it. The remaining door closed and every member of the crew breathed more freely. A moment later the rear gunner reported a large explosion which lit up the blackness below. It was later confirmed that 'Harold's bomb' had landed smack in the centre of Kassel, a large industrial town engaged in manufacturing war weapons, including the V1 rocket.

They were too short of petrol to land at base in Lincolnshire, so put down at Waterbeach, near Cambridge, still with the load of incendiaries on board. Harold was uneasy, wondering if in some way he was to blame for the 'hang-up'. The following day they flew back to Scampton, and their kite, E Easy, was wheeled away for inspection. When Harold heard the official report from the armament officer he was filled with relief. E Easy was a brand new Lancaster. Like all its contemporaries its underside had been sprayed with matt black paint before leaving the factory. A small ball-bearing had become gummed up with paint. When the bomb doors were opened the ball-bearing was supposed to leave the socket and complete the electrical bombing circuit, but in this case it had stuck fast, rendering the system inoperative. On such small items hung men's lives.

This thought was much in Harold's mind when they returned from one raid in the early hours of the morning. As the crew climbed wearily from their bomber they noticed the station ambulance drawn up beside one of the squadron's aircraft. A blood-stained figure was being lifted into the back of the vehicle. On inquiry Harold was told that it was the bomb aimer who had been killed by flak. A fragment of metal had entered below his chin, spiralled up through his skull and sliced off the top of his head. Harold wandered round to the nose of the Lancaster and looked up. There was a hole no bigger than a two shilling (10p) piece in the aluminium underside.

One of Harold's duties was to discharge 'Window' down the flare chute on a carefully timed basis while over enemy territory. The heavy metal strips were packed in compact blocks. From that day on he lined the floor of his cabin with a generous supply of these solid parcels. (Unlike American aircraft, British bombers had a minimum of armour plating.) On more than one occasion after that, he spotted holes underneath the Lancaster when they returned from a mission. Once a sharp sliver of flak penetrated right through the parcels and, although its velocity was much reduced, it cut through his flying boot and buried itself in the calf of his right leg.

Their tally of trips to Berlin should have been ten. One night they were flying across the North Sea, still climbing steadily, when the Lancaster was attacked by a Ju88 night fighter and the starboard outer engine set on fire. Arthur threw the bomber all over the sky while his two gunners replied as best they could with their Brownings. For some reason the German broke off his attack and disappeared into the night. Although the crew managed to get the fire under control their aircraft was in no shape to continue the long journey to Berlin. But Harold had what almost amounted to a phobia about being involved in an 'abortive sortie' – returning to base without bombing. (The Kassel incident had counted as an 'op' because a target had been bombed, even if it was not the primary one.) After some argument he persuaded his skipper to press on the comparatively short distance to Heligoland, and drop their load on the heavy fortifications there. Over the island the Germans opened up at them with everything they had, so Harold aimed at the gun flashes. After the line-overlap photographs had been developed and examined the crew were credited with their 'op'.

Harold was now completely satisfied that Arthur's crew was the finest in 5 Group, if not in the whole of Bomber Command! It was a standing joke that their skipper was also the oldest Sergeant pilot in existence. The Commanding Officer of 5 Group, Air Vice-Marshal The Hon R. Cochrane, accompanied by his chief, Air Chief Marshal Sir Arthur Harris, visited 57 Squadron on a morale-building exercise following heavy losses. After the customary pep-talk, aircrew were invited to express themselves freely. When Cochrane turned to Arthur Fearn and asked him what was in his mind as he approached the target, Arthur, always outspoken, replied, 'Getting through the damn thing as quickly as possible and then heading home like a bat out of hell!' His crew reckoned that this retort had scuppered their skipper's chances of promotion for ever.

Towards the end of their time with 57 Squadron and when the outfit had been transferred to East Kirkby, Arthur was at last made a Pilot Officer. His bomb aimer was now a Flight Lieutenant, but in a few weeks, by an unprecedented promotional leap, Arthur caught him up. After a raid in which the squadron sustained particularly heavy casualties, including the loss of both its Flight Commanders, Harold's skipper, as the longest surviving pilot, took over as one of the Flight Commanders and was immediately promoted to Flight Lieutenant. Engineer Trevor Davies became a Pilot Officer. The rest of the crew remained NCOs.

Harold had a high regard for Sergeant Howard Dewar, the rear gunner. He was a Canadian, a tough ex-lumberjack, who seemed to be without fear. Together with his fellow gunner in the mid-upper turret, Wilson Williams, he had saved the crew from disaster on at least two occasions. Then one night, on yet another trip to Berlin, an extraordinary thing happened. They were approaching the target when they were attacked by a Messerschmitt 109. Arthur went into his usual corkscrewing routine to try to throw the German off his tail. During this manoeuvre the crew temporarily lost communication with each other. Nevertheless the fighter was foiled and they went on to bomb the city.

As they set course for home, the skipper, as was his custom, called up each crew member in turn to ask if they were all right. Everyone replied except Howard. After several unsuccessful attempts to get an answer, Jack Baker, the wireless operator went along the fuselage to investigate. To his astonishment, Jack found the rear turret empty – Howard had baled out over Berlin! No trace of him was ever found.

Dennis Pearson, a West Indian, took over the tail gunner's job and remained in Arthur's crew until the completion of operations, as did all the other NCOs, including Harry 'Johnny' Johnson as navigator, and Trevor Davies, the recently promoted flight engineer.

From the start of their tour, in early September, 1943, until the end of March the following year, Bomber Command lost in the region of 1500 heavy bombers over enemy territory, and many more in crashes in England. Over 10,000 young men's names had been deleted from the command's roll call during this period. Yet, towards the end of January, 1944, and with their missions totalling twenty-eight trips, they were still only just over half way through their operational duties!

A Bomber Command tour with Main Force consisted of thirty operations, after which, for those fortunate enough to reach such a figure, there would be a 'rest' period of six months, normally spent as an instructor, before returning to fly a further twenty-five missions. But for Flight Lieutenant Fearn's crew it was to be altogether different because of the intervention of 617 Squadron.

The astounding exploits of 617 Special Duties Squadron need no retelling in detail here. They have been immortalized in the history of the RAF, in Paul Brickhill's *The Dam Busters*, and in the award-winning film of that name. It was a squadron unique in the annals of war, formed in the spring of 1943 to carry out the audacious raid which breached the Moehne and Eder Dams in Germany. Thanks to the courage of the airmen who undertook this mission and the inventive genius of Barnes Wallis who gave them the 'bouncing bomb' to do the job it was a major success. The price was high, eight out of the nineteen Lancasters taking part were lost, and only three of the fifty-six airmen involved in those losses survived.

Since that time, nearly nine months earlier, 617 had specialized in raiding selected targets with mixed results. They had had a crack at the Dortmund-Ems Canal, a viaduct in Italy, an armaments factory near Liège, a flying-bomb site, and even a leaflet raid – always operating in small numbers, sometimes of not more than nine or a dozen Lancasters. Their original brief to attack at low level had been changed. With the acquisition of the revolutionary Stabilizing Automatic Bomb Sight, they were now bombing from a greater height – sometimes at the maximum of 20,000 feet, similar to Main Force, but, on other occasions, around 12,000 feet.

In need of experienced crews, 617 Squadron canvassed the various squadrons, mostly in 5 Group, asking for volunteers to join them. It may seem surprising that the members of Harold's crew, now with only two trips to go before completing their tour, should even contemplate such a move. Yet they did. Crew loyalty probably accounts for their reaction. They felt that if they split up for six months they might never get together again. Eventually, they argued, they would have to do a second tour anyway. 'Better stay together and get on with it now, rather than risk our necks later with strangers.' So they volunteered – and were accepted.

By this stage, Arthur, Harold and Trevor had each been awarded the Distinguished Flying Cross, while Harry, the navigator and still a Sergeant, got the Distinguished Flying Medal.

Arrival at Coningsby meant a return to rigorous training, but this was a relief from the strain of night operations. Harold revelled in the cunning efficiency of the SABS – the new bomb sight. But, as Paul Brickhill said in *The Dam Busters*:

> It needed more than a hawk-eyed bomb aimer; it called for team work. The gunners took drifts to help the navigator work out precise wind direction and speed, and navigator and bomb aimer calculated obscure instrument corrections. An error of a few feet at 20,000 feet would throw a bomb hopelessly off. Altimeters work off barometric pressure, but that is always changing, so they used

a complicated system of getting ground-level pressures over target and correcting altimeters by pressure lapse rates (with temperature complications). A small speed error will throw a bomb off, and air-speed indicators read falsely according to height and the altitude of the aircraft. They had to compute and correct this, and when it was all set on the SABS the pilot had to hold his exact course and height for miles while the engineer juggled the throttles to keep the speed precise. That, over-simplified, expresses about a tenth of the complications. When the bomb aimer had the cross-wires on the target he clicked a switch and the SABS kept itself tracking on the aiming point by its gyros, transmitting corrections to the pilot by flicking an indicator in the cockpit. The bomb aimer did not have to press the bomb button; when it was ready the SABS did that, and even told the pilot by switching off a red light in the cockpit.

Practising day after day, with help from the rest of the team, Harold's accuracy reached extraordinary levels. His best effort, over the bombing range at Wainfleet Sands on the East coast, was when he dropped six practice bombs from 15,000 feet on to the target with an average error of only 20 yards! The squadron invited units of the Eighth American Air Force, stationed at Mildenhall, to take part in a bombing competition. The Americans were quoted at that time as being able 'to put a bomb in a barrel from 20,000 feet!' The B17 Flying Fortresses flew over on the chosen day and bombed the practice target. They were unable to get anywhere near the pin-point accuracy of 617 Squadron.

The crew's first raid with 617 on 8/9 February was led by the squadron's new Commanding Officer, Wing Commander Leonard Cheshire, when they attacked the Gnome & Rhone aero-engine factory at Limoges. Only twelve Lancasters were involved and, in bright moonlight, Cheshire and his crew went in first at low level. They made three passes over the factory to warn the workers to take shelter, then, at 50/100 feet, on the fourth run they dropped a load of incendiaries on the buildings.

The remaining eleven Lancasters aimed their 12,000 pounders at the factory, ten scoring direct hits, the eleventh bomb falling in the river alongside. No casualties among the French population were reported; in fact, a message was 'smuggled' through to 617 Squadron from the Mayor of Limoges, on behalf of himself and the girls working in the factory, thanking the RAF flyers for the

78

timely warning before the bombing began. This new form of low-level marking became a speciality of the squadron, later refined by Cheshire when he moved on to the faster, more manoeuvrable D.H. Mosquito before eventually transferring to the even speedier, single-engine long range Mustang fighter.

For the next four months they bombed numerous targets of this type, individual manufacturing plants, including the vitally important signals depot at St Cyr, near Versailles, and culminating in the most unusual task of all, when on the night of 5/6 June, 1944, 617 flew meticulously timed legs over the English Channel, while dropping out a screen of Window to simulate a huge fleet of approaching ships. This operation was designed to fool the Germans into thinking the Allied invasion of Europe was taking place further north than it actually was. The ruse worked.

Three nights later they had their first chance to put Barnes Wallis's 12,000 lb Tallboy bomb to good effect. This was a deep-penetration weapon with a sharply pointed nose which 'cork-screwed' into the target. (It bore no relation to the previous 12,000 lb blockbuster). The Allied armies were establishing a toe-hold in Normandy when it was reported that a Panzer Division was approaching by train from the south and would, within hours, be passing through the Saumur railway tunnel.

The raid was mounted with great haste and Arthur Fearn's crew were soon climbing for height, accompanied by twenty-four other Lancasters from 617. As they arrived over the tunnel the target was illuminated by flares dropped by four Lancasters of 83 Squadron and marked at low level by three Mosquitoes. Harold guided Arthur into the bombing run, released the gigantic Tallboy and scored a direct hit on the tunnel entrance. All the bombs were dropped with great accuracy and, as they exploded under the ground, they created small earthquakes which brought down tons of rocks and rubble completely blocking the tunnel.

The squadron only had a limited supply of Tallboys, though 'Butch' Harris' was constantly taking up the cudgels on their behalf, demanding faster delivery. But at the height of the invasion there were pressing demands for war equipment of all kinds. The 617 'Lancs' had been specially converted to accommodate the Tallboys. The bomb doors had been removed and the undersides of the bombers contoured in such a way that the bombs, when winched up into position, formed an integral part of the aircraft's belly. After the bombs had been released, the aircraft looked strangely concave.

Occasionally, when conditions over the target turned out to be unsuitable for bombing, the order would go out for the precious Tallboys to be brought back to base. Harold never forgot one such occasion. They had returned with their 12,000 lb bomb and, on receiving permission to land by their WAAF controller, had actually touched down on the runway. Then there was an urgent call over the R/T, 'Bandits! Bandits in the circuit!' Next moment all the airfield lights were switched off. Harold, who, against regulations, was lying in the nose, saw a dark shape above them. It was another 'Lanc' and it was about to land on top of them.

'Swerve, Arthur! Swerve for Christ's sake!' he yelled. Instinctively Arthur veered off to port; the bomber, with its huge load of high explosive, charged across the airfield. They missed the squadron bomb dump by feet and finally came to rest with the nose of the aircraft overhanging a water-filled Lincolnshire dyke. A female voice from the control tower came over the head-sets, 'Where are you, E Easy? Where are you, please?' Arthur's reply does not bear repeating.

It was indeed fortunate that Arthur was left-handed and left-footed. In the darkness a right-handed man would undoubtedly have swerved the other way – and crashed straight into the control tower.

On 6 July Wing Commander Cheshire led his squadron to attack the V3 gun site at Mimoyecques. This battery of enormous guns, with barrels 400 feet long, and situated underground, had been installed by the Germans to blast London to smithereens. 617's Tallboys put paid to their hopes for ever. When they returned, Cheshire was ordered by Air Vice Marshal Cochrane to leave the squadron and take a rest from operational flying. He would also revert to being a Group Captain, a rank he had relinquished in order to lead the squadron in the air. Shortly after, Leonard Cheshire was awarded the Victoria Cross for sustained courage over four tours totalling 100 operations.

Harold thought him a remarkable leader and quite different

80

from any other Squadron Commander he had known. In the Mess this tall, thin, studious-looking Wing Commander seemed self effacing, almost withdrawn, as if lost in thought. From personal experience he knew him to be sensitive and concerned for the needs of others.

The old lags told Harold that their retiring CO was in complete contrast to Guy Gibson, the original leader of 617. He had been a man of stocky build, a sharp tongue when the occasion warranted, yet with a boisterous sense of humour. Gibson, too, was a holder of the Victoria Cross, awarded for his outstanding conduct during the famous Dams Raid. Yet, apart from the obvious differences of physique and demeanour, these men had much in common. Their courage was unquestioned. Their ability to remain cool, flying with professional efficiency even during the most perilous moments, distinguished them as outstanding leaders in the air. On the ground they shared the intellectual gift of thinking out satisfactory answers to complex problems.

The successor to these rare commanders was a Welshman, Wing Commander Willie Tait. At first the boys of 617 found it hard to puzzle him out. With smooth black hair, a brown face and slim frame, he would stand in a group for long periods of time without saying a word. When he did open his mouth, as often as not it would be to stuff a large black pipe into it. On the occasions when he did speak, it took time for his listeners to interpret his strange brand of dry, Celtic wit.

His reputation was established in the eyes of the crews when they flew to the rocket site at Wizernes. Handling a Mustang for the first time in action, Tait lobbed his smoke markers from ground level in the teeth of fierce flak. Then, climbing steeply to 4,000 feet, he realized that haze and low cloud would obscure the markers from his Lancasters flying at 18,000 feet. Diving down again into the shell fire, and circling immediately above the building in the hope that the light would reflect off his wings, he called up to the bombers above him, 'Try bombing me!'

By the end of the war Willie Tait, who was 26 years old when he took over 617, had been awarded four DSOs and two DFCs—a record.

One morning on air test Arthur was not satisfied with the performance of the aircraft. After executing a series of dives and turns he realized that there was a fault in the fuel feed system, resulting in momentary engine cut-out. A raid had been planned to take place in a few hours' time, and he was far from happy about flying until the fault had been rectified, but there was no time to put things right. As the crew stood in the shadow of the bomber a car drew up and out stepped the CO. 'Listen Fearn', said Tait, 'if you don't want to fly tonight, then I'll take your crew.'

'OK.' replied Arthur, 'They're all yours!' Then, with mock solemnity, he walked round and shook hands with each of them in turn. Finally he said, 'It's been nice knowing you, boys. We've been together a long time, but tonight's the night when you all get the chop!'

Needless to say, they didn't and Harold later flew with Tait to bomb the German battleship *Tirpitz*, then sheltering near the Norwegian port of Tromsö. The target was at the Lancaster's extreme range, a 2,250 mile round trip. Only by removing the mid-upper turrets and other equipment, installing extra fuel tanks and taking off from Lossiemouth, in Scotland, did the bombers stand any chance of getting there and back. In the event they were thwarted by a bank of cloud which hid the ship. The *Tirpitz* was reprieved for two weeks, but was finally sunk by 617 after numerous attempts spread over many months.

Before this, Harold had flown on a mission to Rilly-la-Montage, where the Germans had stored flying bombs in an old railway tunnel. About a hundred aircraft took part, the Main Force cratering the approaches to the site, while 617, with its Tallboys, caved in both ends of the tunnel. Two aircraft were lost on that daylight raid. One was a 617 Squadron Lancaster piloted by Flight Lieutenant William Reid VC, previously mentioned in connection with 61 Squadron. The official record says he was shot down by flak, but Harold, from his vantage point in the perspex nose of his bomber, actually watched the aircraft being destroyed – he is perfectly certain that the tail unit was knocked off by a falling bomb. Miraculously William Reid survived.

Arthur Fearn's crew had diced with death from the beginning of September, 1943; now it was the late summer of 1944 and they were about to fly their final operation. Always a time of nervous

82

apprehension. Having cheated Fate for so long, would she, in the end, have the last laugh? The raid was to be on the U-boat pens at La Pallice, a hot spot for flak well remembered from a number of previous trips.

In broad daylight they flew to the target without any problems. On the bomb run Harold had set up his SABS and the red light was already glowing – the bomb would drop automatically in a matter of seconds. But before those seconds had ticked by, there was a shattering explosion right in front of the Lancaster. The perspex nose was destroyed and pieces of red-hot shrapnel ricocheted back and forth inside the bomb aimer's compartment which was filled with choking smoke. The tubular steel rods supporting the bomb sight were severed like matchsticks.

Fortunately for Harold, he always drew his head back immediately before the Tallboy dropped away from the aircraft. This was because, released from the heavy load, the bomber would leap up several hundred feet, giving an unwary bomb aimer a nasty smack on the back of the head. This time Harold's instinctive reaction saved his life.

For a moment he lay unconscious, then, gathering his wits, he started to crawl up the steps into the main cabin, where he received his second shock. Trevor Davies, the flight engineer, took one look at him and screamed. Harold raised his trembling hands to his face. When he brought them away they were bright red. Small slivers of shattered perspex had cut into his face.

So, with fifty-one operations behind him, more than the rest of the crew because of his extra missions with Wing Commander Tait, Harold's combat career ended. His wounds healed and slowly he came to terms with the fact that he was going to live. Even then, celebration of his 22nd birthday on 14 September was blighted by the news that his school friend Neville Crisp had been shot down and killed in his Beaufighter on that very day, attacking E-boats in the channel.

Leaving 617 Squadron, which had long since moved to Woodhall Spa, Harold did a spell as an instructor. One day he received a signal report to Thorney Island, in West Sussex, to carry out some specialized bombing practice. The war in Europe was over but Japan was still fighting and plans were afoot to send 617 out to the Pacific to bomb the Japanese Navy. Unlike the German capital ships, which had been moored in various docks, the Japanese warships were on the move. The practice therefore involved bombing moving targets – black and white striped drogues towed by motor torpedo boats.

One day he was asked to take some aerial photographs of Thorney Island, where the airfield was due for reconstruction. He was standing in the open doorway at the rear of the Lancaster with a rather cumbersome P4 camera strapped to his chest, taking shots, as his pilot, Wing Commander Brooks, flew back and forth at about 1,500 feet. Harold had grabbed the first parachute harness that came to hand, one adjusted for a man around 6 foot 2 inches. This meant that the lower canvas straps which should have been snugly embracing his crutch were actually hanging down level with his knees. Of course he was not wearing the actual chute pack which was tucked neatly away in its holder.

Brookie called up on the intercom and told him he was going to do a gentle rate 1 turn. The turn must have been so perfectly executed that they hit their own slipstream on the way back. The sudden turbulence pitched Harold straight out of the door.

By a miracle a small metal ring attached to the bottom of the dangling harness caught on some protrusion on the door, a bolt perhaps or a hinge, and stopped him from plunging 1,500 feet on to the concrete runway below. The wireless operator had noticed his unexpected exit and, with the help of the flight engineer, managed to haul him back on board. By this time, not surprisingly, he was out cold.

The force with which the slack in the harness had been taken up on his downward plunge nearly ruined him. In hospital his appendages, which, to use his own words, 'had swelled up like footballs!' were encased in a kind of leather bladder with a hole in the front. He remained in this embarrassing state for several months. His discharge from medical supervision came in time for him to take part in a 'joy ride' to Berlin to see the damage that he and others had inflicted on the German capital. Gazing in disbelief at the acres of ruins brought him no particular pleasure.

Soon afterwards he was granted leave to spend time with his wife, Cynthia, at their home in Nottingham. From Thorney Island it was a long and tedious train journey, so he was therefore pleased to scrounge a lift in a Lancaster to Fiskerton, in Lincolnshire, and in this way cut down his travelling time considerably. With satisfaction he saw that the youthful Pilot Officer planned his route meticulously, and also decided to ignore the stipulated safety height of 4,000 feet, opting to fly at 9,000 feet instead.

They were over the Midlands and Harold was standing in the astrodome enjoying the view. Ready for leave, he was not even in flying kit, but wearing his officer's greatcoat and peaked cap, with a small travelling case at his feet.

Suddenly the aircraft tilted and dived straight towards the earth. With less than 1,000 feet to spare, the pilot managed to pull out of the plunge. If they had flown at the official safety height, they would have finished up several feet into the ground. The cause was simple enough – the aircraft had been on automatic pilot. The Lancaster was new, straight from the factory. Inspectors had failed to detect iron filings in the linkage control ducts; these filings had jammed the controls in the dive position on the automatic device.

His leave completed, Harold returned by train.

SIX

The U/T Pilot

The following is a selection from the daily entries in a diary kept by a U/T Pilot (a pilot under training). It covers the period from the day he joined the RAF up to the unforgettable moment when he received his pilot's wings.

Francis George Kelsey was an unusually mature aircrew cadet. Born in the East End of London on 23 July, 1910, he was 12 or 13 years older than the average trainee flyer. His knowledge of life, and his ability to form a view of the people he met, was greater than that of the majority of those who shared the course with him. This is apparent from some of his written comments. He also shows a refreshing honesty when he assesses his own ability, or lack of ability, to cope.

It would have been a pleasure to have met Francis and had the chance to ask him some questions; particularly why he decided to volunteer for flying duties. He had a wife and small son, and his age would have exempted him from 'front line' service. He was running his own printing business in Ilford, Essex. His father had to come out of semi-retirement to look after the family enterprise for more than five years while his son was away in the RAF. Sadly, Francis died in 1960. I am indebted to his son, Malcolm, for the privilege of quoting from his father's diary.

The Diary of a U/T Pilot

July 7th 1941. Reported to No 1 ACRC London at 3 pm. After filling in numerous forms and having an FFI was marched off in a flight of fifty men to our billets which proved to be 'Stockleigh Hall', a modern block of flats in Prince Albert Road. We received our first meal in the service at 9.15 pm and it was of very poor quality. All our meals are served in the Pavilion in the Zoo at Regent's Park . . . We marched there, about ¾ miles, and upon

86

finishing were allowed to wander around the Zoo until our following parade.

After about a week the Mess Hall was parted from the Zoo and we had to march back to parade in Flights. This was due to the fact that some of the fellows had been teasing the animals.

During the first 14 days we received inoculations, vaccinations, psychological tests, night vision test, and mathematical grading test. We were also kitted out.

July 19th 1941. Posted to 'Viceroy Court' two blocks further along the road. We are now in 'Q' Squadron. This squadron comprises all cadets who either need eye training or require special lenses in their Flying Goggles. While in this squadron we receive lectures in Mathematics and Signals.

July 27th 1941. Had a vision test. Results: Fit Pilot, unfit Observer, fit Wop/AG with special lenses.

August 3rd 1941. Today some of our flight were posted to ITWs. Those of us who are left behind continue with our lectures and after a course of 24 hours I managed to scrape through the ITW Mathematical Examinations with 61%, 60% being a pass, also passed the Signals Exam at 4 words per minute with 100%, 90% being a pass.

September 13th 1941. After 10 weeks in ACRC finally posted to No 1 ITW Babbacombe. Arose at 3 am. Breakfast 4 am. Moved off in trucks 6 am for Paddington. Left 7.15 am and arrived at Torquay at 2.15 pm. Marched up to Babbacombe. After an FFI had our first meal which was a very great improvement in both quality and quantity to that which we had received in London.

September 15th 1941. First parade at 7.25 am. After inspection, started the Initial Training Wing Course. 19 of us finally convinced the Education Officer that we have passed our Maths Exam, so we are allowed to start Navigation immediately. Except for ¼ hour at 10 am and 55 mins break at 12.30 pm and a further ¼ hour at 3.45 pm the whole of the day from 7.25 am until 6 pm is spent attending Lectures, Drill and PT. This course is very hard work and it is necessary to study every night. One afternoon per week is given over to organized games and, within reason, one may choose which sport one would like to indulge in.

September 30th. Issued with Flying Kit.

October 17th 1941. Taken our last examinations this morning . . .

Left Babbacombe at 11 am for my first leave since coming into service.

October 22nd 1941. Back again at 23.59. We now await posting to an EFTS. Have now discovered that most postings are abroad and fortunately any Cadet over 26 years of age or is married or has been transferred from the army is not allowed overseas for training.

November 17th 1941. . . . Had a scrounge round the OC's office and found all my marks for exams which are as follows:
Mathematics 61%. Navigation 87½%. Signals 95%. Law & Administration 52%. Hygiene 56%. Anti- Gas 70%. Aircraft Rec. 64%. Armaments 92%. (Law and Hygiene are both 50% passes). The passing of the exams reclassifies us to LACs with an increase of 3/- per day in pay.

Nov 28th 1941. At last a home posting. About 9 of us to go to Sywell (Northants) to be trained as night fighters. We have been selected because in our night vision test we are average or above average (I am average). We are to go on Dec 5th.

Dec 3rd 1941. Posting postponed until Dec 20th.

Dec 18th 1941. Posting cancelled. All our spirits back to zero . . .

Another Cadet, S Perrin, and myself have been helping in the Orderly Room for some considerable period during which I have managed to get a glimpse of my 1499A (a form that gives all results of examinations, bearing, speech, intelligence, etc). My 1499A is as follows:
PT – average. Drill – average. Speech – average. Bearing – average. Intelligence – average (although at some time there had been a mark against – below average). General Character – A keen reliable type. Not recommended for commission. I have now come to the conclusion that I am a very average person.

Dec 23rd 1941. Done our utmost to secure Christmas leave but all to no avail. At one period it was almost within our grasp, but due to an over-zealous LAC it slipped through our fingers.

Dec 25th 1941. Christmas in the service. Not a very bright prospect. Rather a pleasant surprise was our Christmas dinner. Turkey, roast pork, boiled and baked potatoes, sausage and stuffing balls, brussel sprouts followed by Christmas pudding and custard, soft drinks, beer and cigarettes. Spent Christmas night at a party at the Services Club Torquay, after going to the cinema. Although I have had a very nice Christmas, one always wishes one was a home, and being away at this time pulls at your heart strings.

Handley Page Halifax. A superb four-engine heavy bomber used for a variety of purposes apart from dropping bombs.

THE HALIFAX CREW
(left) Flt/Sgt Thomas 'Tommy' McCarthy, bomb aimer, (aged 19), posing with the crew mascot, Thumper Rabbit. The bomb sight can be seen through the perspex nose.

F/O 'Ben' Bennett, navigator, (aged 21), with his pilot, F/Sgt John Hollander, (aged 20), under the nose of their Halifax Mk 111 bomber, MH-R, of 51 Squadron, Snaith.

THE HALIFAX CREW (continued) (right) Flt/Sgt Douglas Parkinson, flight engineer, (aged 20), perched alongside the astrodome.

(middle) Flt/Sgt Ken Booth, mid-upper gunner, (aged 19), with his four Browning .303 machine guns in a Boulton Paul hydraulically operated turret.

(foot) Flt/Sgt Mick Campbell, RAAF. Rear Gunner, (aged 24), the crew's 'grandad'! On operations, both he and Booth wore electrically heated suits to combat the freezing conditions.

(above) Avro Lancaster. Unlike this 'Lanc', those operated by 101 Squadron differed in having accommodation for a crew of eight instead of the usual seven, and two large aerials pointing upwards from the fuselage, with another pointing downwards from the nose. The rear 'ROSE' turret was larger than standard to accommodate twin .5 Browning machine guns (*RAF Museum*)

AUTHOR'S FIRST CREW
(above left) 'Skipper', Flying Officer, (later Squadron Leader) Jack West. Although severely wounded pressed on and bombed target. Awarded DSO and DFC.

(left) Flight Engineer. F/Sergeant Ken Ward (later commissioned). Seriously wounded.

AUTHOR'S FIRST CREW
(continued)
(right) Bomb Aimer. Canadian
F/Sergeant Jimmy Hutchinson.

(below) Wireless Operator.
F/Sergeant Bruce Lewis (later
commissioned). The author.

(above) Rear Gunner. F/Sergeant
Stan Wright.

Mid-Upper Gunner. F/Sergeant
Ted Morgan. Later killed.

AUTHOR'S SECOND CREW
(below) 'Skipper'. Flight Lieutenant
Jim Bursell. Outstanding pilot.
Awarded DFC.

(foot) Flight Engineer Peter
Clifford (*right*) with his sister and
brothers, after his commission. As
the only regular serviceman in the
crew he remained in the RAF after
the war and rose to the rank of
Group Captain. Awarded DFC.

(top) Navigator Colin Pyle
after his commission.
Awarded DFC.

(above) German speaking
Australian 'Special
Operator' Max Doolette.
Like the author Max served
in both crews.

THE ENEMIES
Messerschmitt 109G.
The ultimate
development of the 109
day fighter carried an
offensive armament of
one 30 mm cannon,
two 13 mm machine
guns and either two
20 mm cannon or two
210 mm rocket
launchers (*RAF
Museum*).

Focke Wulf FW190.
Arguably even more
deadly than the
Messerschmitt 109,
with similar armament
configurations, but
having over three times
the endurance, at 3¼
hours (*RAF Museum*).

UNITED STATES 8TH ARMY AIR FORCE, THE FRIENDS: The North
American P-51 Mustang. The best of a group of three escort fighters
which in 1944 ensured success at last for the 8th AAF (*RAF Museum*).

THE US HEAVIES AND
THEIR CREWS
(right) The Liberator Waist
Gunner – Sergeant Odell
Dobson.

(below) B-17 Flying Fortresses
(*RAF Museum*).

(foot) The Consolidated Vultee
Liberator B-24. The other
'Heavy' of the 8th AAF.
Powered by four 1200 h.p. Pratt
& Whitney radial engines, it was
a rugged war machine (*RAF
Museum*).

8th AAF Air Gunners. A group of typical air gunners, tough and generally of stocky build, but the exception, Sergeant Odell Dobson, was well over six feet.

Odell Dobson's Crew. Typical of many crews who manned the 'Heavies' of the 8th AAF - ten flyers; four officers and six sergeants. From this group, only Odell Dobson, (fourth from left, back row), and radio operator Roger Clapp, (fifth from left, back row), survived an attack by enemy fighters on 10 September, 1944.

THE EARLY BIRDS
Fairey Battle operating in France, Spring 1940. A sleek and 'modern-looking' aircraft, it was completely outgunned and outmanoeuvred by opposing German fighters (*RAF Museum*).

Bristol Blenheim. Three years before the outbreak of World War Two this was the fastest medium bomber in the world. Yet from the start of hostilities it was outgunned by the enemy. Only the useful turn of speed from its twin engines gave crews some chance of survival (*RAF Museum*).

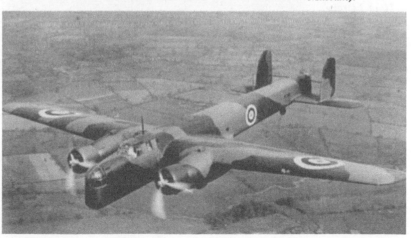

Armstrong Whitworth Whitley. At the beginning of the war it was the only RAF 'Heavy' designed specifically to operate at night (*RAF Museum*).

THE EARLY BIRDS
(continued)
Vickers Wellington.
Designed by Barnes
Wallis and
incorporating a
geodetic
construction of
great strength, this
bomber was by far
the best of the
RAF's earlier
wartime twin-
engine 'Heavies'.
Note the geodetic
framework showing
through the beam
gunport, giving an
almost 'Tudor'
window effect!
(*RAF Museum*).

Handley Page
Hampden. Twin-
engine medium
bomber. With a
crew of four this
was among the
most cramped
aircraft ever
designed (*Robert
Hunt Library*).

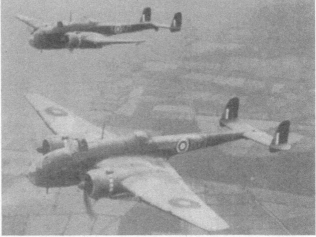

THE ENEMY
BOMBER
(below) Heinkel HE
111. One of three
twin-engine bomber
types used in large
numbers on heavily
escorted daylight
raids by the
Luftwaffe during
the Battle of Britain
(*Robert Hunt
Library*).

THE REAL
HEAVIES ARRIVE
(above) Handley
Page Halifax
similar in app-
earance to
that used by
161 Squadron
(*RAF Museum*).

(left) Short
Stirling. Here
being 'bombed-
up'. First and
biggest of the new
breed of Bomber
Command's four-
engine 'Heavies',
it was inferior in
every way to
either the
Lancaster or the
Halifax but
retained the
affection of the
crews because it
was built like a
'brick hen house',
yet was very
manoeuvrable at
lower altitudes
(*RAF Museum*).

THE UNLUCKY GLIDER (see Chapter 3)
Airspeed Horsa. Troop or freight-carrying glider. Apart
from pilot and co-pilot, this glider could lift fifteen fully-
armed airborne troops (*RAF Museum*).

Sergeant Leslie Biddlecombe.

Sergeant John Roberts DFM.

Flight/Sergeant Reg Scarth.

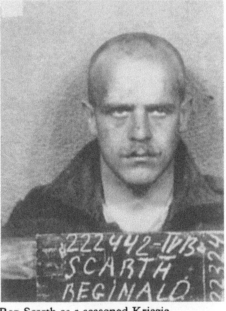

Reg Scarth as a seasoned Kriegie.

RAF TRAINERS
(above) Avro Anson.
Twin-engine Advanced
Training monoplane
(*RAF Museum*).

(left) North American
Harvard. Single-engine
Advanced Training
monoplane.

(below) DH 89B
Dominie – RAF version
of the twin-engine
Dragon Rapide biplane
(*RAF Museum*).

TRAINING
(below right) Hawker Hart. Originally introduced into the RAF in 1930 as a single-engine Light Day Bomber, this biplane was powered by a 525 hp Kestrel.

(below left) Francis Kelsey as a Pilot Cadet.

FULFILMENT Flying Officer Francis Kelsey and crew in front of their Lancaster of 625 Squadron, Kelstern, July, 1944.

(left) Flt/Sgt Bruce Lewis – the author, during training at No. 8 Air Gunnery School, Evanton.

(below) Flight Lieutenant Harold Chadwick, DFC, as a trainee pilot in Canada. He is seated in a Steerman PT17 biplane trainer.

(above) Blackburn Botha. Designed as a twin-engine Torpedo Bomber, the aircraft was a failure in this capacity. Relegated to Air Gunnery training it was still far from ideal (*RAF Museum*).

(right) LACW 'Miki' Smith of 101 Squadron's highly secret Signals Section, Ludford Magna, 1944.

THE WEIGHT LIFTER
Avro Lancaster of
Harold Chadwick's 617
Squadron. Various
modifications were
undertaken at different
periods to accommodate
the special bombs
carried by 617
Squadron. This 617
'Lanc' has a 'cut-away'
under-belly forming a
neat recess for giant
bombs (*RAF Museum*).

THE ENEMY
Junkers Ju 88G.
Luftwaffe Night Fighter.
The enemy 'homed in'
on Bomber Command
'Heavies' by means of
Lichtenstein radar. Note
the aerials installed in
the nose (*RAF Museum*).

THE FRIEND A DH Mosquito Night Fighter Intruder of the type
that came to the rescue of Reg Scarth and his crew (*RAF Museum*).

Jan 1st 1942. Went to a dance last night. It was most necessary for my peace of mind. All day have been thinking of the way I have always spent Old Year's Night and was very homesick . . .

The OC of the Squadron and I do not get along very well together. My civilian occupation brought me in contact with a great many people, and it has become more or less a habit to be able to sum up a person's character after the first conversation with them. My first encounter with him did not impress me at all, in fact it was to the contrary. Incidentally, I think that this has been recipro-cal upon his part. My subsequent association with him has proved my first impression. (I was in contact with him several times a day whilst working in the Orderly Room.)

He hasn't any military bearing or manner but does his utmost to keep on the right side of the Wing Commander. During the whole of my stay never has he addressed any individual flights or given any Cadet encouragement. Neither does he seem very keen upon the work. Providing there is no trouble in the Squadron he doesn't trouble about anything. He has done nothing for us, but nothing against us, in fact his psychological outlook is very poor. All our other officers are real gentlemen. When you do anything wrong you are reprimanded, but also given praise when doing anything outstandingly good . . .

Jan 13th 1942. 23 of us called into the OC's office individually and told we are posted on an overseas posting to a hot climate. It appears the regulation regarding men over 26 years and army transfers has been altered . . . fortunately, we have been given 13 days embark-ation leave . . .

When the aircrew cadets returned, they were posted to Blackpool and, after travelling all night by train, were left standing in a heavy snowstorm outside the RAF HQ from noon until 4 pm. They had not had a meal since 6 o'clock the previous evening. Eventually Francis and four others were found a billet in the attic of a boarding house. That night they froze because of a lack of blankets. On subsequent nights they slept in their flying kit.

They shivered in Blackpool for two weeks and the only practical outcome was the issue of tropical kit – during another snowstorm.

Thursday Feb 12th 1942. Left Blackpool 9 am. Boarded HMT *Ormond* [15,000 tons] at Glasgow at 4 pm. Mac and I have been separated due to the difference in our numbers which have been taken in order.

Friday Feb 13th 1942. Sailed down the Clyde and anchored off Gourock. Conditions on ship very bad. 216 men being placed in a comparatively small space, where they eat, drink and sleep. When sleeping, hammocks are almost touching. Those on mattresses sleep where they can, on tables, under tables, in fact anywhere there is space.

Sunday Feb 15th. Still at anchor.

Monday Feb 16th. Anchor up at 9 pm. Voyage commenced.

Wednesday Feb 18th . . . Dissatisfaction among the men regarding the difference between the Men's and Officers' conditions. The officers have good meals. 2 to 4 sitting at a table, with an excellent lounge for smoking, cards, etc, while men get where they can. One bright spot today, we all received a South African orange. . . .

Thursday Feb 19th . . . boat drill every morning. Have volunteered and obtained mess orderly job. Have to draw meals for our mess (18 men) serve it, and wash and clean up after each meal . . . actually volunteered to kill time, it certainly does. I never seem to get any time at all.

This is a large convoy, ** Troopships, ** Destroyers, ** Aircraft Carriers and a Heavy Cruiser. Some excitement today watching (Fairey) Albacores landing on Carriers.

Friday Feb 20th. . . . tea was made with salt water, consequently none of us could drink it . . . The ship is called 'Slave Ship' and 'Hell Ship' by the men.

Saturday Feb 21st. Sea very rough. The ship is pitching, tossing and rolling all at the same time. One moment you are standing the next you are lying down. It is surprising at what angle the ship will go over without turning turtle . . . Had an altercation with a Squadron Leader regarding conditions and was informed it could be worse. We could have horses down here and have to clean them and still eat and sleep down here, as they did in the last war. My reply was, 'that still thinking in last-war terms was probably the cause of our many mistakes in this war, 25 years later.'

Sunday Feb 22nd . . . Some excitement today when one of the planes from the carrier landed and tore his tail completely off. I actually saw this occur. Fortunately, the main planes and the fuselage stayed on the deck, so we assume Pilot was not killed. The one bright spot today was when 'Bootle' (the other mess orderly) and I shared a tin of salmon. He scrounged a couple of lettuce leaves,

90

leavings from the officers' tables, so had salmon and lettuce sandwiches. (Naturally it was necessary to scrounge the bread also.)

Monday Feb 23nd. Today has been like a tropical summer's day. It has been very warm. . . . Another aircraft cracked up on landing on the carrier, although I did not see this. We are sleeping on the boat deck tonight.

Thursday Feb 23rd. (My wedding anniversary – the 4th) Saw today for the first time flying fish. They appear to be about 8 inches long. They come out of the water, fly along for 10 to 12 yards about 1½ to 2 feet above the water then they re-enter, preferably into a wave. Their appearance in flight is that of a bird with a fish body. Their 'fins/wings' move so quickly that they look just like a model aeroplane gliding in to land. . . .

Friday Feb 27th. Heat getting worse . . . rose at 5.20 this morning, crept into the officers' bathroom and had a good hot sea-water bath (have been able to obtain sea-water soap). . . .

Sunday March 1st 1942. Went on deck first thing this morning and found we were moving slowly into moorings. This proved to be Freetown, Sierra Leone. I should think there are between 60 and 80 ships lying off the town, including our own convoy. . . .

Francis gives a picture of his impressions of Freetown; its smallness, the palm trees lining the sandy beaches, the scrub-covered hills in the hinterland. But, tantalizingly, their ship comes no nearer than 1½ miles to the shore. They hear news of a convoy disaster in the North Sea in which three troopships are reported sunk by U-boats. He wishes he could send his wife a cable to let her know he is safe. After six days the ship up-anchors and continues its voyage south. On 21 March, 1942, after five long, uncomfortable weeks at sea the ship steams into Durban, South Africa. Boarding a train, drawn up at the dockside, the men travel all through the night on a journey lasting twenty hours.

Arriving at No. 75 Air School, Lyttelton, Transvaal, he is reunited with Mac and some of his other pals who shared the attic in Blackpool. He moves, with other cadets, to EFTS at Potchefstroom. Living conditions are excellent. In the mess, meals are served by waiters. The following day they are divided into four flights of twelve men each under the guidance of a Flight Commander and six Instructors. He and Pupil Pilot Holdup are to be trained on Tiger Moths by 23-year-old Lieutenant Slater:

Tuesday May 26th 1942. . . . We go up and contrary to my thoughts I am not afraid but thoroughly enjoy it. I'm given the controls to fly straight and level, climbing, gliding turns and I seem to have got thoroughly at home with it . . . I'm back to my keenness for flying.

Thursday May 28th. . . . When we are about 150 feet he says, 'I can't believe it, we must go down and do it again'. Down we go and go through the same performance again. When we get off, he says, 'It must be true'. I am in doubt as to what exactly he means [good or bad] . . . so ask him . . . he replies, 'It is the first time that I have known a pupil to take off as well as that at the third attempt'. When we come in to land he tells me what to do and gives me some help with the controls . . . he tells me he is very pleased with my flying.

Tuesday June 2nd. Some excitement today. The instructor explained to me the method of recovering from a spin – and not to recover until he says so. I put her in and start spinning down. It seemed a devil of a time before he said recover. I immediately gave her opposite rudder, then centre and put the stick forward. The next thing I hear is, 'I've got her', to which I reply, 'You've got her, Sir', and then we were straight and level . . . When we came down he told me he thought we had 'had it' because I put the stick too far forward and we dived down under the vertical . . . I'm inclined to think he does not like spinning because he told me he would never do them for fun.

Saturday June 6th. I took off as usual and when we were up 1000 feet he asked me if my straps were tight. I replied, 'I think so'. He said, 'Don't think, make sure'. After ascertaining that they were, he said, 'I gave Holdup a slow roll this morning and afterwards his flying was much better, so I'm going to give you one to see what it will do to you'. Up we went and then he started to roll. What a horrible feeling. You roll over on your side very slowly until you are upside-down, and you are then hanging from your straps with the earth above your head. Slowly you turn right over until you are the right way up again . . . throughout the whole manoeuvre I had my hand on the handle of the 'rip cord' of my chute. . . . When I landed she bumped slightly and he said, 'What did you think of that landing?' I replied, 'Not much'. He said he would not like to be my wife because I'm too B—dy fussy.

Wednesday June 10th. . . . My second period was with the Flight Commander for a progress test. I took off and he started grumbling

92

from the time he got in until he got out. First I was doing one thing wrong, then another until I was beginning to think I was NBG. In fact he got on my nerves. He made me land. It was a fair landing but not good. We took off again, and when we were about 500 feet he cut the engine. I immediately started to glide to enable me to keep flying speed. Down we went merrily towards the ground. I did not take her out of the glide and he did not say anything so we kept going down.

I thought, if it was good enough for him to hit the deck at 70 mph, it was good enough for me. He had cut the engine, so let him put it on again. At 30 feet from the ground, he said, 'All right. Take your engine and climb.' By the time I had taken my engine and levelled out we were within 10 feet of the ground.

He told me to make a circuit and land, which I did and came down a perfect 3 pointer as gently as a kitten. He got out and said, 'All right. Make one circuit and landing on your own'. And these were the words that let me go on my first solo. . . . I was the first of the three of us to go solo, my time being 12.50 hours. Frank Henley was 13.20 hours and Perrin 13.50 hours. So I collected the 3/-

Thursday June 11th. . . . Found out that apart from Mac and Dorsie who have both flown solo in England, I have the lowest solo time in the flight of 12 cadets.

This afternoon we had to go on a funeral parade of a Pupil Pilot who was killed when he crashed at SFTS.

Tuesday June 16th. . . . We very nearly had a serious accident. As we were making a landing and gliding down another 'Tiger' flashed in front of us, and our prop very nearly touched his tail. I gave my instructor a thorough shaking and those who saw it wondered how a collision was averted. Incidentally the plane that nearly crashed us was crashed 30 minutes later when it landed upon another plane. Fortunately, no one was seriously hurt.

Wednesday June 17th. . . . Holdup is having some trouble. He has had 3 Flight Commander tests and 1 Chief Flying Instructor test. This morning the CFI took off with him and returned without him. It appears he did not set his tail trim, so the instructor made him get out at the far end of the field and walk back, about ¾ of a mile. 3 of the cadets have been 'washed out' because their progress was not satisfactory.

Thursday June 25th. Holdup finally went solo this morning after

93

having had 9 tests. This means I will not get so much flying in future. . . .

Tuesday June 30th. When taking off this morning I swung and very nearly collided with another aircraft. We passed within 20 feet of each other 30 feet up. For this my instructor said I was to wash an aircraft, later he cancelled it.

Thursday July 2nd. We had two crashes today. Both were due to the same reason, stalling too high. One of the fellows 'dropped it' from 30 feet, smashing the undercart, mainplane, propellor and part of the engine and centre section, leaving the nose on the ground with the tail sticking up in the air.

The pupil, who was solo, climbed out perfectly sound and was brought back to the hangar in an ambulance. The instructor called him a few choice names and told him to run around the flying field three times for being so dozy. The other crash was similar but not quite so much damage was done to the plane.

Francis had the highest regard for his instructor, Lieutenant Slater. He inspired confidence, was very fair, and told his 'star' pupil that he had bet on him getting an 'above average' assessment at the end of the course. Then the blow fell. On Monday, 6 July Francis was transferred to another Flight and came under the supervision of a different instructor, Lieutenant Williams. It seemed that for Williams he could do nothing right. What particularly upset him was that his new instructor, from whom he found it impossible to learn anything, blamed his 'lack of progress' on his previous tuition.

Friday July 10th. Today I went on a dual X Country. I went straight from lectures to the hangar . . . as soon as he saw me he started his moaning. Told me to 'wake up'. Those were not the actual words he used but that was the meaning. I obtained the wind and computed the course and we emplaned. Unfortunately when we were taxiing to the down-wind edge I dropped my pencil in the cockpit and could not find it. This set him off good and proper. He asked me ETAs but as soon as I attempted to work one out he would ask me what particular landmark was this or that. When I had told him, he would ask what the ETA was. I'd reply, I'm just working it out. Off he went again, 'Wake up! We haven't all day,' and so on. This continued all the way and when we arrived and got out he started on me again about my bad ETAs, (The worst

94

one was 3 minutes out.) Coming back the same thing happened, only I had to do the piloting as well.

This time I gave him a really bad ETA, 13 minutes out, so I got it good and strong. I felt like saying, 'Turn this plane upside down and I'll drop out'. Altogether the whole trip took 2¾ hours and he was moaning the whole time. I see I'm going up dual with him on Monday. If he moans all that period I'm going to ask for a change of instructor. I haven't learned a thing since I started flying with him. All I've had is mental torture.

Monday July 20th. Went up with another instructor this morning, Lieutenant Beattie. He complimented me on my steep turns and half-roll off the top of a loop. Took our final exams in Navigation Theory and Plotting, and Signals Procedure.

Saturday July 25th. Passed my Morse Receiving at 10 words per minute. We then had to read the lamp at 8 words per minute. I never could read the lamp, so I got a colleague to read it for me. . . . The reading of the lamp is the first exam I have ever manipulated. This was necessary because, although I can read morse quite well, my eyes water when staring at it. I'm afraid that if my eyes are examined again, I shall be taken off aircrew.

Saturday August 1st. Went to the 'flicks' this afternoon, consequently hadn't anywhere to go tonight. Finally went to a dance at the Jewish Guild. I didn't dance but sat watching. Tea, sandwiches, fruit salad and minerals were issued free. There were about five of us RAF there, and after I left there was the usual fight. Three or four SA Artillerymen beat up one of the RAF lads. The SAAF and the RAF get along well, but the South African Army and the RAF are like poison to each other. Unfortunately we are in the minority and always get beaten. Sometimes it works out 6 to 1. Strangely enough, if there are eight or nine of us together we are left severely alone.

Thursday August 6th. My assessment is Average-Plus and the remarks are as follows – 'Never say die type. Has worked hard and done well.' Altogether in our Flight there are 18 pupils. 2 got Above Average assessments, one of them being Mac. 4 of us Average-plus. The other 12 Average.

Thursday August 13th. The Flight Commander told me he had recommended me for Fighters. Ten minutes later he informed me there was a rule that no one over 25 could go on Fighters – so I'm back on bombers again. Have got friendly with the WAAF Sergeant in the CFI's office and have found out that I have been recommended for a commission. We have been informed that we are to have 15 days' leave commencing Sunday.

Leave for Francis seems to have been a pleasant relaxation. He managed a few days hunting in which, among other things, he bagged a 10-foot python. On return to Potchefstroom the pupils did a little more flying and then left to continue their training at SFTS, Waterkloof.

Sunday September 6th. It appears we have a 24-week course here and the station is very strict on discipline. Have to fill in a form giving particulars of where born, what school attended, educational qualifications, etc. We have been told that our educational qualifications will be taken into consideration during recommendation for a commission. I have put down on the form that I was born in London, and went to Columbia Road Elementary School, E2, and have no qualifications. So I'm pretty certain I shall not be recommended here – especially as this is an RAF station [as opposed to a SAAF establishment].

Monday September 7th. Had my first flip in a Hart. [Originally introduced into the RAF in 1930 as a single engine, light day bomber, the Hawker Hart byplane was powered by a 525hp Kestrel engine]. It's heavy but I think I shall be able to manage it. Lectures have started again (4 hours a day).

Friday September 11th. After two circuits with the instructor he sent me solo. 2.25 hours instruction on these Harts in all, then my solo which consisted of 2 complete circuits and landings. Another pupil and myself share the honours for the least time in which to solo in the Flight.

Friday September 18th. Due to one of the fellows being 'washed out', I have been transferred to another squad and now have an English Squadron Leader for my instructor. He does a good deal of moaning and groaning. Incidentally, he was the instructor of the pupil who was 'washed out'.

Monday September 21st. I honestly felt like turning the course in. There is nothing that disheartens one so much as an instructor who continually grumbles when you are trying. It puts you off far more than the natural or unnatural things you meet in the air. Altogether the X Country flight was a failure. I gained no instruction from it, neither did I fly as I would have done had I been alone.

I feel sure that I shan't do well under this instructor.

96

Friday September 25th. One period of 25 minutes dual to convert me on to 'tail skid' Harts. Had a different instructor for this test and he says I'm OK to go solo on them. Mac today landed in the 'bad ground' at the side of the drome and turned the plane up on its nose. He was unhurt.

Monday September 28th. Did 1.40 hours solo and 20 minutes Instruments with instructor. Even when solo I'm not flying at all well. I'm inclined to think I'm flying on my nerves. Mac has got his punishment for his charge, which is to pay the cost of the damage. £35.

Monday October 5th. There were two crashes here yesterday in one of which a pupil was killed.

Monday October 19th. My flying is now going from bad to worse and I'm beginning to think I shall never finish this course and get my Wings. . . . I'm flying on my nerves. Two planes collided while taking off. They caught fire but all 4 (2 pupils and 2 instructors) got out quite safe. Altogether we have had 7 crashes in 3 days.

Wednesday November 4th. Had an instrument test this morning by my own instructor. Did very badly and he 'striped' both in the air and when we came down. I'm not doing at all well and I'm inclined to think I shall be 'washed out'.

Friday November 6th. If I do not go night solo within the next two periods I think I shall be finished.

Tuesday November 10th. Solo X Country via Loskop to Pietersburg and back – 350 miles. 5 of us flew at approximately the same time. I never saw any of them on the way, but we all landed at Pietersburg within 10 minutes of each other. Steve was one of the 5. We arranged to fly back in formation, which we did, I leading and doing the navigating. We arrived back on ETA. Altogether a flight which I greatly enjoyed.

Tuesday November 17th . . . finally did my first night solo after help from my new instructor. I feel sure if I had been with him from the start I would really be able to fly now.

Friday November 20th. The Flight Commander called me into his office and informed me that Lt/Colonel Bosch the Chief Instructor who examined me on my passenger Test, had given me an Above Average assessment. I am now allowed to take passengers. This was a very pleasant surprise to me. There are only 4 out of 42 of us with this assessment. 'Exceptional' is the only higher assessment and no one has ever been known to get this.

97

One of the pupils was killed today when he force-landed.

Tuesday November 24th. Mac has got an Average and Steve an Average Plus. I am the only one on the course who has got anything over average at both EFTS and ITS. Strange as it may seem, those who got average or above average at EFTS have all received average here.

Monday November 30th. Today we wrote the final exams in Navigation Plotting and Signals Procedure. I feel that I should have managed to scrape through both of these. Another of our course has been 'washed out'. This makes 12 out of 50.

Sunday December 6th. Had first trip in a Hind. [More advanced and powerful supercharged version of the Hart. With a Kestrel 640 HP engine]. Did 1 hour Formation dual and then 1 hour solo general.

Monday December 14th. Our exercise today was Finding Wind Speed and Direction with the aid of the Bomb Sight. Lying down in the 'Dog Box', with the 'Monkey Chain' on, hot air and oil in your face, is not very pleasant, in fact it is torture.

Tuesday December 15th. The list of 'Wings' exam failures was posted up this morning. I was very pleased that my name was not on it. There were 12 pupils' names and between them they failed 22 subjects. One pupil failed 4 of the 6 papers. There were only 39 pupils altogether who wrote the exam.

Wednesday December 23rd. Four days' Christmas leave. Toc H fixed us up to spend our holiday with a family at Roodepoort. Had a marvellous time, house parties, picnics, swimming and boating.

Sunday January 3rd. (1943) So far I am pretty well certain that I have passed all the tests that I have taken. There is a real purge on at the moment in the 'washing out' line. No one feels safe. We now have only 32 of the original 50 who came here. I am sure we shall have some more 'washouts' yet.

Monday January 11th. Had my final assessment today. Did not put up a very good show. Cloud was too low for aerobatics. The examiner gave me Average, but said he was under the impression that it was an 'off day', and if he had time he would fly with me again, if not the Average assessment would have to stand. The examiner was an RAF Squadron Leader. I suppose I must be satisfied that I passed.

Thursday January 21st. Today we had an interview with the Commission Board which consisted of the CO and CFI and a Group

Commander. I've an idea that I rubbed the CO the wrong way. After one of the fellows went before the board he was immediately put up for a 'washout' test.

Thursday February 4th. Those getting commissions have been told today. I am not among the eleven. Mac and Steve have been fortunate enough to get commissioned so we shall now split up.

Friday February 5th. Today we summarized our Log Books, in which our 1499c has been inserted. I see that I have two Above Averages in Distinctive Qualities. They are Persistency and Self Control. All my others are Average. I have been recommended to fly Army Co-operation single-engine planes [i.e. Hurricanes or Mustangs]. The remarks on the sheets are as follows:
'Has tried very hard. Struggles against the natural disabilities of age, inclined to be slow-thinking. Acted very cool and collected in a recent emergency.'
Had the opportunity to see some of those 1499s of the fellows who are being commissioned. Only in about two cases have any of them anything above Average. In at least one case there is a Below Average. Under these circumstances it is very difficult to see how the selection for commissions is made.
We have written in our Log Books – 'Qualified to wear the RAF Flying Badge'. No more flying now until I go on the Conversion Course.

Friday February 19th. [The Great Day]. Up at 6.30 am. Breakfast, wash and shave, then dress in our 'Best Blues'. On Parade at 8 am. where we have an inspection. By 8.30 am. the band arrives and at 8.50 we commence the march.
On the parade ground, the band playing, guests seated in wicker chairs each side of the saluting base. Stand at ease until the Inspecting Officer arrives, when we give a General Salute. He then inspects us when we again march past the base. We, the course passing out, then march off the ground and discard our Webbing, Bayonet and Rifle. Forming up again we march back on the parade ground halting between the Guard of Honour and the base, facing the base. The names of the cadets are then called out with their Wings. The first six are in order of merit after which it is in alphabetical order.
The Wings are presented by Major-General Pool, successor to 'Dan Pienaar'. He murmurs to each cadet, pins on the Wings and wishes him luck.
After the last man has received his wings, Major-General Pool gives a short speech at the end of which we pilots march past,

salute him, march past the Guard of Honour and salute them, and off the parade ground.

While this is going on 3 aircraft are flying in formation and they salute by diving. I am no longer a pupil pilot, but a pilot. Tomorrow I shall be a Sergeant Pilot. So this ends the Diary of a U/T Pilot, 19 months from entering the service.

As far as is known Francis Kelsey wrote no further diaries during his time in the RAF. But it is a simple matter to follow the rest of his flying career from the neat entries in his Log Book. After another two months in South Africa he boarded the *Stratheden* and was back in England just over three weeks later.

Following a stay of a few days at 7 PRC Harrogate, he was posted to 11 AFU, Shawbury, where he remained for two months converting to twin-engine Oxfords. In mid-August, 1943, he joined a bomber crew at 28 OTU, Wymeswold, and progressed to Wellingtons.

Posted to Kelstern on 10 April, 1944, he was fortunate to miss the Battle of Berlin and the disastrous Nuremburg raid by a matter of weeks. He and his crew joined 625 Squadron, and flew on 20 April to Cologne, then to Karlsruhe, Essen and Friedrichshafen on their first four raids. With the exception of four further raids over Germany during their tour, the remaining 22 operations were all to France. After not far short of three years in training, his combat duties were completed in just over three months.

Francis had been given his commission shortly before the start of his operational tour. On completion of his 30 missions he was awarded the DFC. It was only then that his perseverence and determination were rewarded. He had always wanted to be a fighter pilot. When he left 625 Squadron he spent the rest of his career flying Spitfires and Hurricanes, not in battle, but either in short hops from one station to another, or carrying out fighter affiliation exercises giving air gunners in bombers practical experience in coping with fighter attacks.

SEVEN

The Navigator

We have already outlined the extreme difficulties faced by navigators in the early days of the RAF's bombing offensive over Europe. They were obliged to find their way into enemy territory, locate the target, and then, having personally dropped the bombs, attempt to guide their crews safely home – an operation often covering many hundreds of miles, sometimes in total darkness. If the weather was bad, as it often was, with icy conditions, high winds or blanketing fog, then the task bordered on the impossible. At that time more bombers were lost through the intervention of nature than were ever brought down by enemy action. In the days when navigation consisted of little more than 'dead reckoning', luck played a major part in the question of survival.

As the war progressed, the nature of the navigator's work changed and the demands placed upon him increased to a greater degree than on any other member of an aircrew. Starting from a crude base, not much advanced from the role of the 'observer' in the First World War, he became a highly trained professional, using a range of new radar devices, radio aids, and techniques developed from the hard-won experience of his pioneering predecessors.

It became routine for hundreds of bombers to set off into the night from a variety of airfields, each making their way individually to their destination. On a dark night, it was possible to complete the flight without ever sighting another friendly aircraft. Yet such was the standard of accuracy eventually achieved by navigators of Bomber Command that the majority reached the target within seconds of ETA (the estimated time of arrival). One such example of this breed was Vernon Bennett, known to everyone as Ben.

'Ben' Bennett, if not actually born with a silver spoon in his mouth, always seemed to be accompanied by a certain amount of good luck. Born on 9 November, 1923, Ben joined the RAF in March, 1942, at the age of 18 years, 5 months, as a potential navigator. But this was not his first association with the service. He had already completed a course with Manchester University Air Squadron while still a civilian. This wise move was to stand him in good stead on numerous occasions during his time in the RAF.

For instance, his basic grounding with the University Air Squadron entitled him to skip ITW completely and move straight on to the initial stages of actual flying as part of the Empire Air Training Scheme in Canada. Qualifying at No 1 Air Navigation School, Rivers, Manitoba, and receiving his navigator's brevet, he also automatically became a Flight Sergeant. This instant leap up the promotional ladder was another of the perks of his university course. There were more advantages to come.

Posted to Moncton, New Brunswick, Ben and three of his NCO companions decided to stop off at Winnipeg and have a look at the city. The attractions, including four girls, proved irresistible and it was not until the early hours of the following morning that they turned up at Winnipeg station to continue their journey. They were not, perhaps, as flattered as they might have been by the concern of a Railway Transport Officer and a posse of Red Caps all determined to see them off to Monkton on the earliest possible train.

Arriving in due course at the main gate of RCAF Moncton, they were accosted by a corporal: 'What's your names?'

'Bennett, Binns, Cook and Douglas'.

'We've been looking for you four buggers,' says the corporal, 'You're for the bloody 'igh jump. You're all on a charge!'

But, as every ex-serviceman will confirm, justice within the forces can sometimes be tinged with a modicum of unfairness. First Binns, and then Cook were marched before the Squadron Leader, and each awarded 'extra duties' and confined to camp for 14 days. When Ben Bennett and Jack Douglas went in to see the officer matters took a different turn.

'You know what's happened to the other two?' asked the Squadron Leader. 'Well, you can both consider yourselves damn lucky.

Your commission papers came through this morning so I can't do a thing about either of you! Here's a chit for each of you. Go and see the Accounts Officer and he'll give you some money. Then report to the Clothing Officer and he'll issue both of you with more chits. With these chits and your money go down into Moncton and buy your officers' uniforms.'

Yet again the University Air Squadron had come to the rescue. It was an understanding that any cadet who entered the RAF via this scheme would be awarded a commission on successful completion of his aircrew course. Jack Douglas had attended the Air Squadron at Edinburgh University.

Ben and the others had come out to Canada on the *Queen Mary*. They now waited for a return trip to Britain, but because all available shipping was then heavily engaged in ferrying US troops and equipment to North Africa, there was some delay. Ben wasted no time in making the most of the social opportunities available in Moncton. The Canadians showed overwhelming hospitality to the British 'boys in blue'.

After about a month they boarded the *Queen Elizabeth*. Designed to carry around 2000 passengers and 1000 crew in peacetime, on this voyage she crammed 7000 servicemen inside her capacious hull. These great ships not only had the advantage of enormous capacity, they also crossed the ocean at high speed, far faster than any German submarine. In consequence they never needed to travel in convoy.

After a fortnight's leave, he was sent to Bournemouth for a brief course on ship and aircraft recognition and it looked as if he was being prepared for duties in Coastal Command, but he was then sent to Sidmouth where he underwent a toughening-up course conducted by the RAF Regiment. Scaling commando assault courses, running up and down hills with full pack, undergoing daily doses of PT, taking part in escape and survival exercises, he finished up at a peak of physical fitness never reached before, or regained since.

Next he was posted to 15 OTU, Harwell, where he became part of a very cosmopolitan crew. Flying Officer Alcorn, the pilot, was an Australian. The Flight Sergeant bomb aimer came from Canada. The rear gunner was a Scottish Flight Sergeant and the wireless operator, also a Flight Sergeant, was a Cockney. At the completion of their training on Wellingtons, they acquired a Flight Sergeant mid-upper gunner from India!

No flight engineer joined the crew because they were destined to fly Liberators in Burma, and, although a four-engine bomber, they were told this aircraft, when flown by the RAF, did not carry an engineer.

Only at the last moment was it realized that Ben, a qualified navigator, was not trained for the dual role of bomb aiming. Why this should have mattered is not clear, because the crew already had a bomb aimer. But while his crew flew off to Gibraltar, on the first stage of their journey east, Ben went home for some more leave!

During this time, a crew of Flight Sergeants on 51 Squadron, based at Snaith, had struck a difficult patch. So far they had only completed two operations and had been badly mauled on both occasions. On the first trip they had flown to Aachen and after their Halifax had been severely damaged by flak 20-year old Johnny (Dutch) Hollander, the diminutive Cockney pilot, had done well to make an emergency landing on a wire-mesh runway at Gatwick.

The second mission was no less traumatic. They were attacked by night fighters and were fortunate to struggle back to base. They had been briefed for their third raid and were actually standing on the concrete dispersal pan ready to climb into the Halifax when the navigator broke down. He refused to fly on the grounds that 'this is going to be the trip when we all get the "chop". No way will we be coming back from this one'. 'Dutch' and the others argued and pleaded with him, but nothing would persuade him to enter the aircraft.

In the end, reluctantly, they had to call up control and explain the situation. While the other bombers of 51 Squadron were roaring into the air on their way to Germany, a sad little scene was being enacted on the ground. While the crew stood disconsolately in the darkness below the aircraft, the CO arrived. Their comrade was put under arrest and taken away. He later faced a court martial, was stripped of his rank and disappeared from their lives.

Meanwhile Hollander's crew were returned to the Heavy Conversion Unit to await the arrival of a new navigator. He, of course, turned out to be Ben Bennett who had been recalled from leave to join them. This was a similar situation to that experienced by Harold Chadwick, the only officer in an otherwise all NCO crew. Bomber Command gave them plenty of time to shake down together – three or four cross-countries at the conversion unit before rejoining the squadron. Even on the squadron it was only after more than a month of intensive training in air-to-air firing, sea firing, practice bombing over the range, long cross-countries of up to ten hours' duration, that they were considered ready for operations.

Their first raid together was scheduled for the night of 15/16 February, 1944. The target turned out to be Berlin and it was the largest force of bombers sent to the German capital at any time during the war – 561 Lancasters and 314 Halifaxes. Hollander and his crew, complete with new navigator, flew off into the night, following a scheduled course that took them over the North Sea, across Denmark, entering Germany above the Baltic coast between Rostock and Stettin.

As prearranged, they had crossed the North Sea at only 1,500 feet, climbing to 18,000 after passing over Denmark. So far nothing eventful had happened and Ben had kept them meticulously on time. It was while crossing the Baltic that things went wrong. 'Dutch' came on the intercom:

'What's the fuel situation, Douggie?'

'Time to change tanks, Skip,' replied the flight engineer.

'OK. Go ahead.'

Douglas Parkinson made his way amidships, intending to switch over the fuel cocks located under the rest bed. He re-plugged his oxygen tube into the nearest point. Within moments of his departure all four engines started to cough and splutter. This was disconcerting enough, but when they suddenly cut dead and the Halifax started to drop like a stone, the situation became terrifying.

'What the hell shall we do?' someone yelled.

'We can always glide!' suggested Ben fatuously.

'Get back and see what's happening, Tommy, quick as you bloody can!' ordered 'Dutch', wrestling with the controls.

Tommy MacCarthy, a Geordie from Wallsend, scrambled up the steeply diving kite until he reached Douggie who was lying unconscious on the floor. Although Tommy was the bomb aimer he knew exactly what to do. Thrusting his hands under the rest bed he adjusted the fuel controls. The response was immediate as fuel flooded back into the starved engines. The Halifax came out of its plunge and resumed level flight.

They had lost thousands of feet in a matter of seconds. Ben was busy with his calculations:

'Not a chance of getting back to 18,000 feet by the time we reach Berlin, Skipper, not with this bomb load.'

'What do you suggest, Ben?'

'Only one thing to do. Sticking to our 180 mph indicated airspeed, and pressing on at our present height of 10,000 feet, we'll reach the target on time.'

'And have the whole of Main Force dropping their bombs on us from a great height. Sounds healthy!'

'No bloody option, I'm afraid.'

So that is what they did – bombed on time with thousands of incendiaries and hundreds of 4,000 lb high explosive bombs hurtling past them, unloaded by their comrades above. They had no idea at the time that this was the biggest raid ever on Berlin, or that a record 2,642 tons of bombs were to cascade down that night. They came all the way back at 10,000 feet. Later they learned that 43 aircraft, 26 Lancasters and 17 Halifaxes, had been lost. Perhaps Flight Sergeant Hollander's crew had finally taken on board a lucky omen – their new navigator.

Naturally there was an investigation into what had gone wrong on board H for 'Hollander'. Obviously the flight engineer had suffered a blackout due to oxygen starvation. It transpired that, like all other aircrew, he kept his flying gear in a steel locker in the crewroom. His particular locker, though, was the nearest to a large, and very hot, anthracite stove. The metal panel, on the inside of which he hung his oxygen mask and tube, became overheated and the rubber equipment had perished. Parkinson was reprimanded because he had failed to use the oxygen mask testing device provided in the crewroom.

Confidence steadily increased as they welded together into a professional flying team. Their CO was a stickler for training, never missing an opportunity to send them up on fighter affiliation exercises, bombing practice or cross-country jaunts to brush up their navigation whenever there was a lull in operational flying. Although no higher in rank than a Flight Sergeant, Hollander established a reputation as a fine pilot, much respected on the squadron for his outstanding ability. The Wing Commander once said to them:

'You must reach the absolute peak of efficiency in your own particular job, then learn as much as you can about the other fellow's job too – all your lives depend on it. Look how Tommy saved your bacon by knowing how to adjust those fuel cocks. You may find these training flights a bit of a bind, but they are vital if you are going to survive.' He started to walk away, then, struck by an afterthought, he turned, 'Come to think of it, we haven't had a crew yet which has managed to complete a tour!'

Ben, unlike Leslie Biddlecombe, Harold Chadwick or myself, always felt certain of personal survival. It never occurred to him that he would be killed. In spite of the statistical evidence to the contrary he knew he was destined to complete a tour and come through unscathed. This confidence must have been a source of strength to himself and the rest of the crew.

They flew to bomb Stuttgart, but had to return early because of engine trouble. In a later raid they bombed the same target without incident. Operations to Düsseldorf and Essen also passed off comparatively free from trouble. Ben, of course, was two missions behind the rest of the crew. In order to even the score, he flew as navigator for a Warrant Officer Skinner on one raid, and then did another to Le Câteau. This second trip was bedevilled by bad weather. They encountered cloud all the way to the target. The rain was so intense it was driving through the window frames and the joints in the panels of the fuselage, soaking both the occupants and their equipment. All the electronic gear was inoperative as the radio and Gee navigation aid became saturated. Ben had to plot the course by dead reckoning alone. On the return journey he was reasonably satisfied that he had their position worked out.

'Where are we, navigator?'

'Approximately between Beachy Head and Reading.'

But the pilot was not prepared to rely on the word of an

unknown navigator. 'I'm going below cloud to establish our position more accurately.'

'Fair enough, Skipper, but remember the minimum safety height in this area is 1,500 feet.'

Ben watched with growing anxiety as the aircraft descended through impenetrable cloud. Concentrating on his duplicate altimeter he saw the needle fall to 1,500 feet. They were still in cloud. 1,200 feet – still in cloud.

'Skipper, we're below the safety level.'

'Don't worry.'

Down they went – 1,000 feet. Ben knew there was high ground in this locality at around that altitude and his altimeter had been set at sea level. At last at under 800 feet they broke through the cloud base and saw the misty countryside below them. All of a sudden a massive grey structure loomed up to port, perilously close. It had battlements and turrets and an enormous round tower dominating the whole building. Pulling back on the stick, the pilot hauled the Halifax up into the cloud once again.

'OK, navigator. That was a damn good pinpoint. What was it?'

Ben took a deep breath inside his oxygen mask before replying, 'That was Windsor Castle!'

Beyond Nottingham the weather cleared and they landed at base without any problems. As soon as they were on the ground Ben tackled the pilot over his stupidity in disobeying the rules. As a Flying Officer he was outranked by his temporary skipper, but his anger knew no bounds when he thought of the danger imposed on the entire crew, the possibility of wrecking a valuable aircraft, and, most awful to contemplate, how near they might have come to wiping out the Royal Family.

A blazing row developed in which the Flight Lieutenant tried to pull rank. But Ben stood his ground, convinced that he was in the right. In the end he marched off and reported the matter to the Wing Commander. The pilot was severely reprimanded.

He was glad to return to his own crew, stalwart, efficient, cheerful, and yet unbelievably youthful:

| Pilot – John 'Dutch' Hollander. | Age 20 |
| Navigator – Ben Bennett. | Age 21 |

Bomb Aimer – Tommy MacCarthy.	Age 19
Wireless Operator – Harry Bottrell.	Age 20
Flight Engineer – Douglas Parkinson	Age 20
Mid Upper Gunner – Frankie Jones	Age 19
Rear Gunner – Mick 'Aussie' Campbell.	Age 24 Crew 'Grandad'

At the time of their first raid, on Berlin, Ben worked out that the average age of the crew was 20 years and 9 months.

In spite of their youth, there can be no doubt that Bomber Command aircrew took their duties very seriously. Whatever their task in the aircraft they felt a strong sense of responsibility for the welfare of their fellow crew members. It was this intense crew loyalty that enabled the system to work at all. Men would rather have forfeited their lives than let down a comrade. Ben's greatest worry as a navigator was the thought of making an error without realizing it, and then, perhaps, finding he had exposed his crew to extra danger by flying alone, outside the protection of the main bomber stream. He once made what he considered to be a glaring boob. In the navigator's working area some of the appropriate dials used by the pilot were duplicated. The altimeter, as we have already seen, was one of them. They were known as 'repeaters' and included the aircraft's compass – a DR (distant reading) compass – and the API, an integral part of the Air Position Indicator, which enabled the navigator to read out the latitude and longitude of air position, according to the air speed fed into it, and the compass bearing fed into it relative to the point he had set when he started.

Having set the base point of latitude and longitude it would, from then on, always indicate the *air* position of the aircraft at 'the time read', until it was reset. To find the *ground* position, a wind vector was applied to it according to the length of time the aircraft had been flying, and the variation in winds through different levels.

Ben did not realize it at the time (the Station Navigation Officer found out afterwards) that he had wrongly reset the Air Position Indicator after leaving the target by one whole degree of longitude. This meant that he was working on a position 40 nautical miles from where they actually were!

It was when they reached the French coast in the early hours of the morning that they were able to identify a visual pinpoint. If the indications he had been working on had been accurate, then they could only have been flying through a wind of 150 knots, which would have been nonsense.

We have already discussed how busy navigators were. Ben, like the others, followed a set routine to establish the bomber's air position once every twelve minutes, either by DR, visual sighting, a Gee fix, or radio bearings. It took him six minutes to complete his calculations and do the plotting. This left him six minutes free to try to warm his hands on the heater behind him, haul on his various layers of gloves, and then, after a pause, peel them off again in time for the next round of work. This was the procedure carried out continuously over the whole period of a six, seven, eight or nine hour mission.

He was happy in his work and would not have swapped his navigator's job for any other in the aircraft. His sympathy was always for air gunners sitting in lonely isolation in their cramped turrets, remote from the rest of the crew, strained eyes constantly scanning each quarter of the dark sky, constantly on the alert for impending danger, and often frozen almost beyond endurance.

Soon after their Berlin raid, they flew to Schweinfurt on the night of 24/25 February, to bomb the home of Germany's main ball-bearing factories. Bomber Command lost thirty-three aircraft on this mission. It was not until the flight engineer warned that they were consuming far too much fuel on the return trip that they realized the Halifax must have been hit by the flak over the target. Petrol was obviously pouring out of a damaged fuel feed. Ben did some rapid figuring. No chance of getting all the way back to base. Might possibly make the English coast and flop down at Ford or Tangmere:

'How far to the coast, Ben?'

'10 minutes.'

'How much fuel left, Douggie?'

'5 minutes.'

'Looks as though we're going to get our feet wet boys!'

'Mayday! Mayday! Are you receiving us?' No reply.

'Mayday! Mayday! Are you receiving us?' No reply.

'Mayday! Mayday! Are you receiving us?'

'Hello Mayday. Hello Mayday. Receiving you loud and clear. This is Friston. I repeat, this is Friston.'

'Where the hell is Friston, Ben?'

'Well, there's no Friston aerodrome marked on the map. The only Friston I know is a little village up on the top of the cliffs just to the west of Eastbourne.'

'Hello, Mayday! This is Friston. We are putting out flares. Repeat. We are putting out flares.'

The crew of H for 'Hollander' spotted them at once. With fingers crossed, and the notoriously inaccurate fuel gauges showing zero, they came straight in to land. As they rolled to a stop a combined sigh of relief came from seven throats. They learned that Friston was a fighter 'drome being used by a Polish Spitfire squadron.

After a good meal and sound sleep, they strolled out to look at their aircraft the following morning. The bulky Halifax had landed on a short grass runway on top of the cliffs at Beachy Head. 'Dutch' became involved in discussions with Flying Control about the length of the field and the practical possibility of getting the bomber into the air from such a short take-off area. His attitude was, 'We got her down here, we'll get her off again.'

Then bad weather took a hand. Swirling snow and an ice-bound surface closed the airfield, putting take-off out of the question. 'Right,' said Ben. 'This is a golden opportunity. My home is only just down the road in Brighton. I'm taking you all home to see the folks!' They caught the Southdown bus and were soon in town. At that time Brighton was not only a Holding Centre for aircrew but also the home of an Aircrew Punishment Unit in which 'incorrigibles' underwent a period of correction for naughty behaviour while in the air – low flying over girlfriends' houses and the like.

Because of this Ben's home town was infested with service policemen who eyed Hollander's crew suspiciously as they sloped along the pavements in their flying boots, coloured scarves, worn battle-dresses and no caps. The flyers felt certain they would be pounced on at any moment for being improperly dressed, in which case the crew were ready with a first-class excuse. But they were never accosted – some primeval instinct might have prompted the cops not to interfere, or maybe it was the sight of Ben's Flying Officer ribbon that deterred them.

When the weather cleared a little they returned to Friston. A sure-fire scheme had been worked out to get the old 'Hallibag' safely into the air before it ran out of grass at the edge of the cliffs. Substantial wooden chocks were placed under its wheels with ropes attached to a couple of farm tractors. Johnny revved up the four Merlins until the bomber was almost leaping over the blocks. Then, as he signalled to the drivers, the tractors tugged the chocks away and it shot down the field like a stone released from a catapult. By the time it reached the cliff it was already airborne. They set course for base, map-reading their way over a snow-covered England, little realizing what was waiting for them.

Ben's mother had a friend whose husband was a reporter working for the *Daily Mirror* in Fleet Street. He had sussed out the story and, using a fair amount of journalistic licence, had written a piece which appeared with Ben's photograph in that day's edition:

THE MAN WHO CAME TO DINNER
As she prepared dinner in her home at Stanmer Park Road, Brighton, Mrs Edith Bennett heard the roar of a low-flying British aeroplane.
    'Bless 'em all,' she murmured, for her only son, Flying Officer Vernon Bennett, is navigator of a bomber.
    The big bomber passed over the house, dropped towards the downs . . .
    An hour passed . . .
    Mrs Bennett heard the garden gate click and seven young men in flying kit trooped down the path.
    'How do, Mum?' said one of them. 'I thought we'd look you up in passing.'

Predictably, when they walked into the mess after landing at their home base in Snaith, they were greeted by raucous shouts of derision from their fellow aircrew and had to suffer continuous repetition of a ditty hastily composed for the occasion:

'Out of the blue came Hollander's crew! Ta-ra! Ta-ra!
Veteran aces away they flew! Ta-ra! Ta-ra!'

etc., etc., followed by the chorus:
'The Man Who Came to Dinner!'

Their story had earned its place among 51 Squadron's store of legends. On the more serious side, Ben was shaken to find that in

112

the short time they had been away some of his best friends had gone missing. In his diary he noted, 'Poor old Jackson and Love bought it at Schweinfurt. McKenzie's a prisoner of war'.

Normally Bomber Command aircrew were granted a week's operational flying leave every six weeks. The only thing he hated about this was returning to the squadron to find that during his absence more crews had disappeared. On one occasion they arrived back to discover that their own kite, in which they put so much trust, had been flown by another crew while they were away and had been lost.

During these breaks in flying Ben looked up old acquaintances and made the most of the many bars in Brighton. He also put in some time encouraging youngsters who had an interest in flying. His future mother-in-law was the head of the Women's Junior Air Corps. He enjoyed teaching her girl cadets morse, the theory of flight, basics of navigation, and even air traffic control. He illustrated this last function by getting the girls to 'fly' round in circles with their arms outstretched to simulate the wings of the aircraft. Then the 'controller' would bring them in to land in the correct order!

Mother-in-law to be was a born organizer. She knew the mayor and had arranged that, after her daughter Pam's marriage to Ben, the reception should take place in the impressive banqueting hall of Brighton Pavilion. Everything had been set for the great occasion on Saturday, 11 March 1944, right down to the last detail. All the guests had received their invitations and Ben had been granted 14 days' leave.

At 8 am on Friday, 10 March, he got up in preparation for his leave. At 10.30 am came the shock; leave was cancelled and he was told to prepare for operational flying. His diary, written at the time, says, 'If I have to fly, I think I will bale out. Am hopping mad.' Rushing off to see his Wing Commander, he pleaded in vain. 'So sorry Ben. Quite understand how you feel, but I've lost so many crews lately, I can't spare a single bod.'

Ben was desperate and unprepared to let the matter rest. He asked permission to see the Station Commander. Again, a stone wall. 'Sorry Bennett, but I have to support your Squadron Commander's decision.'

113

Still determined that the most important day in the lives of Pam and himself should not be ruined, he tried one last desperate throw. 'Permission to see the Air Officer Commanding, please, Sir.' The Group Captain thought for a moment. 'Fair enough, Bennett. You are entitled to that privilege.'

The Group Captain drove him in his car to Group HQ at Bawtry and they were ushered into the great man's presence. After he heard the story, the AOC looked at Ben. 'You are a very determined young man. I am going to grant you 48 hours' leave to get married.'

The wedding day went off splendidly. The bride looked beautiful, the groom handsome in his uniform. The guard of honour was provided by the girls of the Women's Junior Air Corps. Apart from good coverage in the local papers, the *Daily Mirror* did a follow-up story, a sequel to 'The Man Who Came to Dinner'.

The following Monday evening he was back on 'ops' with a trip to Le Mans. Then on Wednesday Hollander's crew flew to Stuttgart. They were harried most of the way there by fighters, coned by searchlights over the target and attacked by a twin-engine fighter, an ME 210, on the return journey.

By the end of that week new replacement crews had filtered in to the squadron from the HCUs. To Ben's delight, his CO told him he could now get back to enjoying his interrupted honeymoon and granted him 14 days' leave. That stroke of generosity may well have saved his life. During the time he was away, on four raids alone – two to Frankfurt, one to Berlin and one (the most disastrous) to Nuremberg – Bomber Command lost 222 heavy bombers – more than 1550 aircrew.

His leave lasted from 17 to 31 March. When he returned on the Friday morning, he found 51 Squadron in a state of deep depression, a depression shared by all other squadrons on that day. In those two weeks they had lost twelve aircraft, six of them the previous night on the Nuremberg raid. Their own aircraft had gone. Flown by their Flight Commander, Squadron Leader Hill, the crew had included the gunnery and engineering leaders. That night Ben wrote in his diary: 'The whole squadron seems as if it will never get over this last loss; there is an air of despondency over the whole camp.' From then on even his optimistic attitude

114

was tempered by a new realization of the grim game they were playing. Later, after a raid to Düsseldorf, he wrote: 'Coned by searchlights tonight. Really scared for the first time in my life.'

Hollander's crew, now flying in an R Robert, were nearing the end of their tour. It was the night of 5/6 June, 1944. By this time their aircraft was equipped with H_2S, an electronic device for 'seeing the ground' through cloud. As they neared the French coast while returning from the target, Ben was studying the screen. Instead of a reasonably defined impression of the coastline what he saw looked like a violent snowstorm. Puzzled, he switched the set off, after trying unsuccessfully to clear the supposed fault.

A few minutes later, shortly before dawn, Tommy MacCarthy called up from his position in the nose: 'Funny thing. There are masses of white specks all over the sea. It's still too dark to make out what they are.'

Back at base other crews were reporting the phenomenon. The Wing Commander drew them all together and said, 'You have just witnessed the start of the greatest invasion in history!' It was D Day.

When the thirty trips were completed, they opted to become instructors and were all posted to 21 OTU, Moreton-in-Marsh. Ben was promoted to Flight Lieutenant, awarded the DFC and became a senior navigation instructor.

Dutch Hollander and bomb aimer Tommy MacCarthy were both commissioned, and each received a DFC. The crew's 'grandad', rear gunner Mick 'Aussie' Campbell, was awarded the DFM.

There was one exception to this posting: Harry Bottrell, their wireless operator (who received no award or promotion), decided to continue operational flying. Posted to a Lancaster squadron, he completed three trips with his new crew and was then shot down.

EIGHT

The Wireless Operator
and Others

For a long time all wireless operators were also air gunners. It was the practice in the more cramped, twin-engine bombers for the Wop/AG to man, for example, either the beam guns, in the case of the Wellington, or the upper, rear-firing gun in the Hampden. Only after the arrival of the bigger bombers did he hand over his gunnery duties to a full-time air gunner, leaving himself free to concentrate on radio and newly introduced radar equipment. Whereas he had previously worn the AG brevet, he later had his own S (for Signals) brevet. If an NCO, he continued to wear a wireless 'sparks' badge on his upper sleeve.

The wireless operator's course, especially when combined with gunnery training, was longer than that of any other aircrew category. After initial training, which included morse signalling practice up to 12 words a minute, cadets were sent to a 'wireless school' to learn every aspect of signals procedure, including the technical side of radio. In order to pass out successfully, pupils had to achieve a high standard in written examinations, as well as sending and receiving at not less than 22 words a minute. The 'drop-out' rate was high.

Before the introduction of the flight engineer, the Wop/AG was looked on as the 'practical' man of the crew. He was the Mr Fixit of the team, always ready in an emergency with a screwdriver and bits of wire, and, in extreme cases, wielding the axe or smothering a fire. It was his responsibility to set the detonators to destroy secret equipment before the aircraft force-landed in enemy territory. In some ways the wireless operator led a lonely existence in a bomber, mentally isolated from other members of the crew for long periods of time, while he strained to listen through the static in his headphones for faint but vital signals. The wireless operator who flew with a squadron specializing in radio countermeasures led a full and interesting life. It was only over the target that he sometimes had to endure moments of terrifying idleness.

I suppose it was the Junkers that did it. Or at least not so much the Junkers as the Spitfire that was chasing it. We were outside the tuckshop during a mid-morning school break when we heard the grinding growl of unsynchronized German aero-engines. It was the summer of 1940. The Battle of Britain was at its height and schoolboys knew all about these technical matters. The twin-engine Luftwaffe bomber flew low over the school, and then, thrill of thrills, came the shapely little Spitfire in hot pursuit, the distinctive whistle from its Merlin engine sounding almost like the wind itself.

In an instant the two planes had passed from sight over the Wiltshire downs. Later we learned that the Spitfire had shot down the Ju88 on a bleak corner of the Plain to the west of Salisbury. But what really set us boys on fire was the news that the victorious Spitfire pilot was Eric Marrs, who, not so long ago, had been a pupil at our school. As far as Dauntsey's School was concerned, the RAF could not have had a more effective recruiting officer than Marrs. As for me, this was the day I jilted the Royal Navy after a passionate affair that had lasted more than ten years.

I was 16 years old at the time, born on 6 November, 1923. The following year, on leaving school, I started broadcasting as a radio actor with the BBC Repertory Company. The Drama Department had been evacuated from London to Bristol because of the bombing. It was the break of a lifetime, and a great privilege for one so young to be in the company of then famous people doing work that brought me so much pleasure and satisfaction. Under normal circumstances it would probably have been the doorway to an exciting career. However, the 'war was on' and, like many thousands of others, I knew I had to do my bit.

My father, who was a professor, wanted me to give up broadcasting and go to university, where, until I had completed my three-year course, I would have been exempt from war service. To my mind such an existence would have been impossible – to sit studying in complete safety while others of my age were dying for their country was not on. My father himself, as a 20-year-old subaltern

117

in the 8th Devons, had been badly wounded on the Somme in 1916. He had been a fine athlete, but the First World War stopped all that when it took away his arm.

So on my 18th birthday, with visions of that avenging Spitfire of the previous year still clear in my mind, I walked into the RAF recruiting office and volunteered for flying duties. Eventually, called before an Aircrew Attestation Board with thirty others, I spent the morning doing basic written examinations in mathematics and English and filling in intelligence tests. In the afternoon we appeared before a board of officers who fired questions at us of a 'Why do you want to kill Germans?' variety.

From those tested that day, three of us were accepted for aircrew. One, who turned up in ATC uniform wearing gliding wings, was accepted for pilot training. Another, good at maths, was designated as navigator, while I was to become a wireless operator/air gunner – with the promise that I could re-apply to train as a pilot 'at a later date' (something which, in the event, I never did). The Spitfire suddenly seemed a long way off. Oddly, the passing of that dream did not worry me much. I just felt elated that I was going to fly anyway.

It was a bit of an anticlimax when we were given little winged badges to wear in our lapels, and told we were now on 'Deferred Service'. The RAF would call us when it was ready. That call came in March, 1942. It was a shame that a fine service like the Royal Air Force should have tolerated such an unworthy reception camp as Padgate, near Warrington. Enthusiastic young volunteers entered this gateway to their new career only to be cursed at, degraded and insulted by the low-quality types on the permanent staff. I was well prepared for all this bullying nonsense, having tasted the rigours of life in public school, but some of those lads were away from home for the first time. I used to feel sorry for the ones I heard sobbing in our hut at night.

What a contrast when we arrived at Blackpool to start our basic training. Ultra-smart drill and PT instructors; efficient classroom teachers; wizards at morse code – especially two civil servants in striped trousers, one short and portly, the other tall and thin – inevitably known as 'Dot' and 'Dash'. To hear them signalling to each other at well over 25 words a minute was like a symphony.

118

Unfortunately, not every cadet could 'take' morse and those who failed were remustered as 'straight' air gunners. One pupil disappeared for a week and was eventually discovered sleeping rough in an air-raid shelter. He was muttering to himself in morse, having gone completely out of his mind.

At pay parade we received 30/- per fortnight. After deductions for the PSI fund and other mysterious organizations we did not have a great deal left. Nevertheless, entertainment was cheap. We could see a show at the Tower Theatre for 4d. Stars were plentiful – Arthur Askey, Max Wall, Michael Bentine were just a few. I went to have a chat with Arthur in his dressing room and took a couple of my pals along to impress them with my show biz contacts!

On one occasion we were all gathered in the vast Tower Ballroom to hear a lecture about the Poles, of whom there were many in the RAF in Blackpool. The speaker was introduced as a world expert on Poland and its people. Who should walk on the stage in Flight Lieutenant's uniform but Reggie Hill, my former history master. Turning to my mate, Pete Bishop, I said, 'I know him!' My reputation as a chap who knew everything, and everybody, became difficult to refute. During the rest of my stay by the sea, Reggie, who enjoyed a smoke, used to welcome my cigarette ration, while my friends and I never went short of chocolates from the Officers' Mess.

One of my most terrifying experiences ever occurred during this period. We cadets were scheduled in rotation to do 'fire-watch' duty at night in the larger buildings. My turn came to look after Woolworths. The extensive area on the first floor above the store had been converted into a morse instruction room. Bare trestle tables with benches occupied the whole floor space. With careful precision, morse keys were screwed in rows at three-foot intervals along the tops of either side of these tables. The black shiny knobs appeared to stretch into infinity. It was like a parade of soldiers, or the dead straight lines of headstones in a military cemetery.

I occupied my time wandering about the building and climbing up on to the flat roof and staring out to sea. But it was a chilly night and I soon took up position in the instructor's chair facing the tables. Time passed slowly. Only the light on my small desk fought to penetrate the gloom of the vast interior. In diminishing return as they faded away into the shadows the parallel rows of bakelite knobs reflected back the light. As I contemplated these objects, so familiar to me during the day, my mind started to dwell on the hundreds of hands that must have pressed those silent keys. How many of those hands now lay immobile in death? Before long I was 'seeing' those keys moving up and down in unison. Horrified, unable to turn my back as these noiseless messages were being transmitted from another world, I sat transfixed until dawn. Then, when I glanced in a mirror, I saw my face had turned a sickly green. Group Captain Leonard Cheshire once said that aircrew were better off without too much imagination!

After three months those of us fortunate enough to complete the course participated in a grand parade. As we marched along the promenade, toting our heavy First World War Lee Enfield rifles, the salute was taken by Sir Archibald Sinclair, complete with morning coat and winged collar. He was the Minister for Air. 'I suppose you know him,' whispered Pete Bishop. 'No,' I replied, 'and considering how little he knows about aviation, I wouldn't want to.'

One might have supposed, with all the fuss, that this was the culmination of something important. In fact it was only the beginning. The wireless operator's course was longer than any other in aircrew. Still only Aircraftmen 2nd class, we proceeded to No 1 Signals School at Compton Bassett, near Calne, in Wiltshire. In a matter of months we had to try to absorb all the technicalities of radio, virtually double our morse sending/receiving speed to twenty-two words per minute, and cover related subjects including navigation, beam approach, aircraft recognition and radar. Such a course would have been spread over three years in peacetime.

Pete Bishop and I looked at each other with grins of satisfaction when, at the end of it all, we sewed our 'sparks' on our right sleeves. Nothing that we achieved subsequently meant quite as much to us as those 'sparks'. They represented months of unremitting study, and only about a third of our original intake had made it. There was no outward sign of an increase in rank, but an appreciative RAF turned us into Aircraftmen 1st class.

Because of bottlenecks in the system, although we had now been

120

in the service for a year, we had to endure a period of waiting. I was posted as a temporary ground wireless operator to 7 Flying Instructors School, Upavon, Wiltshire. This was a First World War aerodrome, consisting of well-built permanent buildings and a grass airfield with a dip in the middle. By a coincidence I had once flown as a schoolboy from this station on a brief trip in an Avro Anson. If I could avoid it, I was not going to spend my time in a stuffy signals cabin. I badgered every pilot in sight to let me fly with them in their Airspeed Oxfords. Soon I was being allowed to take over the controls in straight and level flight. On one occasion I flew with a Flight Lieutenant Mansell on a cross-country and, although only a cadet, was designated as the crew's wireless operator.

My Signals CO, impressed with my keenness to fly, presented me with the Log Book of a dead airman. 'Keep a record of your trips in there, Lewis, until you get your own Log Book at Gunnery School.' At the time I prized that book above all other possessions.

It was while at Upavon that I saw my first crash. A poor old lumbering Whitley, lost and in trouble, tried to put down in the dark. It finished up in the sunken part of the airfield and burst into flames. The crew were reduced to charred effigies. Later, when it was all over, I remember staring at the melted money spread over the wireless operator's hip-bone. It may be hard to believe, but a handful of General Duties types chose this occasion to look at us aircrew cadets with pitying contempt. One said, 'What price aircrew now? Ten a penny! That's all you're bloody worth!'

Among my happier memories of Upavon were my visits to the station library. The Sergeant 'librarian' would normally be sitting with his feet up on the anthracite stove, reading an American comic. He was the famous Freddie Mills, that most courageous of light-heavyweight boxers. Beating everyone in his own class, he was forced to take on the heavier guys and always gave a good account of himself. His cheerful face had become concave, like the moon, because of the bludgeoning received in many fights. We had many an amiable chat, little realizing that in years to come we would share a television news show together.

The time came to press on. In April, 1943, we travelled to

Madley, in Herefordshire, home of No 4 Radio Flying School. Combined with liberal doses of 'ground tuition', we also took to the air in what can only be described as 'flying classrooms'. The DH Dominie was a 'joke' aircraft, originally designed as a biplane airliner. With a bored pilot flying round in circles, a harassed Corporal Instructor and four miserable pupils trying to tap out morse while on the point of throwing up, as the underpowered kite wallowed about the sky like a one-winged duck, it was all stiflingly claustrophobic.

I was mad about flying, but not in DH Dominies. Messages somehow got transmitted from air to ground, and from ground to air in spite of it all. It was a pity that the transmitter/receivers were obsolete, and bore little relation to the much more sophisticated equipment we were to use in Bomber Command. The station appeared to be run by corporals who laboured manfully to turn us into Wop/AGs. They were supported by a few senior NCOs, but officers, if there were any, obviously had something better to do than take part in the training function.

Again Pete Bishop and I made the grade quite comfortably, thanks to the Corporals, and along with other successful pupils we were promoted to Leading Aircraftmen. This time we did not stitch on our award – the LAC 'propeller'. It hardly seemed worth the effort. We had confidence that in a little over six weeks, after our air gunner's course, we would be sewing on our Sergeant's tapes.

In fact we had overestimated the time it would take. We actually completed the introduction to our second trade in three weeks and five days. No 8 Air Gunnery School was situated in glorious Scottish countryside, at Evanton, north of Inverness. The camp had a backdrop of magnificent mountains, while the runways stretched almost to the edge of the Cromaty Firth.

Each morning at dawn we woke to the sound of pipes. The pipers, in a highland version of RAF uniform complete with kilt, would descend the mountainside or rise out of ditches and other mysterious hideaways and meet at the camp gate. During this period of coming together we cadets had to be up, washed, shaved and dressed ready to fall in behind them for a march down to the hangars. There, mounted on a rostrum, the padre offered a short

122

prayer, the RAF flag was broken to the sound of a bugle, the parade was dismissed and the day's work began. It was unforgettable – the beautiful sunrises, the dark silhouettes of the aircraft, the skirl of the pipes.

If the DH Dominie was a joke, the Blackburn Botha was beyond a joke. Originally designed as a torpedo bomber, this high-wing, twin-engine, underpowered aircraft proved to be useless for its intended purpose. It was relegated to the role of flying back and forth over the sea, while trainee air gunners took pot-shots at canvas drogues towed by single-engine Martinets. The pilots engaged in these exercises were not among the most enthusiastic I had met. They took care never to stray far from base as the 'Bloody Botha' was unable to maintain height on one engine should the other fail.

It was a rule that the pupils had to wear full flying kit as if equipped for a night trip over Germany. This gear consisted of silk under-combinations, 'inner' and 'outer' flying suits, parachute harness, Mae West life-jackets, three pairs of gloves, flying helmet and oxygen masks. In the sweltering heat of a brilliant summer, four sweating pupils stood in the forward cabin, beside a non-communicative shirt-sleeved pilot, waiting their turn to crawl down a narrow tunnel which led to the egg-shaped Fraser-Nash turret.

It was bad enough for all of us, but for 'Paddy' it must have been purgatory. A 6 foot 3 inch giant of a man, 'Paddy' had transferred from the Irish Guards in order to see some action in the air. On one occasion he was scheduled to enter the turret before me. After an inordinate amount of time, during which no firing had taken place, the pilot impatiently told me to go and investigate. I found poor 'Paddy' in the pipe, near the upward bend into the turret itself. What with his size, and the amount of bulky clothing he was wearing, he had stuck fast, unable to move forwards or backwards. Similarly clad, I was almost too exhausted to return and carry out my own air-firing by the time I had managed to drag him backwards along the tunnel. As a weight-losing exercise I never found a better.

In the classroom we had some inspirational guidance in Aircraft Recognition from a tour-expired Flying Officer air-gunner. Armed with a multitude of models he would zoom in and attack us from all angles, coming up from floor level, or standing on a desk and diving down unexpectedly. Using a projector, he would flash perhaps a head-on view of a Ju88 on to the screen for a split second. 'Come on boys! What is it? Quick! Quick! Your life depends on it.' He went to infinite trouble to cut out endless jigsaw puzzles, the pieces made up of characteristic features of a variety of planes. He was a natural teacher, always happy to answer our questions, and we learned a great deal from him. He turned what some of us had considered a dull subject into a topic of endless fascination.

We passed out on air-to-air firing, air-to-ground firing and night firing. It was perhaps strange, but at that school, night firing produced no worse marks than those achieved during the day. The answer was simple. During the 'night tests', which anyway took place during the *day*, cadets were ordered to don goggles fitted with dark lenses. Naturally, with no one in the turret to observe us, we all forgot to do so, that is, with the exception of my great pal, Pete Bishop, whose intrinsic honesty often put the rest of us to shame. He conscientiously wore his blacked-out lenses and drilled neat holes in the tailplane of the target-towing Martinet; the LAC in charge of the airborne winch applied for compassionate leave immediately afterwards.

For a time I feared for Pete's future, but it was all right. All wireless operators passed out 'Average' on air gunnery as far as I could tell. Later on, because of greater specialization in aircrew categories, wireless types ceased to take the gunnery course and were re-classified as signallers, wearing the newly designed S brevet. We, however, were awarded our AG brevets, of which we were particularly proud, being among the last of a breed. We also became Sergeants.

It was a pleasure to go on leave, although it took a long time and several changes of train to travel from Inverness to my home in Aberystwyth in West Wales. To my misfortune, 6 ITW was stationed there. So cadets with white flashes in their caps abounded. Previously, when I had come on leave as a cadet myself, I had frequently suffered the irritation of being stopped in my own home town by Service Police and asked why I was not on parade.

124

Now, as a Sergeant, for the first time I was spared this embarrassment. During the war servicemen were forbidden to wear civilian clothes on any occasion.

But training was by no means over. Next stop was 2 Operational Advanced Flying Unit at Millom in Cumberland. Here we flew on cross-country exercises in friendly old Avro Ansons. The Anson was the workhorse of the RAF, the 'Flying Greenhouse', and, as its nickname implied, offered superb visibility all round. It was so beautifully balanced, with its low wing and twin Cheetah engines, that it was confidently believed the 'Annie-bag' could take herself off, and then come back and land, even if the pilot forgot to turn up. She was designed by Roy Chadwick, the man who gave us the Lancaster.

In such a plane it was easy to concentrate on really learning our job as wireless operators. We navigated our way round Britain by obtaining bearings from ground stations situated all over the country – each one with its individual call sign. We developed the knack of distinguishing where a call was coming from by the note of the morse signal. No two stations sounded exactly the same, just as each operator had a slightly different rhythm when tapping out a message. We progressed from the conscious, deliberate approach to an instinctive level where sending and receiving became second nature. We communicated in morse as in speech, no longer hampered by an awareness of the technique. It was remarkable how we became adept at winkling out faint, distant signals, although they were almost obliterated by crackling static and overriding 'mush'.

At last we were using up-to-the-minute equipment – powerful transmitters and receivers, with dials and switches cleverly colour-coded to indicate the different wave bands. The course lasted less than a month, but, guided by ex-operational wireless operators, it could not have been more valuable.

It was in mid-September, 1943, that I arrived at 30 Operational Training Unit, Hixon, in Staffordshire. For the first time we Wop/AGs were to go our separate ways. After spending our leave together at his parents' place in Carlshalton, Pete Bishop and I parted. He was posted to a different OTU. I missed his company very much.

I have a vivid memory of standing in a room full of aircrew of all categories. We were holding mugs of tea and large sticky buns, so, although this was an introduction exercise, it was physically impossible to shake hands. Apart from the RAF types, there were several Canadians, a few New Zealanders, and some Australians in their darker blue uniforms and enviable black buttons that required no polishing. Not surprisingly, we had formed into distinctive groups, pilots speaking with pilots, bomb aimers with bomb aimers, and so on. Each cluster was comfortably talking their own brand of 'shop'.

It was some while before a young-looking, fresh-faced Sergeant pilot, of medium height and slight build, came over and introduced himself as Jack West. He asked most politely if I was already 'crewed up', and when I replied that I was not, he invited me to join him. He seemed a serious and steady sort of chap so I agreed. Anyway it would have been rude to refuse. From then on, for some time, his fate was my fate.

He led me across the room to meet a stocky little Canadian bomb-aimer. This was Jimmy Hutchinson, who wore his fair hair well over regulation length, and sported a single wing brevet of nearly twice the standard size. He appeared nervy and anxious to make an impression. The other man was a gunner, Stan Wright. Tall, thin, of a shy retiring nature, but with a wry sense of humour, Stan, like our new skipper, appeared to be a responsible type, not likely to panic in an emergency. But who could really tell how any of us would make out? Jack and I were 19 years old, while the other two were only 18. We must have looked like schoolboys in comparison with some of the bewhiskered flyers forming groups in other parts of the room.

At some stage, either then or later, we acquired an equally young navigator. What he looked like, his personality, even his name, has long since gone from my memory. All I remember is that after we had completed a couple of cross-country flights, our first as a crew, he turned out to be incapable of doing the job properly and was removed from the course.

Jack, who had previously flown nothing bigger than an Oxford, settled in happily enough with the Wellington. It was a unique aircraft. Built to a criss-cross geodetic construction, covered in canvas, it heaved its way through the sky creaking and groaning like an old-fashioned schooner – a schooner fitted with exceptionally noisy engines. I remember standing in the astrodome watching the wing-tips flexing as the 'Wimpy' wallowed up and down. Yet this very flexibility was shortly to save our lives.

We acquired another Sergeant navigator. He was not chosen, he was detailed to join us. It was difficult to know what to make of him. Most of his training, he told us, had taken place in South Africa, where 'things had been different'. Communication was not easy, and as the member of the crew who would work most closely with him, I tried hard to find subjects of mutual interest, but without much success. He gave an impression of being listless, and seemed bored with our company. This we thought we understood. While we were a bunch of irrepressible teenagers, he was an old man. Slow in his movements and speech, a hollow haggard face, receding hair, no discernible sense of humour, he appeared to have nothing in common with the rest of us.

Jack, exercising his right as the skipper, went to the office to glance through our new navigator's records. He came back looking worried. 'Do you know, boys, this chap is 27 years old!' I think, more than anything, we felt a sense of pity that someone so advanced in years should be exposed to the perils of life in Bomber Command.

The following day was my birthday. I started celebrating early, when at 10 minutes past midnight, we began a series of circuits and bumps that went on for most of the night. At one stage we were following another Wellington round the circuit. As he came in to land the pilot must have misjudged his height, because he overshot and crashed beyond the runway. Almost immediately the aircraft burst into flames. As we flew over the funeral pyre, consuming five young men and an instructor, I thought how different this birthday was from any I had experienced before. In sensible OTU tradition, the flying exercises continued as if nothing had happened.

Next night our crew was rostered for our first cross-country in the dark. This was to be a trip where we would fly from one well-known location in Britain to another – Base, Conway, Douglas, Mull of Kintyre, South Rock, Land's End, Bardsey Island and back to Base: that kind of thing – wonderful experience for the pilot, wireless operator and particularly the navigator. A veteran pilot was to fly with us, Warrant Officer Rothschild, and our Wimpey, A- Able, BK821, was brand new from the factory.

We took off at 1800 hours and climbed for height. We were soon in thick cloud that persisted for the rest of the trip. At 10,000 feet we set course on our first leg. I hoped that this exercise would establish a good working relationship between the navigator and myself. A forlorn hope. Every time Rothschild called the navigator over the intercom to ask for a position, the man gave a vague answer and told him to 'hang on a bit'. I obtained a series of radio fixes and passed them to the navigator. On each occasion he would look at my figures, then screw up the paper and drop it on the floor. To my astonishment, after we had been flying for some time, he threw his instruments down on the chart with an air of resignation, pulled off his oxygen mask and lit a cigarette – a daft thing to do, fraught with danger in an aircraft reeking with petrol fumes and freshly applied dope. Desperately, I leaned forward, snatched it from his mouth and tweaked it out. After this he took no further interest in the proceedings, sitting as if mesmerised.

From my own estimates we had wandered east across England, at some point done a U-turn, and were now back in the vicinity of our own base near Stafford. By this time we were flying through an electrical storm which played havoc with radio reception. There was no response from Hixon to my urgent calls. Fortunately, I managed to make contact with the people at RAF Cranage [see Leslie Biddlecombe's story], and when they gave us a useful radio bearing we were able to head straight for them.

As we entered the circuit and Jack got through to control on R/T, I went aft to wind in the trailing aerial. This was 300 feet of wire with a row of lead balls on the end – not an object to leave dangling when coming in to land. Having completed my task, for some unknown reason, I sat down on the deck with my back against the bulkhead and plugged in the intercom instead of returning to my radio position. We were on the point of landing when I realized things had gone wrong. Someone was yelling that the throttles had stuck – it seemed they had locked in a position that meant the aircraft was travelling too fast to land, but was left with

128

insufficient power to overshoot and make another circuit. We were going to fly straight on into the unknown – into the darkness beyond the airfield.

Remembering the drill, I linked my hands behind my neck and braced my back against the bulkhead. A vivid image of a Wimpey being consumed by flames engulfed my mind. 'This is *it!*' I thought. There was no shadow of doubt that the end had come. Oddly, I had no feeling of fear, only a deep sense of sadness. I mourned for my poor parents who would tomorrow receive a telegram. I felt pity for myself – to die so soon after my 20th birthday, having achieved nothing in life. No chance to prove myself on 'ops'. No chance to see if I could stand up to enemy fire as my Dad had done in that last Great War.

There were metallic grinding and crunching and tearing noises that went on for an eternity – but no human sounds. Then oblivion.

I first became aware of smells – petrol, dope and oil; but there was, too, the scent of something else that for the moment I was unable to identify. Lying there in the darkness, gradually recovering consciousness, it struck me that heaven was a strange place. It must have been some time before I gathered my wits sufficiently to realize I had not departed this world after all. Slowly getting to my feet I had no idea that the bomber had broken in half just to the rear of where I had been sitting.

Suddenly it struck me that the kite might explode at any moment. I had to get out as fast as possible. But my training made me pause. First it was essential to climb up front and remove the crystals from the TR9 R/T radio – we had been told that these pieces of equipment were particularly valuable and must never be left in the aircraft when it was on the ground. I unscrewed the retaining cover from the set and lifted them out. I also unclipped an inspection lamp from its bracket and stuffed it into my battledress blouse. Then I climbed out of the 'Wimpey' and walked down the sloping starboard wing.

The crew was standing in a semi-circle as I approached. Someone shone a torch on me. There was an exclamation of horror: 'My God! Poor old Bruce has been hurt!' I put a hand to my head

129

and felt sticky rivulets running down my face. 'Blood!' I thought, 'I'm a hero!'

In fact it was not blood at all, and what had happened could hardly have been less heroic. Just opposite where I had been sitting when the aircraft crashed was the crew's Elsan lavatory. This essential feature was attached to the deck with strong rubber bands. On impact the bands had broken, the steel-drum convenience had taken off, hit the roof, turned over and crashed down on to my head, knocking me out and covering me in its contents. Later, after we had been medically examined by Cranage's MO, who was amazed that we did not have an injury between us, apart from the bump on my head, the rest of the crew retired to bed. But I had to stay up and endure several baths treated with a special stain remover. As I explained to my disbelieving companions the next day, because the aircraft was new, the contents of the Elsan were not what they would normally have been, but only a potent, creosote-like chemical.

When we inspected the route we had taken the previous night, we could hardly believe our eyes. Our plane had shot over a main road beyond the airfield's boundary fence, flown through a gap between a copse of trees and a farmhouse, gone straight over a quarry half-full of water, hit a stone wall which tore off a wheel and one leg of the undercarriage, ploughed into a field and spun round and round breaking its back in the process. An engineering officer said it was probably this spinning, caused by only having one wheel, which had saved our lives.

'Normally,' he said, 'on heavy impact the fuel is thrown forward over the hot engine nacelles, and the Wimpey goes up in flames. In this case, the petrol was flung clear because of your gyrations.' I tore a foot-square piece from the aircraft's tattered side and wrote on it: 'The age of miracles is not dead. 7/11/43.' That brittle piece of canvas, and the little copper inspection lamp, are still in my possession.

Jack noticed a long, low, modern-looking factory over to our right. 'Lucky we missed that,' he said. 'What do they make there?' The engineering officer looked at us with a quizzical expression. 'You're not going to believe this,' he said. 'That's a Wimpey repair factory!'

There was the usual inquiry, of course, and it was fortunate W/O Rothschild had been with us. His word carried more weight than that of a 'sprog' crew. Navigator No 2 disappeared from sight in no time at all. We sighed with relief when No 3 came along. Let's call him Tim. He was a pleasant, fair haired 20-year-old of athletic build and, as we soon discovered, a 'gen' man at navigating accurately. 48 hours after our crash we were in the air again and feeling much happier.

I had a friend at Hixon. He was really old in years, yet vitally young in spirit. We called him 'Carstairs' because, with his drooping grey moustache he looked like a colonel in the Indian Army. He had told the RAF he was 38, the maximum age permitted to scrape in as an air gunner. We were convinced he was over 60! Whatever his age, unlike the rest of us, he had already 'lived'. A fund of stories about big game hunting, fishing with the inventive genius Marconi in Cornwall, and taking glamorous ladies to dinner in Hollywood kept us enthralled.

'Carstairs' and I entertained the crews while waiting to fly. We played 'snooker tournaments'. The table was imaginary, so were the cues, the balls, the chalk, even the score-board on the wall. We sustained this elaborate mime either until the match had been 'won', or we were called to our aircraft. The silent concentration of our audience was a great spur to our improvised performances.

One morning a few of us visited a barber in Stafford. 'Carstairs', who had been flying the previous night, fell deeply asleep in the chair. The proprietor managed to cut his hair without disturbing him, then asked us if the Sergeant might like his moustache trimmed. The magnificent grey growth was his pride and joy – he enjoyed demonstrating that when the drooping ends were pulled out horizontally, they could be seen either side of his head when viewed from behind.

The temptation was too great. We told the hairdresser that our friend had recently seen a film starring Clark Gable. He had much admired the actor's 'toothbrush' moustache and intended having his own wild bush cut down to similar proportions. In fact this was the main purpose of his visit. We stressed that he must avoid waking him as he was very tired. The kindly barber snipped and snipped, and trimmed and trimmed, until there was only a slim

131

shadow of bristle under his nose. As a finishing touch he applied a subtle shading of mascara to add emphasis to the masterpiece. We thought 'Carstairs' looked years younger.

At this point we left. Later, we learned there had been an ugly scene when 'Carstairs' woke up. Glimpsing his new image in the mirror, the old air gunner had gone berserk. Grabbing the poor barber, he threatened him with his own cut-throat razor and demanded immediate reparation. It was only when the man explained how he had carried out the work by 'special request' that our infuriated friend relented. As for the rest of us, we tended to move about in threes for some time after that incident.

According to his crew, 'Carstairs' hated wearing his helmet. Because of this, he would sometimes sit in his rear turret in a state of incommunicado, sucking his empty pipe. On one occasion they were obliged to land at a strange 'drome to check their position. Having established where they were, they taxied to the end of the runway in preparation for take-off. 'Carstairs', believing they were back at base, reversed his turret and jumped out, making for the nearest hedge. He suffered a little from bladder trouble.

Having finished what he had to do, he was surprised to see his aircraft roaring down the runway and then climbing into the sky without him. Back at base we were all in a state of semi-shock, thinking that our old mate must have fallen out over the Irish Sea. We were immensely relieved when he turned up the next day having returned by rail. He had had no money on him, and when the train's ticket collector came round, 'Carstairs' had to pretend he was one of our brave Polish allies, unable to speak a word of English. Friendly people in the compartment contributed towards his fare. He noticed, however, as the journey drew to an end, that a fellow passenger was eyeing him a little suspiciously. He was puzzled by this 'Pole's' obvious absorption in an English copy of *Reader's Digest*.

I salute 'Carstairs', and all the characters of Bomber Command, who made life fun in spite of it all.

There is no accounting for the ways of officialdom in times of war. It was mid-November, 1943. Men like Harold Chadwick were engaged in the Battle of Berlin. Losses were to mount all through the coming campaign. It seemed certain we would soon

132

be rushed to a squadron to fill the ever-widening gaps. But not a bit of it. Having finished at OTU we did not fly again for the rest of November, or December, or January. It was the second week in February before we continued our training at 1667 Heavy Conversion Unit, at Lindholme.

Meanwhile, apart from generous doses of leave, we, as a crew, were sent to Dover on an 'inter-services PR exercise'. This turned out to be a week on a destroyer, HMS *Southdown*, patrolling the Channel in rough winter seas. Being Sergeants, we took up quarters with our naval equivalents, the Petty Officers. The Ward Room had been made as un-ship-like as possible. It even had a non-functional fireplace complete with mantelpiece. Most of the POs looked old enough to be our grandfathers. It was just before the festive season, and they reminded me of a bunch of benevolent Father Christmases sitting around in long-johns, sewing teddy bears and dolls for youngsters back home. They were amiable men, showing us every hospitality and plying us with more than regulation quantities of rum. A memorable week, different from anything we had struck before. The on-duty aspect left us full of admiration for the way the Royal Navy went about its work. Even so, I came away content that I had chosen the air rather than the sea.

About this time I grabbed the opportunity to visit my girlfriend who was studying at the veterinary college in Edinburgh. It was disastrous. Our lives had taken different courses. Conversation, once so free and easy, was now strained and stilted. We no longer spoke the same language. It was the end of a friendship that had lasted for five years. At a college dance I was filled with disdain for the male students, a lot of them older than my friends who had volunteered to fly. To them the war was something fought by other people. All they understood was the importance of preparing for a career that would set them up in life when peace returned. It seemed unjust.

Eventually moving on to Halifaxes at Lindholme, we were joined by Ken Ward, a cool, competent flight engineer, while a wiry little Welshman, Ted Morgan, came into the crew to man the mid-upper turret. Jack was commissioned at this time and became a Pilot Officer.

In the Halifax the navigator, wireless operator and bomb-aimer were all located in the nose. It seemed to me an ill-thought-out arrangement, because one burst of flak could wipe out the whole navigation team. Also the heating arrangement was odd. Coils of flexible pipes festooned the deck emitting hot air. We cradled them in our laps, stuffed them up our trouser legs, or pushed them down our shirts. One day we were flying at 20,000 feet. It was cold. I felt liquid dripping down my neck. Assuming this discomfort came from a leaking hydraulic pipe, I called up Jack on the intercom. He sat immediately above me in the pilot's position:

'Jack, I think we've got a leak somewhere.'

Silence.

'Jack can you hear me? I think there's a leak somewhere in the hydraulic system. It's running down my bloody neck.'

'Bruce.' A long pause. 'Bruce. Don't quite know how to put this.' [Rest of crew very silent]. 'You know our crew "piss-tin"?'

'Oh God!'

'Well, Ken forgot it. He's just lent me his brown paper sandwich bag, and I'm afraid the bugger's burst!'

In our early training in Blackpool an irate Corporal O'Mally was fond of telling me: 'You, bloody Lewis, should be shat on, and pissed on, from a great height!' When, by coincidence, we met years later, I was able to tell him his dream had come true.

Inexplicable things happened sometimes. Once, after a cross-country of just over six hours, we landed at base in mid-afternoon. The aircraft had behaved impeccably. After a quick refuel a fresh crew climbed aboard, accompanied by a Flight Lieutenant 'screen' pilot. We watched the Halifax roar down the runway, climb into the air, then dive into the ground and explode.

On another occasion we had engine trouble and put down at Fulbeck, a USAAF station. A swarm of jeeps tore towards us, disgorged over a score of GIs full of enthusiastic curiosity. They clambered all over our Halifax exploring every nook and cranny, but showed no interest in us. Later, a Top Sergeant took us in tow and looked after us very well. We asked him why his chest was bare of medals, unlike the other American servicemen. In reply he pulled open a drawer in his cabin. It was stuffed with 'gong's. 'Yer see boys, I'm what they call a veteran. After a time

134

yer kinda git tired of these goddam things. Why, I got three for crossin' the Atlantic!'

Lunch in the mess was a curious experience. We sat at long trestle tables and rank seemed of no consequence. Unshaven, grease-covered fitters rubbed shoulders with captains and majors. The Colonel was admittedly at the head of the table. He was a lean young man, with close-cropped hair and dressed in a leather jacket. In a moment he began to lose patience. Banging his fork on the table-top he yelled:

'Cam on! Cam on! What's keepin' yer, Wilmer? Let's eat chow!'

The kitchen hatch flew up and the face of a fat, sweating man in a singlet and a chef's hat appeared in the frame. Addressing his Commanding Officer, he said: 'Hold yer water, bud! It's a' cumin'!'

Jack leaned across and whispered: 'Imagine us yelling at "Groupy" like that!'

When the 'chow' did arrive we stared at it in wonder. Huge steaks hung over the edge of every plate. Each plateful represented more than an Englishman's meat ration for a month. We waited eagerly for the arrival of the 'two veg'. Instead, big cans of peanut butter were dumped in front of us. This was plastered thickly on the steaks which were then surrounded with pineapple chunks. A dressing of sugar, liberally sprinkled over the lot, completed the main course. Pudding was a choice of exotic-flavoured ice-creams, the like of which we had never tasted in our lives. As I ate, I thought of my young brother and sister and felt guilty.

We stayed overnight and continued to enjoy the hospitality of our kind American hosts, while their engineers generously sorted out the fault in our aircraft. When we flew the forty-minute trip back to base the following day, I believe it was the only occasion when we all felt airsick!

A few evenings later I went to the cinema with a Land Girl, attractive in tight green sweater and riding breeches. After the show she kindly invited me back to her place. Here the food on offer was a little different. She set in front of me a bowl of what looked like a mixture of cold ground rice and porridge. As I was eating it, more out of politeness than enjoyment, I asked her what she did in the Land Army. 'Oh,' she said, 'I'm a rat exterminator.

135

I mix in poison with the sort of stuff you're eating there. It soon gets rid of them!' Always ready to take a hint I was on my bike and pedalling furiously back to base without waiting to see what other delights were in store.

Completing 55 hours 35 minutes on Halifaxes, we moved on to No 1 Lancaster Finishing School, Hemswell. The mighty Lancaster at last. At Hemswell we learned the difference between a good aircraft and an outstanding one. It took Jack West and the rest of us only four days to familiarize ourselves with the bomber that flew like a bird.

On 22 April, 1944, our last day at LFS, we flew night circuits and landings from 0330 until 0600. Fighter Affiliation exercises, with attacking fighters, were laid on from 1610 until 1655 in the afternoon. Then our course finished with a spell of bombing practice from 1735 until 1850 that evening. This businesslike urgency convinced us we would soon be on missions over Germany (Francis Kelsey had passed through here less than two weeks previously on his way to 625 Squadron).

Being sent to a particular squadron was, I suppose, every bit as chancy as being picked to fly with a certain crew. Although we did not realize our luck at the time, we had the good fortune to be posted to 101 Squadron. It had a fine reputation, particularly for bombing accuracy, dating back to the First World War. Now it was doing a unique job. Apart from playing its full part in bombing raids, it also carried a device known as ABC, 'Airborne Cigar'.

The Lancasters on this 'Special Duties' squadron carried an eighth crew member, a second wireless operator known as a 'Special Operator'. These 'Specials' spoke German and operated powerful radio transmitters that interfered with the instructions being sent out by German ground controllers to their night fighters. 101 [pronounced One-Oh-One] Lancasters had two substantial aerials pointing upwards forward of the mid-upper turret, and a third, pointing downwards below the nose. Inside the fuselage the rest-bed, amidships, had been removed to make room for the bulky ABC equipment. The 'Specials' worked in isolation in the body of the aircraft and saw nothing of what was going on outside from the time they took off until they landed back at base. As

136

wireless operator I had a warning button which I pressed to bring the 'Special' on to crew intercom in moments of emergency.

When I had joined the RAF more than two years previously, and shambled through the gates of Padgate camp with an odd assortment of fellow civilians, the first person who had spoken to me was a little, thick-set man with black curly hair. Clutching a battered fibre suitcase in one hand, he had raised a clenched fist under my nose and said: 'Greetings Comrade!' He was Ron Herschkovitch, a Russian Jew. All his family had disappeared into Nazi concentration camps. The best way he could think of getting back at the Germans was to join Bomber Command.

We had gone different ways during training, but now here he was again, a 'Special' at 101. He had already established himself as a 'squadron character' with a boisterous sense of humour. When he flew, he always wore running shoes strung round his neck. 'Well look at me,' he would exclaim, raising his arms, shrugging his shoulders, and turning sideways to emphasize his profile. 'If I'm shot down, what chance would I have against those Nazi bastards? All I can do is don these plimsolls – and run like hell!'

Because of its role in Bomber Command, 101 was often operating, to give protection to the rest of the stream, when other Lancaster squadrons in 1 Group were resting. It sustained a greater number of casualties than any other squadron in the RAF during World War Two according to Andrew Brookes whose book *Bomber Squadron at War* is a full account of the work of 101 Squadron.

There were compensations. 'Bomber' Harris himself, fed up with trying to get things done through official channels, arranged for a small Lincolnshire firm, Rose of Gainsborough, to provide rear turrets sprouting heavier twin .5 Browning machine guns, in place of the usual .303s, as increased protection for 101 Lancasters.

We also had FIDO [Fog Investigation Dispersal Operation]. Two metal pipes with upward-facing holes, running along either side of the runway, had petrol pumped through them and ignited when visibility was poor. The resulting blaze effectively dispersed low-lying fog. Coming home from a raid at night and looking down through the hole in the clouds was like peering into the flaming mouth of hell. It was sometimes hard to 'sit the aircraft down' because of the rising heat – but it was a welcome facility.

137

We did two practice cross-countries when we arrived at Ludford Magna, the Lincolnshire home of 101 Squadron. It was the beginning of May. These trips were completed smoothly enough, but I was worried about Tim, our navigator. He appeared nervy, and looked as though he was finding it difficult to concentrate on his calculations while we were flying. I decided to keep this to myself for the present, but to have a private word with him if things did not improve.

The opportunity never came. An evening later Tim walked into our crew hut and said straight out: 'I'm sorry boys but I can't go through with this. I'm having nightmares about going on "ops" and being shot down in flames. I can't do my work properly, and that's not fair on all of you.' Nobody said a word. He put his head in his hands, and that was that.

LMF (Lack of Moral Fibre) cases were treated very harshly by the RAF. They were stripped of their rank, if they were NCOs, and sent away to carry out the most menial tasks that those who had never placed themselves in danger could devise. Within hours Tim had disappeared from our lives.

Now we had to wait for navigator No 4. During this enforced idleness we were offered the chance to volunteer for Pathfinders in 8 Group. Lacking a navigator at the time of the offer, we opted to stay with 101.

It was 2 June before we finally took off on our first 'op'. Rarely can a crew have been so delayed before flying into action. Our new navigator was a Canadian Flying Officer. We reserved judgement. Our task was to bomb a radar-jamming station at Berneval-le-Grand in France. This, we later learned, was achieved with great accuracy and without loss. Our morale was boosted by the presence of the Squadron Commander, Wing Commander R. I. Alexander, who flew with us in our Lancaster to see how we got on. This was typical of the man.

After this we were on our own. We flew on two or three daylight raids to attack V1 rocket sites. Our first night operation was to Villeneuve. Here is a quote from my log book:

Owing to a misunderstanding between pilot and navigator – missed target. Bombs jettisoned. Came back late.

138

The following night we were off on a long trip to bomb the marshalling yards at Dijon. This went reasonably well, but a couple of nights later a trip to Vaires turned into a shambles. Owing to a succession of navigational errors we arrived late and alone at the target. On the way back we received a pasting from flak over Paris and flew home on three engines.

18 July was scheduled to be our first trip to Germany – a synthetic oil plant at Wesseling. But we never got there. On the outward journey Stan's rear turret became u/s (unserviceable) and Jack decided to abort the sortie. Returning to base over the sea, we were fired on by an allied convoy.

By this time I was convinced we were leaping from one crisis to the next and had no hope of completing a tour. Our crew had every confidence in Jack as skipper, but he seemed fated to suffer from duff navigators. We had now made our judgement on the latest one. What made matters worse was his arrogance – an unusual trait in a Canadian. They were normally such jolly fellows.

Jack was promoted to Flying Officer and I became a Flight Sergeant. These were automatic promotions after serving a certain time in the previous rank. At the end of the month we completed a mission to Hamburg. Losses on this raid were high due to the activity of enemy fighters, but we were not attacked. As I was eating my post 'op' breakfast, I was handed a telegram, it read: 'PETE MISSING. HOPE YOU ARE SAFE.' It was from Pete Bishop's mother.

I was stunned. I passed the message to Stan sitting next to me. 'My mate', I said, '4 Group. Halifaxes'. He studied it, slowly nodding his head, 'Tough,' he replied. Then added, 'Nice sort of Mum'.

Gentle, thoughtful, patient, quietly cheerful Pete. Gone. But it was unfair to expect members of my crew to grieve over a stranger, so I folded the telegram away and said no more about it. After all, we had twenty-four gaps of our own in the mess that morning.

Yes, she was a nice Mum. To my undying shame I never replied. I had no idea what to say.

On 2 August we, who already qualified as one of the ten most experienced crews on the squadron, were briefed to attack a V-rocket launching site at Coquereaux in daylight. The methods adopted were unusual. In a letter to my parents later I said:

> The plan was for us to follow the [2] Mosquitoes. We were in two lines of five behind them. Our Lancaster was last in line to port. When they opened their bomb doors we had to open ours. On seeing the bombs drop from the 'Mossies', the first six Lancs were to follow suit. Then, when the last four, which included us, drew level with a smoke puff, the idea was for us to drop our load.

In practice things worked out rather less neatly. Mosquitoes were tearing around the skies over bomber bases in northern England, looking for their particular group of 'Heavies'. When the flying cavalcades eventually formed up and set course for France, the fast Mosquitoes were throttled right back, almost falling out of the sky, while the heavily laden Lancasters vibrated on full power, trying to keep up.

Bomb doors were opened well before the target was reached, and our aircraft, P Peter [PB256], not the best machine on the squadron, was lagging further and further behind. Then it happened. A burst of predicted flak exploded between our port inner engine and the fuselage. The interior of the Lancaster was filled with choking black smoke and we dipped forward into a steep dive. I remember reaching for my chute. It was my 13th operation!

At that moment we did not know it, but Jack had been wounded. Apart from metal fragments in various parts of his body, half the base cap of an 88mm shell had torn into his groin, missing his genitals by a fraction. After losing precious height, he managed to pull the aircraft out of its dive. 'Right,' he said, 'I've got her. We'll go on and bomb.' From the tone of his voice, we could have been on a cross-country exercise. Jimmy, the bomb-aimer, did not like the idea and said so. Who could blame him? But Jack had made his decision; 'Behave yourself, Jimmy, we'll go on and bomb.'

And that is what happened. Jack kept the Lancaster straight and steady for the run in, while Jimmy bombed the small target visually. Still on our way in, we could see the rest of the Lancasters heading for home and the Mosquitoes just dwindling dots in the distance. As we too turned for home, the daylight sky seemed a lonely place.

Jack, who was losing a lot of blood in spite of our emergency bandaging, was determined to hang on till he got us safely back to base, but Ken, the engineer, told him that because of damage to the aircraft we were leaking fuel, and must put down at the nearest available airfield on England's south coast. We called up the Squadron Commander who was flying somewhere out ahead:

'P Peter calling. P Peter calling. Pilot wounded. Intend landing Ford.'

Back snapped the reply: 'Maintain radio silence.'

But then you could almost hear the wheels turning inside the CO's head. It was daylight – radio silence was hardly that important when aircraft could be seen. A wounded pilot? Then who was flying the kite?

'Hello P Peter. Good luck!'

Jack brought us all the way back, made a perfect landing at Ford and fainted as soon as the wheels stopped rolling. As he was being lowered from the aircraft on a stretcher, his delicate, schoolboy features as pale as death, a group of American flyers standing near, asked:

'Whose that little guy?'

'He's our Skipper.'

'Yeh? So the co-pilot brought this ship back?'

'No. Our Skipper brought it back. We don't have co-pilots.'

Ford was full of Polish, French, American and British flying types who had all put down temporarily for a variety of reasons. The place was cluttered with aggressive-looking Thunderbolts, Mustangs and Typhoons. It seemed ironical that these single-seat fighters should *each* be carrying more effective fire-power than a squadron of Lancasters.

As early as mid-1941 Marshal of the Royal Air Force Sir John Slessor, DSO, MC, [who was then Air Vice Marshal] was commenting on British bombers:

Ever since those big "Heavies" appeared on the horizon I have been convinced we must arm them with cannon. If it means a drop in the bomb load – well that's just too bad; but it's better to carry 7,000 pounds and get to the target and back than to carry 8,000

141

pounds and get shot down. The Americans think we are crazy to go on quite happily with .303s in bombers; and I'm sure they are right.

Making the most of the opportunity, and taking Max Doolette, our stalwart Australian 'Special' with me, I nipped on a train and went to call on an uncle and aunt who owned what would now be called a garden centre in the middle of Chichester. They were surprised to see us stroll in, dressed in our flying gear, and made us warmly welcome. It was good to relax in a 'normal' atmosphere for a few hours.

Jack finished up in No 1 Ward, St Richard's Hospital, in Chichester. My uncle kept an eye on him while he remained there and took him fruit each day. Meanwhile, the rest of us returned to Ludford Magna. I wrote to my mother and father about part of our journey:

> The following day we travelled back by train in flying kit. The Londoners are marvellous. Sirens blowing and no one pays any attention. They just carry on with their work as if things are quite normal. We didn't see anything of the Flying Bombs, and damage was slight except coming up from the South to Victoria where things are pretty devastated, I'm afraid.
>
> The London taxi drivers are a grand bunch of blokes. We exchanged comments with many of them as we passed in transport provided from Victoria to King's Cross. Nelson still stands undaunted in Trafalgar Square. To me he has *always* been London.

Back on the squadron I had a conversation with our Station Commander, Group Captain King. This most approachable of officers wanted to know in precise detail exactly what had happened on our trip to Coquereaux. As a Lancaster pilot himself he appreciated how magnificently our skipper had behaved. Shortly afterwards it was announced that Jack had been awarded the Distinguished Service Order – the only DSO to be won by 101 Squadron that year.

Sadly, after only a few days, the rest of Jack's team, with the exception of Max and myself, were posted away from the squadron. Max, as a 'Special', was in an aircrew category unique to 101, and waited, like me, to be absorbed into another crew. I was

142

left feeling lonely and isolated – losing a crew was like being severed from a family.

However, being a gentleman of leisure for two or three weeks set in train events that were to affect the rest of my life. I met a beautiful young WAAF who was involved with Signals Duties on 101 Squadron. Miki had previously seen front-line action on a fighter 'drome when stationed at Biggin Hill, during the desperate Battle of Britain days. She knew all about the terrors of being bombed and strafed while still carrying on her work. Our experiences, emotions, the way we lived and our language led to a shared understanding. These alone would have been enough to bring us together, but of course there was much more. An overwhelming attraction, each for the other, soon meant we were in love.

We arranged a date for the day after our first meeting, but I nearly failed to keep it. I was asked to accompany a Pilot Officer Bateman and a ground staff Engineering Officer on an air test. Only the three of us were detailed to fly. Apparently a seasoned crew on a raid the night before had failed to get the Lancaster (I Item RV293) above 8,000 feet and had returned to base before reaching the target. The CO was dubious. We had to give a second opinion on the aircraft's performance.

We flew west over the Welsh mountains. To simulate operational conditions, the aircraft carried a full bomb load. Impatient to get the test over, (it was already late afternoon), I stood in the astrodome dressed in my best uniform ready for the evening date with the marvellous WAAF I had met the previous day. It soon became obvious that the previous night's veteran crew had done well to get as high as they did. After half-an-hour's flying we were barely over 3,500 ft. I Item was patently unfit for service.

The Engineering Officer was making careful notes when the starboard inner engine spluttered and stopped. Bateman was astounded to find the bomber would not maintain height on three engines – unheard-of for a Lancaster. He suggested we might jettison the 4000 pound 'cookie' over the Welsh mountains. With a clear vision of my Aunt Annie, I protested strongly and gave him a course to steer across England to the Wash. This would also bring us into the vicinity of Ludford Magna. As we crossed the east coast we were down to 1000 feet and I had positioned myself

143

in the nose, trying to remember the many things that Jimmy had told me about releasing bombs. All the switches on the panel had been flicked to 'on', everything seemed set. Flying out over the Wash, Bateman opened the bomb doors and said, 'Let the bloody things go, Bruce. Quick!' I pressed the tit. Nothing happened. Again and again – still they would not unstick. It was the Engineering Officer who twigged what was wrong. 'Because this is an air test, the bombs are not wired up. We'll have to get them away manually.' Remembering Jimmy's instructions, I looked in the holder for the 'bomb toggle', a long piece of wire with a loop on the end specially fashioned for dislodging bombs by hand. It was missing. From Bateman: 'We're down to 800 feet, for Christ's sake!' The odds on survival when plunging into the sea with a fully laden Lancaster would not be looked on with much optimism by bookies or insurance actuaries.

Having removed the small, oblong hatch-covers located on the deck above the bomb bay, I was lying flat on the floor, bathed in sweat and covered in grease and oil, trying to unhook the 'cookie' with an improvised contraption made up of a short length of wire cable, a pair of pliers and a screwdriver. Looking down the sides of the stubbornly resisting 4,000-pounder it was all too evident the sea was frighteningly close. The white crests that topped the green waves almost seemed to be splashing the underside of the Lancaster.

Just as the moment of despair overtook me, the monstrous drum of explosive broke away and plunged into the sea. Relieved of its weight, the aircraft eased out of its downward journey. Later, Bateman told me we had been at 300 feet when it went. It continued to be a tricky business, because, although we were now flying level, I Item still lacked the power to climb. We sent a message to base and obtained permission to come straight in. As we touched down a second engine started to splutter. The Engineering Officer looked as though he might be glad to get back to his desk!

After a lengthy report, and our heartfelt suggestion that this new aircraft should be sent back from whence it had come, I was still in time for my important date. But my appearance hardly lived up to the debonair image I had hoped to present. The image was, in fact, rather closer to that of a fitter's grease rag. Miki, who looked stunning in her beautifully pressed WAAF uniform, affected not to notice.

A little more than three weeks after Jack West's misfortune I flew to Kiel with a new crew. There was heavy opposition over the target, the starboard elevator was holed, but otherwise it was a good trip. The skipper, 32-year-old Flight Lieutenant Jim Bursell, apart from being mature, also had a streak of the 'swashbuckler' in him, which prompted him from time to time to perform some 'daring deeds' well beyond the call of duty. On a later occasion we went to Neuss, near Düsseldorf in the Ruhr, and flew three times over this heavily defended target just to get our line up 'absolutely right', before dropping the bombs. Another time we continued over the target, although recalled by the Master Bomber because of poor visibility, in order to take line-overlap photographs proving that we could have bombed in any case. That was the time we were struck by lightning.

Jim Bursell, a tall New Zealander, was hero-worshipped by his young crew. They made no bones about telling me he was the best pilot on 101, the only one who had the guts to take off with a full load and then do a *double* climbing turn! Although, at the beginning, I did not share their enthusiasm for the skipper's eccentricities, I eventually came to appreciate his outstanding abilities both as a pilot and a leader. From then on I was convinced we were in sure hands.

By mid-August Bomber Command was ready to return to attacking German cities, especially some of those that had proved difficult to eliminate earlier in the war. We had just completed a period about which the Bomber Command War Diaries say:

Operations during this period consisted of a multitude of small or medium-sized raids. The planners never worked harder, nor did the aircrew and the ground staffs. Sometimes aircrew flew two sorties in twenty-four hours. By day, they might be bombing targets only a few yards from the battle lines in Normandy; a few hours later they could be bombing an oil refinery in the Ruhr. Bomber Command flew approximately the same number of sorties in an average week during this period – more than 5,000 sorties – as in the first nine months of the war! No one who flew in those weeks and survived will ever forget them.

And of course, for reasons already explained, 101 Squadron flew with even greater frequency than the rest!

Later, in October, we were still hard at it. On the 5th we air-tested a new machine, a G George, (the same designation as our previous one, which by now was worn out). That was around 1100. It proved to be satisfactory so at 1850 that night we flew it to Saarbrücken and bombed military concentrations. We did not return to base, having being diverted to Witchford.

The following morning we flew back to base from Witchford. Then at 1741 we took off for another night raid, this time on Bremen. On return there was hardly time to close our eyes before being called to a briefing for an urgently mounted mission support-ing the army at Emmerich, and were airborne by noon. Within a brief period we were testing yet another new machine, because our 'recently new one' had been damaged by a bomb that had hit us when it fell from one of our own aircraft flying above us in the target area.

On our night 'ops' we flew around 20,000 feet above large German cities, while daylight targets were sometimes attacked by our heavy bombers at hair-raisingly low altitudes. For example, we bombed a coastal battery at Cap Gris Nez, near Calais, at only 2,700 feet.

Our longest trip had been to Stettin on the German/Polish fron-tier at the end of August. We had taken off as daylight was fading, flown over the North Sea, across northern Denmark, then found our way south to the target flying high above the Baltic. After bombing, we came back by the same route, and landed at base just as dawn was breaking – the trip had lasted 9 hours and 5 minutes.

Yet the most memorable moment on that mission was when our bomber stream flew over Malmö, blatantly breaking through the air-space of neutral Sweden. What a sight it was! After nearly five years of total 'Black-Out' both at home and on the Continent, it is almost impossible to describe the wonder of looking down on a city bathed in light. Houses with twinkling windows, streets lined with illuminated shops, highways picked out by marching rows of lamps, traffic with headlights blazing, neon signs, illuminated docks, and perhaps most strange of all, an airport aglow with light. It was a fairyland in a world at war.

The Swedes made a gesture, as they had every right to do. They fired obsolete flaming onions that burst 10,000 feet below us. We spotted some ancient biplane fighters that wisely kept their distance from our 402 Lancasters, but flashed their Aldis lamps in 'warning'. On the way back, around 0300, it seemed most of the inhabitants, including the Swedish armed forces, had gone to bed. The activity had died down, and the lights extinguished.

Moments later, over Denmark, the dream ended for over twenty Lancaster crews, as waiting Luftwaffe fighters tore into the bombers and sent them tumbling from the sky. We, as on other nights, were lucky.

The three raids mentioned earlier, on the 5th, 6th and 7th October, completed my 30 'ops'. Still not quite believing I had actually survived I sat down and penned a letter to my parents telling them it was all over for the present, and that some leave should follow shortly. Then Miki and I went for a walk. As we wandered through the beautiful autumnal woods that overlooked the lovely little village of Tealby, where we had spent so many off-duty hours, I proposed to her and she accepted me. Danger was behind us. The future, whatever it held, looked bright and exciting. That night, lying on a haystack, we watched 101 Squadron taking off. As our Lancasters climbed for height my heart went out to all the crews, but with special thoughts for Jim Bursell and the boys who still had six trips to do to complete their tour.

The following morning, with a light step and a new sense of freedom, I was making my way to the Adjutant's office to sort out some leave when Jim Bursell waylaid me. 'Bruce,' he said, coming straight to the point as always, 'as you know we flew last night, and the boys are not happy with the new chap. They don't want to fly with him any more. We've had a chat about it and they've asked me to ask you if you'll carry on with us – fly with us on our last five trips.'

'Bloody hell, Jim, you're asking a hell of a lot!' That was my immediate reaction. Then I looked at him, lean, reliable, like an older brother, his eyes anxious for my answer. I thought of the crew. The two inseparable Canadian gunners: Larry Robinson, tall, boyish and fair in the rear turret; Chuck Austin, in the mid-upper, chunky-square dark as a bear, an ex-lumberjack; George Woolridge, the steady, calm bomb aimer; Peter Clifford, utterly reliable as our flight engineer; and Colin Pyle, the unflappable, skilled navigator from Newcastle-upon-Tyne, with whom I had worked so harmoniously. Then, of course, there was my old friend, Max Doolette who flew with us many times as special operator. These were the men who had accepted me as part of their team. Now they were calling on me again. My emotions were a mixture of pride, frustration fear, and a certainty that, having 'diced with Jesus' and miraculously won, yet now, after all, it was only going to be a temporary victory.

It was blackmail of course. If I refused, there would be a lifetime to ponder on my decision, whatever happened. Yet, if I agreed to carry on and we got the 'chop', what about Miki? What about the shock to my parents? Having received my letter, they would assume I was safely through. But from that first second when Jim asked me, I suppose I knew there could only be one answer: 'OK Jim. I'll do it.' And somehow managing a grin, 'I'll hold you personally responsible if I get the "chop"!'

Jim's relief was obvious. 'I'm bloody pleased, Bruce. If you hadn't agreed I think I'd have had a mutiny on my hands!'

'The bastards!' I muttered with a mixture of resentment and affection.

Almost at once we flew off to a Fort Fredrick Heindrik, near Breskins, to destroy some heavy guns, attacking them at low level. Next it was Duisberg, where the Germans threw up intense heavy flak wrecking our starboard outer engine. This was the fourth time I had flown in Lancasters with less than the full complement of engines. Then there was a daylight raid on Cologne. This time the heavy flak blew a hole in the front of the aircraft. The return trip was uncomfortably cold and draughty. Three down, two to go.

Raid No 4. Another mission to Cologne. A night job this time. Again we lost an engine, but on this occasion within minutes of taking off. Let me quote from my log book:

148

30.10.44 Operations: Cologne. A trip of snags! Starboard Inner Engine U/S from Reading on outward journey. Intercom U/S before target. No brake pressure. Fuel shortage. Sent message to base. Lightning flashes from aerial connections. Earthed all aerials. Target bombed OK. Landed Woodbridge.

Woodbridge, in Suffolk, was a specially established 'crash drome' for bombers in trouble. Twin searchlights pierced the sky vertically. They were like the gateway to heaven. Enter between those beams of light and you would touch down on concrete – stretching away into infinity and three times the width of a normal runway. Jim brought our wreck of a machine to a halt and she never flew again. He was awarded the Distinguished Flying Cross for this effort. Next day we went back to 101 by train. One to go!

The Bursell crew flew their final operation three days later. It was in yet another brand-new Lancaster, our *third* G George, the other two having literally been shot to pieces under us. The raid on Düsseldorf was almost an anti-climax. We bombed an armament centre supplying the front line, and only encountered moderate flak in our wave. As we crossed the Dutch coast on the way home, Jim called me up on the intercom: 'Well, that looks like it for real this time, Bruce. Will you and Miki be getting married now?' 'That's the intention,' I replied. 'What are you going to do, Jim?'

We were roughly above The Hague at that moment. Jim said, 'Before the war I used to be an executive with the Shell Oil Company. I've got an office down there somewhere. I'd like to think that when this lot is over, my chair will still be waiting!' Normally, when flying, this well-disciplined crew only spoke when it was vital to do so. But now, with the tour all but over, each member in turn talked of what he hoped to do after the war. I thought I knew them well, but at this moment they were adding a new dimension to their personalities – drawing an image of what sort of people they might be in the future. Now they felt certain there was going to be a future.

We celebrated in style the following evening, and with us, of course, was the 'other' crew, the one who had kept our kites flying trip after trip. Never grumbling, working in all weathers, they had performed near-miracles. We pulled each others' legs unceasingly:

'We'd no sooner fixed up the poor old kite when you buggers bent it again!'. 'It's a wonder we ever got there, the way you bodged it up!'. 'You had more G Georges, Jim, than me and the lads have had hot dinners!' Magical, memorable moments, never to be repeated. Soon we would shake hands and not meet again.

Next day Jim cornered me as I was on my way to Signals. Grinning, he said, 'A couple of your high-level contacts want to see you right away.' Sensing a trap, I replied, 'Oh, yes?' 'Yes,' he insisted, 'The Air Commodore and Groupy King.' Now I knew he was having me on. I had had a couple of informal chats with the Group Captain, but the Base Commander? That was like an appointment with God! But I was wrong; they *had* requested to see me!

Group Captain King interviewed me first. After some preliminary chat, he suddenly said, 'By the way, Lewis, you are recommended for an immediate commission. Get washed and shaved. Polish your buttons and shoes. Then, in your best blue, report to the AOC in half an hour. He's expecting you. Good luck!'

Air Commodore Blucke, soon to become an Air Vice-Marshal, and the last wartime AOC of 1 Group, Bomber Command, looked at me disapprovingly. 'You've been a bad lad in your time, Lewis.' He had a thick file open on his desk – my service career to date. All at once I remembered various 'crimes' I had committed in my training days. Breaking out of camp; being improperly dressed; showing disrespect to a corporal. There was no chance that this stern-looking man would consider me as suitable officer material. Then he stood up. 'Coming up through the ranks as you have, Lewis, should stand you in good stead now you are about to become an officer. Don't let me down.' He held out his hand. 'Well done. Congratulations!'

I cannot imagine that anyone flying with 101 Squadron would knowingly let down either Air Commodore Blucke or Group Captain King. Officially, because of their rank, neither was supposed to fly on operations. Yet both men considered morale and esprit de corps of paramount importance. They maintained these vital qualities in the squadron by personal example. They were the living embodiment of the 101 Squadron spirit. From time to time when the going had been rough, and the losses high, King picked a crew and flew as pilot, while Blucke, an experienced Lancaster pilot himself, chose to fly as a rear gunner, invariably with an all-sergeant crew. Had they become prisoners of war, the puzzlement on the face of the German interrogating officer would have been great indeed. An Air Officer gunner taking orders from a Sergeant pilot must have been unique in the annals of air war!

At 2400 hours that night I ceased to be a Flight-Sergeant and one minute later became a Pilot Officer. It was my 21st birthday. Remaining on the squadron until Christmas, I managed to eat three Christmas dinners on the festive day, two with Miki and friends living in the village, and an official one in the mess that evening where, as the most junior officer, I had to propose the 'Loyal Toast'. I was pleased to find that I could still rise to my feet!

Regretfully posted away from 101 Squadron in the new year, (the rest of my crew had long since gone), I became first an Instructor, then an Intelligence Officer, working in 8 Group HQ, at Huntingdon, for Pathfinders. I flew with some of them in a Lancaster to Berlin immediately after the war ended to view the awful devastation; and finally rounded off my service as the RAF's first radio newsreader in Europe, broadcasting from the Telefunken House in Hamburg. In a way, events had gone full circle.

Most important, I returned to 101 Squadron in the Spring of 1945. Miki and I were married in the little church of Ludford Magna. Max Doolette, the Australian 'Special', gave the bride away There was no confetti, but a Canadian crew climbed on the porch and showered us with 'Window'.

Note: The author and Colin Pyle met again recently after nearly half a century. During this happy reunion, Bruce Lewis, glancing through his former navigator's log book, noted an operation that he had omitted to enter in his own log – a raid on 29 September, 1944, in which they participated in a concentrated attack on Omberg dam on Walcheren Island, below cloud at only 1,500 feet in daylight. He thinks he probably forgot to record this event at the time through tiredness. Anyway, it brings his total up to 36 operational missions.

NINE

The Co-Pilot

The courageous aircrew who flew the B-17 Fortresses and B-24 Liberators of the United States 8th Army Air Force stationed in Britain followed a policy of bombing only by day, in the belief that strength in numbers and collective fire power would see them through to the target and back. The RAF had found this policy disastrous in the early days of the war, and the Americans, too, suffered bitter disappointments and grim losses during their initial daylight missions.

Flying first to Rouen on 17 August, 1942, it was well over a year before the Americans were really able to get into their stride. Britain, whose factories were fully stretched in supplying her own forces, was unable to help beyond providing the USAAF with air bases. Every bomber, every nut and bolt, in fact all material, including food, had to cross the Atlantic from the USA. It was a gigantic logistic exercise. Eventually they won through, but only after a long and bloody struggle. Mastery over the German Luftwaffe came with the development of the long-range escort fighter and improved tactics born out of hard experience.

Lieutenant-Colonel Beirne Lay, Jr. left his desk as a staff officer to fly with his comrades on missions over Germany. There could be no better description than his of how the 8th AAF went to war:

In the briefing room, the Intelligence Officer of the bombardment group pulled a cloth screen away from a huge wall map. Each of the 240 sleepy-eyed combat-crew members in the crowded room leaned forward. There were low whistles. I felt a sting of anticipation as I stared at the red string on the map that stretched from our base in England to a pinpoint deep in Southern Germany, then across the Alps, through the Brenner Pass to the coast of Italy, then past Corsica and Sardinia and south over the Mediterranean to a desert airdrome in North Africa. You could have heard an oxygen mask drop.

'Your primary,' said the Intelligence Officer, 'is Regensburg. Your aiming point is the centre of the Messerschmitt 109G aircraft and assembly shops. This is the most vital target we've ever gone after. If you destroy it, you destroy thirty percent of the Luftwaffe's single-engine fighter production. You fellows know what that means to you personally.'

There were a few hollow laughs.

After the briefing, I climbed aboard a jeep bound for the operations office to check up on my Fortress assignment. The stars were dimly visible through the chilly mist that covered our blacked-out bomber station, but the weather forecast for a deep penetration over the Continent was good. In the office I looked at the crew sheet, where the line-up of the lead, low and high squadrons of the group is plotted for each mission. I was listed for a co-pilot's seat.

While I stood there, and on a chance suggestion of one of the squadron commanders who was looking over the list, the Operations Officer erased my name and shifted me to the high squadron as co-pilot in the crew of a steady Irishman named Lieutenant Murphy, with whom I had flown before. Neither of us knew it, but that Operations Officer saved my life right there with a piece of rubber on the end of a pencil.

At 5.30 am, 15 minutes before taxi time, a jeep drove round the five-mile perimeter track in the semi-darkness, pausing at each dispersal point long enough to notify the waiting crews that poor local visibility would postpone the take-off for an hour and a half. I was sitting with Murphy and the rest of our crew near the 'Piccadilly Lily'. She looked sinister and complacent, squatting on her fat tyres with scarcely a hole in her skin to show for the twelve raids behind her.

The postponement heightened, rather than relaxed, the tension. Once more I checked over my life vest, oxygen mask and parachute, not perfunctorily, but the way you check something you're going to have to use. I made sure my escape kit was pinned securely in the knee pocket of my flying suit, where it wouldn't fall out in a scramble to abandon ship. I slid a hunting knife

153

between my shoe and my flying boot as I looked again through my extra equipment for this mission: water canteen, mess kit, blankets and English pounds for use in the Algerian desert, where we could sleep on the ground and might be on our own from a forced landing.

Murphy restlessly gave the 'Piccadilly Lily' another once-over, inspecting ammunition belts, bomb bay, tyres and *oxygen* – it's human fuel, as important as gasoline – at the height where we operate. Gunners field-stripped their .50-calibres again and oiled the bolts. Our top-turret gunner lay on the grass with his head on his parachute, feigning sleep, sweating out his 13th start.

We shared a common knowledge which grimly enhanced the normal excitement before a mission. Of the approximately 150 Fortresses who were hitting Regensburg, our group was the last and lowest, at a base altitude of 17,000 feet. That's well within the range of accuracy for heavy flak. Our course would take us over plenty of it. It was a cinch also that our group would be the softest touch for the enemy fighters, being last man through the gauntlet. Furthermore, the 'Piccadilly Lily' was leading the last three ships of the high squadron – the tip of the tail end of the whole shebang. We didn't relish it much. Who wants a Purple Heart?

The minute hand of my wrist watch dragged. I caught myself thinking about the day, exactly one year ago, on 17 August, 1942, when I watched a pitifully small force of twelve B-17s take off on the first raid of the 8th Air Force to make a shallow penetration against Rouen, France. On that day it was our maximum effort. Today, on our first anniversary, we were putting thirty times that number of heavies into the air – half the force on Regensburg and half the force on Schweinfurt, both situated inside the interior of the Reich.

For a year and a half, as a staff officer, I had watched the 8th Air Force grow under Major-General Ira C. Eaker. That's a long time to watch from behind a desk. Only ten days ago I had asked for and received the order to go on combat duty. Those ten days had been full of the swift action of participating in four combat missions and checking out for the first time as a four-engine pilot.

Now I knew that it can be easier to be shot at than telephoned at. The staff officers at an Air Force headquarters are the unsung

154

heroes of the war. And yet I found myself reminiscing just a little affectionately about that desk, wondering if there wasn't a touch of suicide in store for our group. One thing was sure: Headquarters had dreamed up the biggest air operation to date to celebrate its birthday in the biggest league of aerial warfare.

At 7.30 am we broke out of the cloud tops into the glare of the rising sun. Beneath our B-17 lay English fields still blanketed in the thick mist from which we had just emerged. We continued to climb slowly, our broad wings shouldering a heavy load of incendiary bombs in the belly and a burden of fuel in the main and wing-tip Tokyo tanks that would keep the Fortress afloat in the thin upper altitudes for eleven hours.

From my co-pilot's seat on the right-hand side I watched the white surface of the overcast, where B-17s in clusters of six to each squadron were puncturing the cloud deck all about us, rising clear of the mist with their glass noses slanted upward for the long climb to base altitude. We tacked on to one of these clutches of six. Now the sky over England was heavy with the weight of thousands of tons of bombs, fuel and men being lifted four miles straight up on a giant aerial hoist, to the western terminus of a 20,000 feet elevated highway that led east to Regensburg. At intervals I saw the arc of a spluttering red, green or yellow flare being fired from the cabin roof of a group leader's airplane to identify the lead squadron to the high and low squadrons of each group. Assembly takes longer when you come up through an overcast.

For nearly an hour, still over Southern England, we climbed, nursing the straining Cyclone engines in a 300-feet-per-minute ascent, forming three squadrons gradually into compact group stagger formations – low squadron down to the left and high squadron up to the right of the lead squadron – groups assembling into looser combat wings of two or three groups each along the combat-wing assembly line, homing over predetermined points with radio compass, and finally cruising along the air-division assembly line to fall into place in trail behind Colonel Curtis E. Le May in the lead group of the air division.

Formed at last, each flanking group in position 1000 feet above or below its lead group, our 15-mile parade moved east towards

Lowestoft, point of departure from the friendly coast, unwieldy but dangerous to fool with. From my perch on the high squadron in the last element of the whole procession, the air division looked like a huge anvil-shaped swarm of locusts – not on dress parade, like the bombers of the Luftwaffe that died like flies over Britain in 1940, but deployed to uncover every gun and permit manoeuvrability. Our formation was basically that worked out for the Air Corps by Brigadier General Hugh Kneer 20 years ago with 85 miles per hour bombers, plus refinements devised by Colonel Le May from experience in the European theatre.

The English Channel and the North Sea glittered bright in the clear visibility as we left the bulge of East Anglia behind us. Up ahead we knew we were already registering on the German RDF screen, and that the sector controllers of the Luftwaffe's fighter belt in Western Europe were busy alerting their *Staffeln* of Focke-Wulfes and Messerschmitts. I stole a last look back at cloud-covered England, where I could see a dozen spare B-17s, who had accompanied us to fill in for any abortives from mechanical failure in the hard climb, gliding disappointedly home to base.

I fastened my oxygen mask a little tighter and looked at the little ball in a glass tube on the instrument panel that indicates proper oxygen flow. It was moving up and down, like a visual heartbeat, as I breathed, registering normal.

Already the gunners were searching. Occasionally the ship shivered as guns were tested with short bursts. I could see puffs of blue smoke from the group close ahead and 1000 feet below us, as each gunner satisfied himself that he had lead poisoning at his finger tips. The coast of Holland appeared in sharp black outline. I drew in a deep breath of oxygen.

A few miles in front of us were German boys in single-seaters who were probably going to react to us in the same way our boys would react, emotionally, if German bombers were heading for the Pratt & Whitney engine factory at Hartford or the Liberator plant at Willow Run. In the making was a death struggle between the unstoppable object and the immovable defence, every possible defence at the disposal of the Reich, for this was a deadly penetration to a hitherto inaccessible and critically important arsenal of the *Vaterland*.

156

At 10.08 we crossed the coast of Holland, south of The Hague, with our group of Fortresses tucked in tightly and within handy supporting distance of the group above us, at 18,000 feet. But our long, loose-linked column looked too long, and the thin gaps between combat wings too wide. As I squinted into the sun, gauging the distance to the barely visible specks of the lead group, I had a recurrence of that sinking feeling before the take-off – the lonesome foreboding that might come to the last man about to run a gauntlet lined with spiked clubs. The premonition was well-founded.

At 10.17, near Woensdrecht, I saw the first flak blossom out in our vicinity, light and inaccurate. A few minutes later, at approximately 10.25, a gunner called, 'Fighters at 2 o'clock low'. I saw them, climbing above the horizon ahead of us to the right – a pair of them. For a moment I hoped they were P-47 Thunderbolts from the fighter escort that was supposed to be in our vicinity, but I didn't hope long. The two FW-190s turned and whizzed through the formation ahead of us in a frontal attack, nicking two B-17s in the wings and breaking away in half-rolls right over our group. By craning my neck up and back, I glimpsed one of them through the roof glass in the cabin, flashing past at a 600-mile-an-hour rate of closure, his yellow nose smoking and small pieces flying off near the wing root. The guns of our group were in action. The pungent smell of burnt cordite filled the cockpit and the B-17 trembled to the recoil of nose and ball-turret guns. Smoke immediately trailed from the hit B-17s, but they held their stations.

Here was early fighter reaction. The members of the crew sensed trouble. There was something desperate about the way those two fighters came in fast right out of their climb, without any preliminaries. Apparently, our own fighters were busy somewhere further up the procession. The interphone was active for a few seconds with brief admonitions: 'Lead 'em more'. . . . 'Short bursts'. . . . 'Don't throw rounds away'. . . . 'Bombardier to left waist gunner, don't yell. Talk slow'.

Three minutes later the gunners reported fighters climbing up from all round the clock, singly and in pairs, both FW-190s and ME-109s. The fighters I could see on my side looked too many for sound health. No friendly Thunderbolts were visible. From now on we were in mortal danger. My mouth dried up and my buttocks pulled together. A co-ordinated attack began, with the head-on fighters coming in from slightly above, the 9 and 3 o'clock attackers approaching from about level and the rear attackers from slightly below. The guns from every B-17 in our group and the group ahead were firing simultaneously, lashing the sky with ropes of orange tracer to match the chain-puff bursts squirting from the 20mm cannon muzzles in the wings of the Jerry single-seaters.

I noted with alarm that a lot of our fire was falling astern of the target – particularly from our hand-held nose and waist guns. Nevertheless, both sides got hurt in this clash, with the entire second element of three B-17s from our low squadron, and one B-17 from the group ahead falling out of formation on fire, with crews bailing out, and several fighters heading for the deck in flames or with their pilots lingering behind under the dirty yellow canopies that distinguished some of their parachutes from ours. Our 24-year-old group leader, flying only his third combat mission, pulled us up even closer to the preceding group for mutual support.

As we swung slightly outside with our squadron, in mild evasive action, I got a good look at that gap in the low squadron where three B-17s had been. Suddenly I bit my lip hard. The lead ship of that element had pulled out on fire and exploded before anyone bailed out. It was the ship to which I had been originally assigned.

I glanced over at Murphy. It was cold in the cockpit, but sweat was running from his forehead and over his oxygen mask from the exertion of holding his element in tight formation, and the strain of the warnings that hummed over the interphone, and what he could see out of the corners of his eyes. He caught my glance and turned the controls over to me for a while. It was an enormous relief to concentrate on flying instead of sitting there watching fighters aiming between your eyes. Somehow, the attacks from the rear, although I could 'see' them through my ears via the interphone, didn't bother me. I guess it was because there was a slab of armour plate behind my back and I couldn't watch them, anyway.

I knew that we were in a lively fight. Every alarm bell in my brain and heart was ringing a high-pitched warning. But my nerves were steady and my brain working. The fear was unpleasant, but it was bearable. I knew that I was going to die, and so were a lot of others. What I didn't know was that the *real* fight, the *Anschluss* of Luftwaffe 20mm cannon shells, hadn't really begun. The largest and most savage fighter resistance of any war in history was rising to stop us at any cost, and our group was the most vulnerable target.

A few minutes later we absorbed the first wave of a hailstorm of individual fighter attacks that were to engulf us clear to the target in such a blizzard of bullets and shells that chronological account is difficult. It was at 10.41, over Eupen, that I looked out the window after a minute's lull, and saw two whole squadrons, twelve ME-109s and eleven FW-190s, climbing parallel to us as though they were on a steep escalator. The first squadron had reached our level and was pulling ahead to turn into us. The second was not far behind. Several thousand feet below us were many more fighters, their noses cocked up in a maximum climb. Over the interphone came reports of an equal number of enemy aircraft deploying on the other side of the formation.

For the first time I noticed an ME-110 sitting out of range on our level out to the right. He was to stay with us all the way to the target, apparently radioing our position and weak spots to fresh *Staffeln* waiting further down the road.

At the sight of these fighters, I had the distinct feeling of being trapped – that the Hun had been tipped off or at least had guessed our destination and was set for us. We were already through the German fighter belt. Obviously they had moved a lot of squadrons back in a fluid defence in depth, and they must have been saving up some outfits for the inner defence that we didn't know about. The life expectancy of our group seemed definitely limited, since it had already appeared that the fighters, instead of wasting fuel trying to overhaul the preceding groups, were glad to take a cut at us.

Swinging their yellow noses round in a wide U-turn, the 12-ship squadron of ME-109s came in from 12 to 2 o'clock in pairs. The main event was on. I fought an impulse to close my eyes and overcame it.

A shining silver rectangle of metal sailed past, over our right wing. I recognized it as the main exit door of a Fortress. Seconds later, a black lump came hurtling through the formation, barely missing several propellers. It was a man, clasping his knees to his head, revolving like a diver in a triple somersault, shooting by us so close that I saw a piece of paper blow out of his leather jacket. He was evidently making a delayed jump, for I didn't see his parachute open.

A B-17 turned gradually out of the formation to the right, maintaining altitude. In a split second it completely vanished in a brilliant explosion, from which the only remains were four balls of fire, the fuel tanks, which were quickly consumed as they fell earthward.

I saw blue, red, yellow and aluminium-coloured fighters. Their tactics were running fairly true to form, with frontal attacks hitting the low squadron and rear attackers going for the lead and high squadrons. Some of the Jerries shot at us with rockets, and an attempt at air-to-air bombing was made with little black time-fuse sticks, dropped from above, which exploded in small grey puffs off to one side of the formation. Several of the FWs did some nice deflection shooting on side attacks from 500 yards at the high group, then raked the low group on the breakaway at closer range with their noses cocked in a side slip, to keep the formation in their sights longer in the turn. External fuel tanks were visible under the bellies or wings of at least two squadrons, shedding uncomfortable light on the mystery of their ability to tail us so far from their bases.

The manner of the assaults indicated that the pilots knew where we were going and were inspired with a fanatical determination to stop us before we got there. Many pressed attacks home to 250 yards or less, or bolted right through the formation wide out, firing long 20-second bursts, often presenting point-blank targets on the breakaway. Some committed the fatal error of pulling up instead of going down and out. More experienced pilots came in on frontal attacks with a noticeably slower rate of closure, apparently throttled back, obtaining greater accuracy. But no tactics could halt the close-knit juggernauts of our Fortresses, nor save the single-seaters from paying a terrible price.

Our airplane was endangered by various débris. Emergency

160

hatches, exit doors, prematurely opened parachutes, bodies and assorted fragments of B-17s and Hun fighters breezed past us in the slipstream.

I watched two fighters explode not far beneath, disappear in sheets of orange flame; B-17s dropping out in every stage of distress, from engines on fire to controls shot away; friendly and enemy parachutes floating down, and, on the green carpet far below us, funeral pyres of smoke from fallen fighters, marking our trail.

On we flew through the cluttered wake of a desperate air battle, where disintegrating aircraft were commonplace and the white dots of sixty parachutes in the air at one time were hardly worth a second look. The spectacle registering on my eyes became so fantastic that my brain turned numb to the actuality of the death and destruction all around us. Had it not been for the squeezing in my stomach, which was trying to purge, I might easily have been watching an animated cartoon in a movie theatre.

The minutes dragged on into an hour. And still the fighters came. Our gunners called coolly and briefly to one another, dividing up their targets, fighting for their lives with every round of ammunition – and our lives, and the formation. The tail gunner called that he was out of ammunition. We sent another belt back to him. Here was a new hazard. We might run out of .50 calibre slugs before we reached the target.

I looked to both sides of us. Our two wing men were gone. So was the element in front of us – all three ships. We moved up into position behind the lead element of the high squadron. I looked out again on my side and saw a cripple, with one prop feathered, struggle up behind our right wing with his bad engine funnelling smoke into the slipstream. He dropped back. Now our tail gunner had a clear view. There were no more B-17s behind us. We were last man.

I took the controls again for a while. The first thing I saw when Murphy resumed flying was a B-17 turning slowly out to the right, its cockpit a mass of flames. The co-pilot crawled out of his window, held on with one hand, reached back for his parachute, buckled it on, let go and was whisked back into the horizontal

161

stabilizer of the tail. I believe the impact killed him. His parachute didn't open.

I looked forward and almost ducked as I watched the tail gunner of a B-17 ahead of us take a bead right on our windshield and cut loose with a stream of tracers that missed us by a few feet as he fired on a fighter attacking us from 6 o'clock low. I almost ducked again when our own top-turret gunner's twin muzzles pounded away a foot above my head in the full forward position, giving a realistic imitation of cannon shells exploding in the cockpit, while I gave an even better imitation of a man jumping six inches out of his seat.

Still no let-up. The fighters queued up like a breadline and let us have it. Each second of time had a cannon shell in it. The strain of being a clay duck in the wrong end of that shooting gallery became almost intolerable. Our 'Piccadilly' shook steadily with the fire of its .50s, and the air inside was wispy with smoke. I checked the engine instruments for the thousandth time. Normal. No injured crew members yet. Maybe we would get to that target, even with our reduced fire power. Seven Fortresses from our group had already gone down and many of the rest of us were badly shot up and short-handed because of wounded crew members.

Almost disinterestedly I observed a B-17 pull out from the group preceding us and drop back to a position about 200 feet from our right wing tip. His right Tokyo tanks were on fire, and had been for a half-hour. Now the smoke was thicker. Flames were licking through the blackened skin of the wing. While the pilot held her steady, I saw four crew members drop out the bomb bay and execute delayed drops. Another bailed from the nose, opened his parachute prematurely and nearly fouled the tail. Another went out the left waist-gun opening, delaying his opening for a safe interval. The tail gunner dropped out of his hatch, apparently pulling his ripcord before he was clear of the ship. His parachute opened instantaneously, barely missing the tail, and jerked him so hard that both his shoes came off. He hung limp, whereas the others had shown immediate signs of life, shifting around in their harness. The Fortress then dropped back in a medium spiral and I did not see the pilots leave. I saw the ship though, just before

162

it trailed from view, belly to the sky, its wing a solid sheet of yellow flame.

Now that we had been under constant attack for more than an hour, it appeared certain that our group was faced with extinction. The sky was still mottled with rising fighters. Target time was 35 minutes away. I doubt if a man in the group visualized the possibility of our getting much further without 100 percent loss. Gunners were becoming exhausted and nerve-tortured from the nagging strain – the strain that sends gunners and pilots to the rest home. We had been the aiming point for what looked like most of the Luftwaffe. It looked as if we might find the rest of it primed for us at the target.

At this hopeless point, a young squadron commander down in the low squadron was living through his finest hour. His squadron had lost its second element of three ships early in the fight, south of Antwerp, yet he had consistently maintained his vulnerable and exposed position in the formation rigidly in order to keep the guns of his three remaining ships well uncovered to protect the belly of the formation. Now, nearing the target, battle damage was catching up with him fast. A 20mm cannon shell penetrated the right side of his airplane and exploded beneath him, damaging the electrical system and cutting the top-turret gunner in the leg. A second 20mm entered the radio compartment, killing the radio operator, who bled to death with his legs severed above the knees. A third 20mm shell entered the left side of the nose, tearing out a section about 2 feet square, tore away the right-hand nose-gun installations and injured the bombardier in the head and shoulder. A fourth 20mm shell penetrated the right wing into the fuselage and shattered the hydraulic system, releasing fluid all over the cockpit. A fifth 20mm shell punctured the cabin roof and severed the rudder cables to one side of the rudder. A sixth 20mm shell exploded in the No 3 engine destroying all controls to that motor. The engine caught fire and lost its power, but eventually I saw the fire go out.

Confronted with structural damage, partial loss of control, fire in the air and serious injuries to personnel, and faced with fresh waves of fighters still rising to the attack, this commander was justified in abandoning ship. His crew, some of them comparatively

163

inexperienced youngsters, were preparing to bail out. The co-pilot pleaded with him repeatedly to bail out. His reply at this critical juncture was blunt. His words were heard over the interphone and had a magical effect on the crew. They stuck to their guns. The B-17 kept on.

Near the initial point, at 11.50, one hour and a half after the first of at least 200 individual fighter attacks, the pressure eased off, although hostiles were still in the vicinity. A curious sensation came over me. I was still alive. It was possible to think of the target. Of North Africa. Of returning to England. Almost idly I watched a crippled B-17 pull over to the curb and drop its wheels and open its bomb bay, jettisoning its bombs. 3 ME-109s circled it closely, but held their fire while the crew bailed out. I remembered now that a little while back I had seen other Hun fighters hold their fire, even when being shot at by a B-17 from which the crew were bailing. But I doubt if sportsmanship had anything to do with it. They hoped to get a B-17 down fairly intact.

And then our weary, battered column, short 24 bombers, but still holding the close formation that had brought the remainder through by sheer air discipline and gunnery, turned in to the target. I knew that our bombardiers were as grim as death while they synchronized their sights on the great ME-109 assembly shops lying below us in a curve of the winding Blue Danube, close to the outskirts of Regensburg. Our B-17 gave a slight lift and a red light went out on the instrument panel. Our bombs were away. We turned from the target toward the snow-capped Alps. I looked back and saw a beautiful sight – a rectangular pillar of smoke rising from the ME-109 plant. Only one burst was over and into the town. Even from this great height I could see that we had smeared the objective. The price? Cheap, 200 airmen.

A few more fighters pecked at us on the way to the Alps, and a couple of smoking B-17s glided down toward the safety of Switzerland, about 40 miles distant. A town in the Brenner Pass tossed up a lone burst of futile flak. Flak? There had been lots of flak in the past two hours, but only once do I recall having seen it, a sort of side issue to the fighters. Colonel Le May, who had taken excellent care of us all the way, circled the air division over a large lake to give the cripples, some flying on three engines and

164

many more trailing smoke, a chance to rejoin the family. We approached the Mediterranean in a gradual descent, conserving fuel. Out over the water we flew at low altitude, unmolested by fighters from Sardinia or Corsica, waiting through the long hot afternoon hours for the first sight of the North African coastline. The prospect of ditching, out of gasoline, and the sight of other B-17s falling into the drink seemed trivial matters after the vicious nightmare of the long trail across Southern Germany. We had walked through a high valley of the shadow of death, not expecting to see another sunset, and now I could fear no evil.

With red lights showing on all our fuel tanks, we landed at our designated base in the desert, after eleven hours in the air.

TEN

Gunners of the United States 8th Army Air Force

The B-17 Flying Fortress was just that – a flying *fortress*. It bristled with guns and was weighed down with protective armour plating. Half its crew of ten were gunners, if you include the radio man. In addition, the engineer, bombardier and navigator all had guns to fire when not otherwise engaged! It was a 'labour intensive' operation involving the services of forty aircrew in four B-17s to carry much the same load of bombs as one Lancaster flown by seven men.

Yet, because American policy decreed that their heavy bombers would fly by day, those aircraft just had to have the maximum fire-power if they were to survive the onslaughts from the vicious guns and cannon of the German single-engine fighters. What is more, it was essential that the fire power from each B-17 Fortress formed part of a concentrated onslaught against the fighters. To achieve this, they flew in protective formation.

Even with all this armament, the early raids into Germany resulted in catastrophic losses for the US 8th Army Air Force. As we have said, it was only after the introduction of the long-range fighter escorts that the situation changed. Then, in the end, through guts and determination the 8th finally won mastery of the daylight skies over Germany.

The B-24 Liberator was the 8th Air Force's other 'heavy'. It was not quite so strongly protected as the Fortress although superior in some other ways. It carried more bombs, had a greater range and was slightly faster. Yet the Fortress crews welcomed the presence of 'Libs' with a cynicism born of combat; on a mission they would say, 'The B-24s are our best escort. When they're around the fighters always go for them, and leave us alone!'

There is no doubt that it was the gunners who made the 'daylight' policy work. It is impossible to pay sufficient tribute to their

166

skill and fortitude while fighting in the most fearsome air battles the world has ever known.

Harry Slater of the 94th Bomb Group gives a comprehensive picture of the 'aerial gunner' in the 8th AAF during World War Two:

The typical profile of the gunner was that he was young, carefree, adventurous and fearless. It is worth noting, however, that the true profile encompassed a much wider range. Many of them were as young as 17, but there were also many from all age groups with varying backgrounds and inner emotions. S/Sgt. Cole of the 385th Group was 48 years old, and our own Albert Herndon at 44 served as engineer and top gunner on Arthur Allen's crew. Herndon was a World War One veteran and hard of hearing, but Allen never considered replacing him because he excelled in duty performance and crew dedication. . . .

Each gunner position on the B-17 had its own characteristics. The tail gunner was likely to be young, small and wiry, though this wasn't always the case. . . . Once at his station the man could only see to the rear. He could not see any of his fellow crewmen from this position. Consequently, when emergencies were encountered, he was on his own with the loneliness of the proverbial Maytag repair man.

A fighter coming in from the rear was an easy target, with accurate determination of the instant he came within range the most important. Luftwaffe pilots soon learned of this deadly tactic and altered their approach so as to attack in a turn from above or below.

The two waist gunners working in their close quarters enjoyed a sense of togetherness, but without any comforts. The designers of the B-17 had given little thought to comfort except for the pilots. The waist position was bare aluminum with a narrow walkway from which the gunners worked. There was no place to sit down. Sitting or lying on the cold walkway was a rustic rest to say the least. In the early B-17 models, the open windows were opposite each other. During battle the men were constantly bumping rears. It was like operating two jack hammers in a phone booth. On later E models the windows were staggered. This helped the situation.

The waist was one of the most dangerous positions during battle. With the open windows, there was no structural protection available. The cold was almost as hazardous as enemy flak and fire. Shell casings were ejected on the floor. During a prolonged fight the footing was like walking on marbles. Every shot from the waist required deflection skills. . . .

The radio operator's life was morse code and static-ridden high frequency radios. This, in itself, was a full-time job and vital to crew and formation welfare. For most of the war the radio operator had a top gun in his rather comfortable compartment. In the great battles it was often necessary for him to man his gun and he was not immune to the flak and fighter threats that might penetrate his area while deciphering an important message.

The ball turret was a position given many descriptions by gunners of the day. It was deadly against low attacks and was probably a little safer than the other positions. It was a glass ball with two fifty-calibre guns, extended in flight to hang below the belly of the aircraft. It was electrically operated and could be rotated in every direction below the aircraft. The gunner entered from the top, assumed the foetal position, closed the hatch and was on his own. There were no comfort facilities, so once in the turret, it took a great determination to endure the threats and pains of nature's call.

Mechanical malfunction could render the turret inoperative and, if not aligned with the escape hatch, it was a frightening circumstance. There are no official recordings of a ball turret gunner being left at his position during bale out or other emergency, but it was a horrifying possibility.

The top turret, located behind the pilots, was manned by the engineer. Aside from his gunner duties, this man was the technical expert on the aircraft. He monitored every system, including the pilots', at all times. Turret time during battle was just an added duty. But the top turret was deadly, versatile and necessary in fighting off enemy attacks from any direction. During firing it was an aural chorus of humming gears and chattering fifties that could be heard and felt throughout the aircraft. It was routine to fire at a passing fighter, leave the turret to switch fuel tanks and synchron-

168

ize the props, and be back in the turret in time to counter the next pass of a fighter.

In the nose section, the bombardier and navigator each had a gun, and, on later models, the deadly chin turret. But their duties were so demanding, especially in lead positions, that they did not man their guns until absolutely necessary. After a few months of the war, the bombardier was not supposed to leave his bomb sight for any reason during the bomb run. But once the bombs were dropped, many bombardiers and navigators scored well against the onslaughts of the Luftwaffe.

The Waist Gunner

Odell Franklin Dobson was born in Virginia on 11 March, 1922. He had wanted to fly from an early age, and, as soon as he was old enough, volunteered for the Army Air Corps and was accepted for a pilot's course. For reasons he was never able to understand, he was 'washed out' after initial flying training. Swallowing his disappointment, he wangled himself onto a course as a 'ball turret' gunner – for which one of the physical requirements was a height not exceeding 5ft 6in – Odel was 6ft 1½in! Fortunately for him, he finished up as the left waist gunner on a B-24 Liberator.

After a number of missions over Europe, the bomber in which Odell had been flying became too battle-damaged to be repaired. As a replacement they were offered 'Ford's Folly' by their CO. The old girl had quite a history. She was the first B-24 Liberator to be built by the Ford Motor Company of America. Early into battle, she had flown more missions than any other American bomber in the European theatre – seventy-nine raids at that time. She was a wreck and should have been written off. Yet when the 'Old Man' offered her to First Lieutenant C. A. Rudd, Odell's pilot, he accepted her. The bait was just too tempting to be ignored. 'Push her total up to a hundred missions,' said the Squadron Commander, 'and you and your crew can take her back to the States on a War Bonds Tour.' The idea appealed to the men very much. They would be wined and dined and feted like heroes by their fellow countrymen – and women!

After all they had made enough fuss of the 'Memphis Belle' –

starred her in a movie and all that kind of stuff – and she had only done twenty-five missions when they sent her home. So 'Rudd's Ruffians', as the crew were known, figured old 'Ford's Folly' would go over real big in the States when the time came.

The following is what happened to Staff Sergeant Odell Dobson, waist gunner, on what turned out to be the last mission flown by 'Ford's Folly'. This is a passage from my book *Four Men Went to War:*

It was the second Sunday in September, 1944. All the enlisted men from the crew of 'Ford's Folly,' with the exception of Odell, were away from base on day pass. Odell had decided to stay around and take it easy, so he was far from pleased when pilot and navigator, Lieutenants Rudd and Dawson, strolled into his hut late in the afternoon and asked him if he would help them swing the compass and calibrate the instruments on their bomber. Irritably he threw down his book and followed them out to the hard stand where 'Ford's Folly' was parked. It was dark long before they had finished their work, yet they were not particularly concerned, because it was after 5 o'clock and no battle order had been posted, which normally meant no operational flying on the following day.

On this occasion they were wrong. At 10 o'clock that night they were told that 'Ford's Folly' was scheduled for a raid in the morning. Earlier that day it had been too cloudy to verify the sun compass, there had been no chance to carry out a flight test and guns and turrets had not been checked. As Odell said later, 'If Rudd had been smart, he would have refused to fly the ship on that mission.' The First Lieutenant would not have been alone in backing down – the Group had called for maximum effort, but only twenty-four out of forty-eight aircraft took off the following morning.

As usual, after pre-flight breakfast, they were briefed. Here they were told that their target was an ordnance manufacturing depot near Hannover. It was still very early in the morning when Odell went over to the flights to oil and install his guns in 'Ford's Folly'. Sergeant Modlen, the nose-turret gunner, was a 'washed-out' navigator who acted as standby for Lieutenant Dawson, the regular navigator, in the event of an emergency. Part of Odell's duty was

170

to check the nose-turret guns for Modlen while he attended the navigators' briefing. Odell fixed Modlen's guns, but did not bother to check the electrical circuit to the nose-turret. Then, feeling tired, he took a blanket and went for a nap in an adjoining wheat-field while he waited for the rest of the crew to show up. Just before take-off, always a time of tension, the flyers were more than usually apprehensive – it was mission 13.

Nervousness was cloaked by flippant observations; Maynard, upper turret gunner and engineer, said 'This is not mission 13, it is mission 12a.'

'No,' cut in Roger Clapp, the radio operator, 'Don't kid your-self, we are taking off on mission 13, and this is the one where we go down.'

On a superstitious impulse Odell slid through the 3×5 feet camera-hatch back onto the ground. He scrubbed his feet several times on the grass at the side of the runway before climbing once more into the aircraft.

Shortly after take-off, as they were forming up, Modlen, the front gunner, called up, 'Dobby, the radical on my gunsight won't light up. Did you pre-flight my turret?'

'Sure I did,' Odell lied, knowing the pilot and all the rest of the crew were listening on the interphone. The crew had always taken great pride in its operational efficiency. Back in the Overseas Training Unit at Casper, Wyoming, the previous March, they had been awarded their own bomber on completion of the course, one of only three crews, out of a total of forty, to receive this privilege. Since then, as operational experience increased, there had been a tendency to back off on some of the routine checks, to become slipshod. Odell cursed himself for being a stupid, lazy slob. He advised Modlen to take the small bulb out of his 'trouble light', (the movable inspection light) and use that to replace the defective one. In a moment Modlen was speaking again: 'Dobby, there ain't no bulb in the "trouble light".' So on that trip there were no sights on the aircraft's front guns. Afterwards, Odell's only conso-lation was that, as far as he knew, there had been no head-on attacks by fighters that morning.

Odell started to get his own gun ready. On a B-24 Liberator the 50mm flexible machine guns mounted in the waist of the

171

bomber were fired through open windows on both sides of the aircraft. The ammunition boxes had belts of 500 rounds and these rattled along flexible metal chutes to feed the guns. During firing the noise and vibration were unbelievable. Odell discovered that the hooks that attached the chute to his gun were missing. He had some safety wire in his 'para bag' and used that to fix up the chute. Then he checked his gun and got it firing satisfactorily. Meanwhile, Sergeant Hoganson, the right waist gunner, was having problems of his own. The chute fitted on his gun all right, but the apparatus that kept the gun steady while firing came off in his hand. Odell had a precious spool of nylon cord, the first he had ever been able to acquire. He used this to bind up the contraption as firmly as possible. By this time Odell was in an ugly mood, cursing the lousy job done by armourers when supposedly preparing an aircraft for a raid.

He was relieving his frustration by swinging his gun around with considerable violence when, all of a sudden, he knocked his front sight off. To top it all, just as 'Ford's Folly' crossed the Belgian coast, the electrical motor operating the tail turret caught fire and burned out. This put the most effective gun position out of action. Odell was shocked by this latest mishap. If all this could happen to the guns, he mused unhappily, what about the state of everything else connected with this wreck of an airplane? The motors themselves sounded pretty rough to him.

As they flew over the Ardennes, Odell knew they would soon be swinging north, heading up towards Hannover. He was sitting on one of his 'personal bombs', an empty ammunition box. He usually carried one or two of these heavy wooden containers to chuck out over the target. As he stared out of his open gun position, he realized they were stationed in one of the most vulnerable sections – lower left squadron, with only 'Tail-end Charlie' behind them.

Suddenly someone yelled 'Fighters!' They were all around. ME109s – the sky seemed to be black with them. Odell fired at one enemy plane. It broke away right under the Liberator, so close he could see the German in his cockpit. The enemy pilot was wily enough not to finish up on the bomber's tail where the gunner would normally have the best shot at him. Tail-gunners had no worries about deflection; they just laid the sight on the fighter's nose and blazed away. Their attacker was not to know Sergeant Place was sitting impotently behind his guns, the tail turret useless.

The Messerschmitts kept coming in on a pursuit curve. They started their attack about three or four thousand feet ahead and a thousand feet above, then rolled over and started firing as they closed in. Odell thought he had hit the next ME109 that came in. As the fighter broke away it was trailing thick black smoke and he felt sure it was going down. Then he recalled being told about the synthetic fuel the Germans were using, apparently made from coal and God knows what. When their pilots hit the throttles for maximum power while breaking away it was no wonder they made smoke with that stuff in the cylinders.

'Hoggy', the other waist gunner, was doing well. He exploded an attacking fighter and punched Odell on the shoulder to look round and see it so he could verify it later at squadron interrogation. Odell had already seen him blow another one out of the sky just a few seconds earlier.

The next one looked as if it was coming straight for Odell; the yellow nose cone was pointing directly at him. This time he was certain his shells had smashed home; the fighter was burning all along the wings. He waited for the enemy to explode. Then, as it came closer, he realized that the flames were only flashes from the ME109's wing guns as it fired at him. Next moment a 20mm shell, maybe from the gun in that yellow nose cone, hit Odell's gun and exploded. Most of the white-hot metal fragments hit him in the chest, but one piece struck him clean between the eyes. It cut through his hard rubber goggle frame and entered his head right at the top of his nose. The force of the explosion knocked him down on the deck. Although he did not know it at the time, the shell had smashed both his legs. Everything went black. He could not see, but was still aware of what was going on. Over his headphones he was conscious of Spencer, the bombardier, telling Rudd that he should salvo the bombs to lighten the aircraft, because by that time both motors on the right wing were out of action; No 3 was feathered, while No 4 was windmilling and burning. Try as

173

they could, they were unable to get the prop to feather completely on No 4.

Every few moments Odell heard someone on the interphone yell out, 'More fighters coming in!' In fact there was a continuous babble of voices and Hoggy said several times, 'Dobby's been hit. Dobby's been hit.' Then Dawson, the navigator, cut in: 'Get off the damned interphone, Hoganson.' He wanted everyone to be quiet so no essential orders would be missed. Unknown to Odell, Mainard, the upper-turret gunner, had been hit and possibly killed in the first fighter attack. His canopy was shot away and Roger Clapp, the radio operator, saw him slump forward and then slither out of his turret, down onto the floor below. Roger put Mainard's head in his lap and tried to put a bandage over a gaping hole in his skull, but the gunner never spoke, or even opened his eyes.

The situation was more than desperate – two engines knocked out and only Hoganson's waist gun still firing. Odell could not figure out how Hoggy kept going the way he did. After a while, Odell was able to see out of his right eye. There was blood running out of his head and dripping into the severed half of his goggles dangling on his left cheek. He tried to raise himself up, but did not get very far. Hoggy was still firing, but then he was hit and fell down on top of Odell. He struggled back up, holding on to his shoulder, turned round and tried to charge Odell's gun to get it firing again, but it had been completely knocked out in the explosion. Then Odell watched Hoggy swing back to his own gun and fire at another fighter. He hit it for sure. In a moment Hoggy was struck again and collapsed onto Odell a second time. Incredibly, he got back up.

His oxygen mask was hanging off and blood was pouring down his face. He fired at the plane he had just hit as it dived past the Liberator's right wing. The Messerschmitt was burning from its wing roots all the way past the cockpit. It was heading straight down to earth. Then a 20mm shell hit Hoggy in the head and he fell down for a third time. He did not get up after that. Odell could see the flames streaming out of No 4 motor. He was sure the bomber was going to blow any second. Struggling out of his flak suit, he clipped on his parachute and crawled to the camera hatch which he managed to open. Lying close to the opening,

174

Odell prayed that, if the airplane exploded, he would be blown clear. Still connected to the interphone, he heard Rudd, his Captain, saying: 'Hang on boys. I'm going to hit the deck.'

As they started to descend, Odell guessed they were around 27,000 feet. The big bomber was diving steeply, when, for some reason he could not understand, 'Ford's Folly' began to climb at an acute angle. It stalled with all the power coming from the two remaining motors on the left wing. It rolled over to the left and started spinning. The first two or three turns of the spin were fairly flat, but then it nosed over and began to go down fast with the flames streaming from the right wing.

Odell knew that, if he were to get out at all, this was his last chance. The centrifugal forces were pinning him to the deck, but he managed to pull himself over the hatch. Just before the slip-stream caught him and pulled him out, he had time to take one last look inside the aircraft. Back near the tail, Place had climbed out of his turret and was sitting with his back to a bulkhead; his oxygen mask was off and blood streamed down his face. Hoggy was lying where he had fallen, his eyes glazed, but, as Odell looked at him, his friend half-raised his hand for a moment, then it fell back to his side. There was nothing that Odell could do to help. The next second he was gone.

The Ball Turret Gunner

It would be remiss to leave the subject of air gunners without relating the unique story of 'Snuffy' Smith. Staff-Sergeant Maynard H. Smith from Caro, Michigan, was the son of a circuit judge, who sadly did not live long enough to learn of his son's outstanding courage during the course of his first mission on 1 May, 1943.

Below is the 32-year-old old 'Snuffy's' own account of what happened, as he told it the day after he had flown with the 306th, of the 8th AAF, and bombed enemy installations at St Nazaire. He was a small man who fitted snugly into the ball turret of his B-17 Fortress:

We had left the flak behind us and were heading out to sea – with the Focke-Wulf 190s trailing right along. About half an hour after we had left the enemy coast I was watching the tracers from

175

a Jerry fighter come puffing by our tail when suddenly there was a terrific explosion, 'Whoomph', just like that. Boy, it was a pip. My interphone and electrical controls on my turret went out, so I decided that the best thing to do was to get up into the waist section and see what was going on.

I hand-cranked myself up and crawled out of my turret into the ship. The first thing I saw was a sheet of flames coming out of the radio room and another fire by the tail-wheel section. Suddenly the radio operator came staggering out of the flames, made a bee-line for the gun hatch and dived out. I glanced out and watched him hit the horizontal stabilizer, bounce off and open his chute. The poor guy didn't even have a Mae West – it was burned off. He was a veteran of 22 missions.

By this time the right waist gunner had bailed out over his gun and the left waist gunner was trying to jump, but was stuck half in and half out of his gun hatch. I pulled him back into the ship and jokingly asked if the heat was too much for him. All he did was stare at me and say, 'I'm getting out of here.' I helped him open the escape hatch and watched him go. His chute opened OK.

The smoke and gas were really thick. I wrapped a sweater around my face so I could breath, grabbed a fire extinguisher and attacked the fire in the radio room. Glancing over my shoulder at the tail fire I thought I saw something moving and ran back. It was the tail gunner painfully crawling back, obviously wounded. He had blood all over him. Looking him over I saw that he had been hit in the back and that it had probably gone through his left lung. I laid him down on his left side so that the wound would not drain into his right lung, gave him a shot of morphine and made him as comfortable as possible before going back to the fires.

I just got started on this when the FW 190 came diving in again. I jumped for the waist gun and fired at him, and as he swept under us I turned to the other waist gun and let him have it from the other side. He left us for a while so I went back to the radio room fire again. I got into the room this time and began throwing out burning débris. The fire had burned holes so large in the side of the ship that I just tossed stuff out that way. Gas from a burning extinguisher was choking me, so I went back to the tail fire. I took off my chute so I could move easier. I'm glad I didn't take it off sooner because afterwards I found it had stopped a .30 calibre bullet.

Another quick burst with the guns and back to the radio fire. Then back again to the wounded gunner to comfort him when on asking, 'Are we almost home yet?' I lied and told him we were. All during this time that damn FW kept coming in and I had to drop whatever I was doing and hop to the guns to keep him off. You have to show these babies that you mean business or they are supposed to finish you off real quick.

By now it was so hot that the ammunition was exploding all over the place and making a terrific racket. I didn't dare to throw all of it out because I had to keep some for the visits of the FW.

Back to the radio room with the last of the extinguisher fluid. When that ran out I found a water bottle and emptied that on it. After that was gone I was so mad that I pissed on the fire and finally beat on it with my hands and feet until my clothing began to smoulder. Again that Focke-Wulf came in and again I answered him. This time he left us for good.

The fire was slowly dying out and the room was beginning to clear. Only then could I see the damage. The room was absolutely gutted. The radio operator's seat was simply burned away and his gun just a melted mess. Most of the ceiling was gone and where the side walls should be were gaping holes.

I want back to the tail and put out the fire there. Talked to the wounded gunner and saw that we were approaching the coast of England. With the ship in the condition it was, I was sweating out three things. It might explode, or break in half, or I might be killed by exploding ammunition. It was lucky I paid particular attention to the control cables so the pilot could bring us home.

I could tell that the ship was acting tail-heavy so I tossed overboard everything I could. Guns, ammunition, clothes, everything. I really had a time with the ammunition cans, they weight 98 pounds and I weigh 130, [9 stone 3 pounds], but I managed to get them out. The tail-wheel gear was gone and I was afraid the shock of landing would break the ship in half. Our pilot brought the ship in OK and by the time she stopped rolling I had the fires completely out.

All I know is that it was a miracle that the ship didn't break in two in the air, and I wish I could shake hands personally with the people that built her. They sure did a wonderful job and we owe our lives to them.

The following was the condition of the 'ship' after it had landed:
Radio room gutted. Tail wheel section gutted. Control cables shot up. Oxygen system gone. Intercommunication system gone. One prop hit. No 4 engine nacelle gone. Tail-wheel gear damaged. Ball turret out of commission. 20mm hit on flaps. Electrical system out from ball turret to tail. One gun in top turret out. Both waist guns out. Radio gun burned out. Radio system burned out. Sides of radio room burned out. Fuel tank in left wing burned out. Nose hit heavily by flak – the nose gunner and bombardier had been wounded. Nine holes from 20mm shells in waist section. Entire ship peppered by .30 calibre holes.
For his outstanding bravery on that first day of May, 1943, 'Snuffy' Smith was presented with the Congressional Medal of Honor, the American Nation's highest award for courage.

ELEVEN

Pilot v Pilot

On 20 February, 1944, the 8th AAF mounted four major raids. Three were into the heart of Germany, and the fourth was an exceptionally long trip to attack the Focke-Wulf assembly plant at Poznan in German-occupied Poland.

Second-Lieutenant Orlin H. Markussen of the 100th Heavy Bombardment group was stationed at Thorpe Abbott, south of Norwich. The 'Bloody 100th' they were called, because of their unenviable reputation for losing more bombers than any other unit. They retained this record for the whole twenty-two months in which they operated. Orlin was a 21-year-old co-pilot about to embark on his twentieth mission. After that, only five more raids to go and he would be posted back to the States. No one before him had made it – not from the 100th. In the less than two years the 100th was in action in Europe the unit lost 229 Fortresses; 177 listed as 'missing in action', and fifty-two from 'other operational losses'.

The 1st Fortress Division and 2nd Liberator Division were to take care of the German targets, both with heavy fighter escort, while the 3rd Division consisting of 300 'Forts' was assigned to the Polish trip. This latter venture, of which the 100th was to be a part, would not have any fighter protection. It was felt that all German fighters would be too fully occupied with the first two American groups to have anything left to attack the more northerly raiders. As so often happens in war, this turned out to be a tragic miscalculation.

'I had a premonition about that mission, one I never had before or after,' said Markussen. 'General Doolittle had just taken command of the 8th Air Force, and 20 February was the first day of massive air attacks against German aircraft production plants and facilities. I may have been apprehensive because of the length of the mission – 13½ hours. I just don't know. Something's going to happen today, I kept telling myself.

'After the early morning briefing, I went back to my room and, for the first time ever, wrote a "To whom it may concern" letter about what to do with my belongings. I also wrote to my wife. I had won some money playing cards and asked my crew chief to make sure my wife got it. I had always worn low-quarter shoes before on missions. This time I wore combat boots. I even attended church service, although I'm not a religious man.'

A Luftwaffe fighter group had moved the previous day from Husum to Oldenburg on the North German coast, German radio monitors having concluded that the entire American 'birdcage' would be opened for multi-pronged assaults on key industries. 24-year-old Luftwaffe fighter pilot, Leutnant Heinz Hanke, was also trying to suppress a sense of foreboding on that 20 February. He had survived two years of war in the air. In his first battle he had fought off twelve RAF Spitfires and landed with a 'frozen engine' and a standing propeller. Since then he had downed four Allied aircraft. This day was to bring him his fifth victory. It would be Hanke's 1,089th flight.

'Funny, on this day I expected something bad to happen,' he said. 'Never before had I entered my cockpit with "dull thoughts".' He had even told his squadron commander that a 'big dog' [bad time] would come today. Yet their fighter base at Oldenburg was covered in a dense ground fog, and this natural blanket, under normal circumstances, should have been enough to exclude any thoughts of taking-off.

But even as the breakfast eggs arrived for the Luftwaffe pilots the airfield's alarm siren howled through the late morning cover and Hanke heard rockets in the distance. The massed force of American bombers was already nearing the German coast.

In spite of what they had been told to the contrary during briefing back in England, Orlin and his companions had been pounded practically all the way on the target.

'They hit us over Denmark, the Baltic Sea, over North Eastern Germany, over Poland, and all the way back toward England,' said Orlin. 'It was just one tremendous air battle that lasted for

180

hours, with many aircraft from both sides going in. I had never seen so many FW-190s, ME-109s, Ju-88s, ME-110s, and He-111s. Flying at 12,000 feet didn't help either. This was the perfect altitude for the fighters.

'We Americans had always respected the German pilots, and were impressed by the courage they displayed. It seemed to us, though, that it was almost suicide for them to press head-on attacks against the colossal firepower generated by our massed bombers.'

Heavy cloud cover had obscured the target in Poland, and because the Americans were not permitted to bomb occupied territory unless the sky was clear, the formation had turned towards its secondary target at Stettin, in Germany. The 300 'Forts' of the 3rd Division, under the command of Brigadier General Curtis Le May, and led by radar-equipped pathfinder aircraft, climbed to 20,000 feet, the lowest Orlin had ever bombed a major German city.

As he and his crew began their bomb run, their aircraft, 'Miss Behavin', was blasted by flak which ripped into No 2 [left inboard] engine.

'I tried to feather the engine,' he said. 'It was my job but I couldn't. It was like having a big brake – like a speed brake on a jet – windmilling out there.'

Reginald Smith, 'Miss Behavin's' commander, called up the squadron leader for help. Normally a formation would slow down to keep 'cripples' under protection. But the squadron leader panicked, according to Orlin, and directed 'Miss Behavin' to fall out of formation and head for the overcast clouds below. Sweden was some seventy miles away.

'As we were diving, the enemy was coming up.' Orlin said. 'I saw them straight away.' Leutnant Heinz Hanke in his Focke-Wulf 190, the 'Mule', and his pickup flight of German fighters were on to Markussen's B-17 in an instant.

Tracers blinked everywhere. 'I was calling out fighter attacks when there was this huge explosion.' said Orlin. 'They had shot off the whole of the top turret. When I turned to look over my shoulder there was just a big hole in the roof.

'I got up, took off my flak vest, and went to see about the gunner, Tom Egan. I was sure he must be in shreds. The con-

181

cussion had thrown him back, but he wasn't even in shock. He didn't have a scratch!'

The Luftwaffe pilots were now slashing away at the derelict B-17 almost dead in the sky, but the German fighters were not without problems of their own. Of the 140 interceptors that had taken off from Oldenburg to meet the American assault force as it returned across the Baltic from Stettin, only seven remained in flight. The others had either been shot down or were on the ground being refuelled and rearmed.

Hanke said: 'About 45 minutes after take-off we lost ground visibility, and a short time later lost ground radio contact as well. I thought the six other fighters were squadron leaders and began the attack.'

As the young German made his first approach towards 'Miss Behavin', a warning light flicked on, indicating he had eight minutes flying time left at reduced power. He decided to press home his attack, hoping that as a last resort he might be able to crash-land on one of the beaches by the Baltic Sea. It would be a hairy experience without radio contact, navigation homers, visibility or fuel.

On his own now after a head-on open formation attack, Hanke roared in at high speed from the rear, splintering the B-17 with his four 20mm cannons and two heavy machine guns. Dodging pieces of the aircraft, he rolled in under the tail toward the left wing.

Too late he realized he was coming too fast and too close. Left waist gunner Ed Britko had him.

Hanke flipped his 'Mule' over on its back and tried to dive to safety. As he started down, Britko raked his plane with bullets. The cabin filled with oily smoke and aluminum dust and the engine screamed like a circular saw.

With his throttle linkage shot away and a foot-long piece of his left wing gone, Hanke's only thought was to get out. Another round of fire pierced the armoured ring above the oil cooler.

'That was the end of it.' Hanke said. 'I couldn't see out of the cabin. It was now blacked out with dark brown oil.'

Releasing the canopy and protected now only by the windscreen, the *Jagflieger* tried three times to work himself out of his fighter.

182

He could barely see for the oil that had smothered his face. At last he managed to struggle free, and his shoulder and ankle brushed against the rudder as he tumbled away from his whining Focke-Wulf.

Meanwhile, Orlin hardly had time to notice. By the fourth German pass, 'Miss Behavin' was an inferno. The No 2 engine and its 700-gallon fuel tank were ablaze, and the fire roared back into the bomb bay, radio room and the waist gun positions. The left horizontal stabilizer was gone, shot away by Hanke, cutting all manual control cables to the tail section.

Except for single 50-calibre guns at each waist position and the twin 50-calibre tail guns, 'Miss Behavin' was defenceless, her turret guns rendered useless after the first attack. The radio was out of action, but crew members could still communicate with each other via the interphone. While Smith worked the elevator control button on the auto-pilot to keep the plane from spinning in, Orlin manoeuvred the ailerons by hand.

Somehow the bomber limped through the sky, but not for long. She was about to career away, completely out of control, but not before taking her toll. Another FW-190 blew up in a hail of bullets, a victim of tail gunner Mike Udick's accuracy. Right waist gunner Bob Dunbar was certain, too, that he destroyed an onrushing attacker, who almost rammed the B-17. The other German flyers were forced to 'belly in' on the Danish beaches out of fuel.

Miraculously not one of the crew of 'Miss Behavin' was hit, but the aircraft was completely afire, its left wing melting. One by one the crew bailed out over the Danish island of Fyn.

Orlin thought as he floated down that after all that noise, 'It was the most beautiful sound I'd ever heard – dead silence.' He landed safely in the standing position and was immediately arrested by German soldiers. Eight other members of the crew were also apprehended, but the radio operator, Ira Evans, managed to evade capture, aided by the Danish underground.

After initial interrogation at an anti-aircraft site where he was held overnight, Orlin was taken to a German military HQ in Odense, the birthplace of Hans Christian Andersen. Oddly enough, his mother had also been born there.

Heinz Hanke had also parachuted safely on to the island, landing between a fence and a flagpole, just missing telephone and high tension lines. Once on the ground, he lit a cigarette. 'Terrible though it tasted, it was surely the best of my life.'

The Danes who surrounded him were not over-friendly when they realized he was a German, but their attitude was soon to alter. He was taken to a large farm and asked what should be done with his plane, embedded deeply in the ground some 50 yards behind the house. 'When I looked into the hole, I knew the ammunition and oxygen bottles would explode at any moment. Frantically I waved the people away and they began to run. Within four or five seconds there was a huge explosion. Luckily no one was hurt. From that moment the people seemed to change their minds about me.'

Hanke arrived at the Odense HQ and there he met Orlin Markussen. The American and German pilots discussed the merits of various aircraft and Hanke remembers treating Orlin to a Danish beer. When the time came to part, all the pilots shook hands. Orlin's leather flying jacket was taken away from him and was later acquired by Hanke. It had 18 bombs painted on the back representing the missions he had flown. He had not had time to stencil on the 19th; the 20th, of course, was never completed.

He was taken by train to Oberursel where he endured about a week in solitary confinement before being moved to Stalag Luft I on the Baltic coast in Pomerania. He spent nearly 15 months as a prisoner of war. Although not mistreated, he lost about 50 pounds over a 3-month period when he subsisted on a daily bowl of dehydrated turnips, 'boiled to a gooey mess', and 3 ounces of meat a week. He and his fellow POWs were liberated by the Russians.

Orlin Markussen left the service in 1946, completed his studies at the University of Minnesota, and returned to the Air Force in time to fly in the Korean War. After that he held various flying and administrative jobs, including ferrying aircraft to NATO countries. He spent a year as an operations officer in Vietnam and retired from the Air Force in 1971 after 28 years service.

Heinz Hanke returned to combat after being shot down by the crew of 'Miss Behavin'. Before the war ended he downed four more aircraft confirmed, totalling nine, plus two unconfirmed. After the German surrender, he worked for the Munich Criminal

184

Investigation Department and Radio Free Europe before rejoining the German military. Retiring in 1972 after 18 years service he took up security work for a large company in Munich. Having contacted Malta fever, he ended up 70 percent disabled with hepatitis.

An item appeared in the August, 1975 issue of an American publication known as the *Veterans of Foreign Wars*. It read as follows:

A former German fighter pilot, now in Munich, Heinz Hanke, is seeking a former American bomber pilot who bailed out over the Baltic Sea on 20 February, 1944, and was taken to Odense, on the Danish Island of Fyn, for interrogation.

The American was known to the German only as Lieutenant 'Mark' from Minneapolis. On the back of his jacket were the words, 'Miss Behavin' and below that, pictures of 18 bombs. Before he was taken to a prison camp in Oberursel, the two men had a Danish beer and parted wishing each other good luck.

If anyone has information about the American, please contact . . .

Orlin, although he regularly received the VFW magazine, missed the notice from Hanke. However, it was brought to his attention by an old friend. Letters were then exchanged and six months later Orlin flew to Munich to meet Hanke.

Hanke gave the American a well decorated walking stick that represented his combat history. It includes nine front view silhouettes of his aerial victories. Orlin also received a Luftwaffe flying jacket to replace the one taken from him.

Orlin presented Hanke with a shield-like plaque with mementoes of his career – hat insignia, wings and other emblems. It is inscribed:

February 1944 – February 1976. To Heinz Hanke. Once a Foe, now a Friend.

Epilogue

Pierre Clostermann, DSO, DFC, a fighter pilot, shall have the last word on those aircrew who flew in heavy bombers in World War Two:

Here and there in the Fortress formations there were gaps. From close to you could see machines with one, sometimes two, stationary engines and feathered propellers. Others had lacerated tail-planes, gaping holes in the fuselages, wings tarnished by fire or glistening with black oil oozing from gutted engines.

Behind the formation were the stragglers, making for the coast, for the haven of refuge of an advanced air base on the other side of the Channel, flying only by a sublime effort of will. You could imagine the blood pouring over the heaps of empty cartridges, the pilot nursing his remaining engines and anxiously eyeing the long white trail of petrol escaping from his riddled tanks. These isolated Fortresses were the Focke-Wulf's favourite prey. Therefore the squadrons detached two or three pairs of Spitfires, charged with bringing each one back safe: an exhausting task as these damaged Fortresses often dragged along on a third of their total power, stretching the endurance of their escort to the limit.

On this occasion Ken sent Carpenter and me to escort a Liberator which was only in the air by a miracle. Its No 3 engine had completely come out of its housing and hung on the leading edge, a mass of lifeless ironmongery. The No 1 engine was on fire, the flames slowly eating into the wing and the smoke escaping through the aluminium plates of the upper surface, buckled by the heat. Through the tears in the fuselage the survivors were throwing overboard all their superfluous equipment – machine guns, ammunition belts, radio, armour plates – to lighten their machine, which was slowly losing height.

To crown it all, there was a burst in the hydraulic system,

freeing one of the wheels of the undercart which hung down and increased the drag still further.

Throttled back to only 1,800 revs, and flying at 200 mph, we had to zig-zag to keep level with him. We had been hunched up in our uncomfortable cockpits for two hours already, and we were still over France, twelve miles behind the main formation. Then Focke-Wulfs began to prowl around us, at a respectful distance, as if suspecting a trap. Anxiously Carp and I kept an eye on them.

Suddenly they attacked, in pairs. Short of juice as we were, all we could do was to face each attack by a very tight 180 degree turn, fire a short burst in the approximate direction of the Hun, and immediately resume our position by another quick 180 degrees. This performance was repeated a dozen times but we succeeded in making the Focke-Wulfs keep their distance. They eventually tired of it – or so we thought.

Over Dieppe the fighters gave way to the flak. We were flying at about 10,000 feet. The German light flak opened fire with unbelievable ferocity. An absolute pyramid of black puffs charged with lightning appeared in a fraction of a second. Violently shaken by several well-aimed shells, Carp and I separated and gained height as fast as we could with our meagre reserves of petrol. The poor Liberator, incapable of taking any sort of violent evasive action, was quickly bracketed. Just as we thought it was out of range there was an explosion and the big bomber, cut in half, suddenly disappeared in a sheet of flame. Only three parachutes opened out. The blazing aluminium coffin crashed a few hundred yards from the cliffs in a shower of spray, dragging down the remaining members of the crew.

Note to Chapter Eight

The author has been reminded by his former skipper, Jack West, now living in Australia, of a further coincidence relating to the crash at Cranage. We were not the only crew to 'deliver' a Wellington at the doorstep of a 'Wimpey' repair factory. A second Wellington had 'pranged' in the next field within minutes of our untimely descent. Emerging

187

out of the night we encountered the crew of this other bent aircraft during our weary trudge back to the airfield.

Secondly, it came as a shock to learn that W/O Rothschild, the 'experienced' pilot, was not actually on the OTU staff. He was a fighter pilot who, visiting Hixon, had been persuaded to fly with us due to a shortage of instructors at that time.

Apparently, although familiar with single-engine fighters, he had little or no knowledge of multi-engine bombers!